Designing for Learning

Creating Campus Environments for Student Success

C. Carney Strange
James H. Banning

Second Edition

JB JOSSEY-BASS™
A Wiley Brand

Published by Jossey-Bass
A Wiley Brand
One Montgomery Street, Suite 1000, San Francisco, CA
94104-4594—www.josseybass.com

Jossey-Bass books and products are available through most bookstores. To contact Jossey-Bass directly call our Customer Care Department within the U.S. at 800-956-7739, outside the U.S. at 317-572-3986, or fax 317-572-4002.

Wiley publishes in a variety of print and electronic formats and by print-on-demand. Some material included with standard print versions of this book may not be included in e-books or in print-on-demand. If this book refers to media such as a CD or DVD that is not included in the version you purchased, you may download this material at http://booksupport.wiley.com. For more information about Wiley products, visit www.wiley.com.

Library of Congress Cataloging-in-Publication Data

Strange, Charles Carney, author.
[Educating by design]
Designing for learning : creating campus environments for student success / C. Carney Strange, James H. Banning. — Second edition.
1 online resource.
Includes bibliographical references and index.
Description based on print version record and CIP data provided by publisher; resource not viewed.
ISBN 978-1-118-82347-7 (epdf) — ISBN 978-1-118-82350-7 (epub) — ISBN 978-1-118-82352-1 (cloth) 1. College environment—United States. 2. Campus planning—United States. 3. College facilities—United States—Planning. I. Banning, James H., author. II. Title.
LB2324
378.1'9610973—dc23

2015015888

Cover design by Wiley
Cover image: © irinap/Shutterstock

Printed in the United States of America

SECOND EDITION

HB Printing 10 9 8 7 6 5 4 3 2 1

Contents

Preface ix

Acknowledgments xvii

The Authors xix

Part One: Components and Impacts of Campus Environments

1. Physical Environments: The Role of Place and Design 9
2. Aggregate Environments: The Impact of Human Characteristics 49
3. Organizational Environments: How Institutional Goals Are Achieved 79
4. Socially Constructed Environments: Different Views Through Different Eyes 113

Part Two: Designing Campus Environments That Foster Student Learning and Success

5. Promoting Inclusion and Safety 143
6. Encouraging Participation and Engagement 187
7. Building Communities of Learning 213
8. Learning Through Mobile Technology 239

9. Assessing and Creating Designs for Student Learning and Success 271

References 301

Name Index 335

Subject Index 343

List of Exhibits, Tables, and Figures

Figure 1.1:	Hierarchy of Learning Space Attributes	30
Exhibit 2.1:	Holland Vocational Interest-Personality Types	54
Exhibit 2.2:	Kolb Learning Styles	58
Exhibit 2.3:	CIRP Freshman Survey Typology of Students	64
Exhibit 2.4:	Types of Engaging Institutions	67
Table 2.1:	Demographic Groups by Student Engagement Types	69
Figure 2.1:	Holland Personality Vocational Interest Types	72
Exhibit 3.1:	Organizational Archetypes – Selected Examples	84
Exhibit 3.2:	Overview of the Four-Frame Model	85
Exhibit 3.3:	A Synthesis of Organizational Models	100
Exhibit 3.4:	Static Organizations Versus Developmental Environments	103
Exhibit 4.1:	University Residence Environment Scale (URES) Dimensions and Subscales	121

Exhibit 4.2:	Classroom Environment Scale (CES) Dimensions and Subscales	122
Exhibit 4.3:	Social Climate Dimensions and Subscales Across Environments	123
Figure II.1:	Hierarchy of Environmental Design	140
Exhibit 5.1:	Principles of Universal Design	166
Table 6.1:	Cluster Centers (z scores) on Engagement Benchmarks for Seven Student Types	193
Exhibit 8.1:	A Framework for Using Social Media to Support Self-Regulated Learning in Personal Learning Environments (PLEs)	258
Figure 9.1:	Campus Design Matrix	276
Exhibit 9.1:	Five Conceptions of Environmental Impact	277
Figure 9.2:	Ecology of Individual Students	280
Figure 9.3:	Real (Form R) Versus Ideal (Form I) Work-Environment Scale Profile	293
Exhibit 9.2:	Work Environment Scale (WES) Dimensions and Subscales	294

In memory of
Martin Bernard Strange, MD
(1907–1949)
Mary Patricia Gardner Strange
(1912–2005)
and
Harriet Vaughn Strange Chalfant
(1937–2006)
whose loving care
shaped the learning designs of my own life
for these many years.

CCS

To Sue

JHB

Preface

Universities are institutions of *purpose* and *place*. Being purposeful, they generate, preserve, and transmit knowledge; nurture the development of students; and serve the communities that support them. As places of distinction, they also aim to create spaces that are both memorable and facilitative of those who use them. Questions about what designs best achieve these ends have long been and continue to be debated as campuses evolve in response to student and institutional needs.

The connection between educational purposes and places lies deep in the history of higher learning in Western culture. From the earliest medieval institutions (e.g., Bologna, in 1088) to the current complex of college and university systems, educators have pursued designs to advance human achievement, the most successful template for which is the experience of *community*. Monastic in origin, the communal model of learning is what first guided the establishment of the great English-speaking universities at Oxford (c.1167) and Cambridge (c.1209) and gave rise to the familiar English collegiate system, most often associated with the layout of a green "quad" framed by a chapel and faculty and student living quarters. This is the vision John Harvard, a graduate of Emmanuel College (Cambridge), brought to the founding of his namesake institution in the New World in 1636, and this is the framework Thomas Jefferson used to create his academical village (Wilson, Lasala & Sherwood,

2009) at the University of Virginia (1819). The parameters of the learning community continue to inform the designs of great institutions intent on the growth and development of students.

In American society, heading off to college—whether by flying across country, driving across town, or getting online at home—is an event that marks for many a significant change in life. For traditional-age students, college attendance coincides with the transition from late adolescence to early adulthood (Chickering & Reisser, 1993). For increasing numbers of mature students, the choice to pursue higher education often marks a change in career interests or relationships (Aslanian & Brickell, 1980; Cross, 1981; Levinson & Levinson, 1996) that requires further training or the exploration of new goals and personal networks. Regardless, this experience is an immensely powerful one, and the selected institution becomes an important place to test new aspects of identity and autonomy, establish new relationships, explore value commitments, sample the wealth of human knowledge and culture, and pursue vocational interests and goals.

Not all college experiences are successful though, as retention studies often indicate. Anywhere from 30 to 60 percent of the students who enter college, depending on the type of institution, decide to leave prior to completing a degree or program certificate. At times this decision to drop out of school is highly appropriate, given the developmental status and needs of some students. At other times the decision to leave a particular institution might result from its failure to offer a sufficiently supportive educational environment or one consistent with its stated purposes and goals.

Student behavior, whether in the form of leaving a college or university or persisting and succeeding, must be examined in terms of characteristics of the person and characteristics of the environment, a differential interactionist perspective first articulated by Kurt Lewin (1936). By inference this perspective suggests a variety of questions the higher education community must ask: What distinguishes a college or university that is successful in attracting, retaining, and challenging students? What are the patterns and design characteristics of supportive educational settings? Are certain environmental characteristics essential for all students? Are some designs appropriate for only certain students? These are concerns of profound significance for any institution proposing or affirming the centrality of student learning, growth, and development, as it occurs in classrooms, residence halls, student organization meetings, at service learning sites, on the intramural fields, or now online.

The capacity of any postsecondary institution to carry out its educational mission depends, in part, on how well its principal features are understood and designed accordingly. This volume focuses on the status of the literature on human environments and the implications this holds for the policies and practices of higher education. Educators in the classroom and beyond, and those in various administrative posts, will find here a comprehensive framework of ideas for structuring their work and ultimately for improving the learning outcomes of the students they serve. All participants in any college or university setting—from physical plant operators and maintenance personnel to faculty members, academic administrators, and student affairs staff—can benefit from a broader understanding of how campus environments, in all their dimensions and features, serve to shape and influence the behavior of those who pursue their opportunities. The purpose of this book is to assemble, synthesize, and orient the many disparate pieces in the literature that address the definition, description, and dynamics of campus environments. Hopefully readers will return to their work with greater purpose toward and greater influence over the environments within which they create and function.

This volume is organized into two parts. Part One: Components and Impacts of Campus Environments offers an overview of concepts and models of human environments, focusing on their manifestations in college and university settings and their implications for the design of educational facilities, systems, and practices. Chapter One examines the physical dimensions of human environments, including campus architectural features, layout, and spatial designs, with emphasis on understanding how such features influence students' behavior and experiences of campus life. Chapter Two explicates the dynamics of campus environments as reflections of the collective characteristics of individuals who inhabit them. Through the lens of human aggregate theories, this unit incorporates a review of models that share an emphasis on understanding how people create characteristic features of any environment through the influence of dominant types. Chapter Three discusses campus environments in terms of the organizational structures or patterns they create in response to, and in support of, the specific goals they pursue. It draws from the sociology of complex organizations and other related frameworks as they inform decisions about how various campus units are organized to achieve certain ends and ultimately influence, for good or ill, the functioning of students within them. Chapter Four explores the nature of campus environments as socially and collectively constructed by those who inhabit and observe them. Included in this review are models of campus environmental press, social climate, and campus culture. Together, these four chapters establish a broad foundation for understanding and assessing the key components of any human environment—physical dimensions, collective personal characteristics, organizational structures, and collective social constructions—as well as environments created more specifically in the service of higher education.

Part Two: Designing Environments That Foster Student Learning and Success focuses on the conditions thought to be important for the design of effective educational environments. In one of the first comprehensive volumes on human environments, Rudolf Moos (1986) raised a critical question in that respect: "What are the criteria by which an environment can be judged as favorable?" (p. 4). We propose that educational environments are most powerful when they offer students these fundamental conditions:

a feeling of inclusion and a sense of security, engaging mechanisms for involvement, and the experience of community. Accordingly, Chapter Five discusses how environments can contribute to or detract from a sense of inclusion and safety on campus, with a focus on various campus design features, including the importance of territoriality and defensible space, effects of dominant groupings, organizational size, and campus culture. Chapter Six characterizes and discusses features of campus environments that encourage student involvement and engagement in learning, both within and beyond the classroom, emphasizing the importance of human scale design, differentiated aggregate groupings, a dynamic organizational structure, and a supportive cultural milieu. Chapter Seven follows with an overview of the nature and characteristics of human communities, with implications for the design of educational environments, particularly in regard to their capacity for including, securing, engaging, and ascribing to participants the status of full membership in the learning community. Chapter Eight opens a discussion of digital forms of human environments as they apply to the postsecondary educational setting and focuses on the design and potential of these new technologies to effect the inclusion, security, engagement, and experience of community among students. Finally, in Chapter Nine, we pull together the various strands of environmental theory and design presented here and offer possible strategic initiatives for institutions to engage students more successfully in achieving their education goals.

This book is meant to be neither an exhaustive nor definitive critical review of extant research on the effects of campus environments. The literature is both too unwieldy and disparate to submit to such a synthesis. What we have attempted to offer, though, is a select sampling of concepts and models, organized around a distinctive framework and reflective of themes critical to the successful functioning of higher education institutions today. We trust that we have unearthed a rich harvest of ideas for educational researchers and practitioners who will further evaluate their validity and their application. We hope these ideas will help to construct an institutional agenda that will stimulate changes in policies and practices to improve colleges and universities as places of learning. Institutional resources should focus on questions of whether or not current practices are effective, as they relate to the ideas presented here. If they are not, changes should be considered.

We complete this preface with the belief that if postsecondary educators had had access to many of these concepts about effective educational environments, especially over the past fifty years, a number of features taken for granted today on many campuses (such as high-rise residence halls and large, theater-style lecture halls) might never have been proposed in the first place, assuming that student learning is the primary goal. We also believe that within the next fifty years many of the features of the higher education systems and facilities we do take for granted today must be transformed or risk disappearing altogether.

Finally, we contend that American higher education may be at a tipping point (Gladwell, 2006) in its history once again, where the future of the enterprise doesn't extend easily from what is most familiar to us today, as perhaps it once did. For one, physical campuses are no longer necessary for access to information and understanding. For another, our use of the physical campuses we do maintain leaves much room for improvement when it comes to supporting student learning. Numerous disruptive innovations (Christensen & Eyring, 2011) are challenging traditional methods of delivery in all that we do (e.g., online learning systems). Given the sharply rising costs of it all, consumers are beginning to question more carefully the feasibility and outcome of what goes on in our postsecondary institutions. In the face of alternatives now available, is it worth the price to dedicate four to six years of one's early adulthood to the experience of traditional campus life in the pursuit of learning? Does it work? Such concerns should command the priority of institutions as they consider their future in the American higher education landscape. Whether colleges and universities, as we know them today, will survive intact is uncertain. We've experienced tipping points before that have led to radical changes in how we implement our mission. The small, private, recitation-of-the-canon-based system of the early nineteenth century evolved, in a matter of forty or so years, into the larger, public, elective-driven, experimentation-based system we know as the modern university. Such seismic changes then altered significantly our way of thinking about education and the means of delivering it. Are we at a similar moment today? Time will tell.

Since publishing the first version of this book, *Educating by Design: Creating Campus Learning Environments That Work* (Strange & Banning, 2001), the discussion of campus environments has been enriched by numerous new concepts and applications, suggesting to us that a revised treatment of the topic is in order. This is our intent with the present volume, *Designing for Learning: Creating Campus Environments for Student Success*. While the basic conceptual framework remains intact, this volume accounts for many new contributions (e.g., universal design, multicultural environments, social networking, mobile learning, student engagement, and residential learning communities) that have added to the mix of understandings about how colleges and universities work to support student learning. Again, the literature informing these topics is vast and disparate. Our work here attempts to synthesize, contextualize, and illustrate many of the key constructs that further influence postsecondary institutional design today. Readers are encouraged to explore how these treatments apply to their own campuses insofar as they respond to the needs of the students they serve. Certainly, multiple purposes are served by and compete for our institutions' resources. Questions of institutional efficiency can be overwhelming, especially at a time of diminished resources, and can lead to policies and practices that are less than desirable or effective in their intended outcomes. Concerns of this kind cannot be ignored, yet when they dominate the discussions of institutional planners and administrators they often risk the core of what we do: supporting students in their learning. This volume promises to focus selectively on two basic educational concerns: How do students learn, develop, and grow? How do we design campus environments to enhance that process? While answers to these two questions will not rule the day every time they are posed, they must nonetheless be brought to the table as institutional decision makers engage in their work, for no other reason than to remind them of why colleges and universities exist in the first place.

Although the particulars of campus design have evolved over the history of American higher education, the fundamentals of student success have not changed; students deserve nothing less than an educational environment that is affirming, energizing, challenging, and productive. It is our hope that the concepts contained herein can be helpful in rising to such a challenge.

December 2014

C. CARNEY STRANGE
JAMES H. BANNING

Acknowledgments

In the first edition of this book I mused on the intersecting circles of my life—family, friends, and professional colleagues, all part of the rhyme and reason in my spending the past four decades as an educator. Although intact, my circles continue to evolve. My family circle has changed, with young ones moving on as adults in the world and elders completing their turns in the cycle of life. My friends and colleagues have also advanced along their paths, moving on to what life has to offer: for some, new locations and new opportunities; for others, like me, retirement—a time to place a coda on what has transpired and move on to new adventures and discoveries. Needless to say, the grind of professional commitments has not been missed. In fact, working without a job now has become one of the new pleasures of this adventure for me and has offered me opportunity to refresh some of my previous contributions—such as this book. It has also provided occasion to reflect on what a gift this long career has been to me.

To serve in a place of ideas—a university—has been an incredible privilege, to write about these ideas has been a fulfilling challenge, and to share and explore the meaning of them with others has been an immense joy. Among my most memorable companion explorers have been the many students I have had the pleasure of accompanying on their own learning journeys over the years. In particular I wish to acknowledge what I have dubbed my Roosevelt

Crew, whose spirit and excitement for these ideas energized my own enthusiasm for their renewal at a time when it would have been easy to just walk away. They were a special group of graduate students at Bowling Green State University who joined me as I took my last turn at the academic till in spring 2013, pursuing these concepts in a course on campus environments. It was their willingness to consider and challenge this material—through reflective readings, active class sessions, and a special road trip—that properly sealed my long-held passion for teaching and spurred me on gently to the finish line. They know who they are; they all contributed to this project in their own ways. Among them though I wish to recognize in particular for their special role in preparing and proofing original chapter drafts: Kristen Anthony, Kate Branstetter, Kyle Fassett, Chelsea Greene, Mariamne Harrington, Patricia Helyer, Tara Milliken, and Elizabeth Yale. I am grateful for the fond memories all of these students have imprinted me with, both as one special group and also as an archetype of the kind of generative experience that has meant so much to me as an educator these many years.

Finally, needless to say, the support of a publisher's editorial cast in a very challenging business is indispensable. From the first edition of this book to the present one, I owe much to my Jossey-Bass team over the years, including the late Ursula Delworth (1934–2000), Gale Erlandson, Erin Null, and Shauna Robinson and crew. Their well-placed pats and prods brought all of this to final fruition. Indeed, it was the spontaneous gift of a book (about the impact of college on students) to a curious graduate student at a professional conference in 1977, by Allen Jossey-Bass (1928–1996) himself, that perhaps first inspired me to consider this work. Once again, my sincere gratitude goes out to all of them.

C. Carney Strange
Bowling Green, OH
December 2014

The Authors

C. CARNEY STRANGE is professor emeritus in the Higher Education and Student Affairs graduate preparation program at Bowling Green State University, Bowling Green, Ohio, where for thirty-five years he taught courses on college student development, the impact of educational environments, student spirituality, and methods of qualitative research. Dr. Strange received his BA in French Literature from Saint Meinrad College, St. Meinrad, Indiana, in 1969; his MA degree in college student personnel from the University of Iowa in 1976; and his PhD in student development in postsecondary education from the University of Iowa in 1978. Dr. Strange has been an active teacher-scholar for thirty seven years, authoring publications on college student development, campus environments, and student services in Canadian higher education. He has served on the editorial boards of the *Journal of College Student Development*, *National Association of Student Personnel Administrators Journal*, *Religion and Education*, and CASE *International Journal of Educational Advancement*. He was the recipient, in 1978, of the Ralph F. Birdie Memorial Research Award from the American Personnel and Guidance Association. Dr. Strange was recognized as an ACPA 75th Anniversary Diamond Honoree in 1999 and a NASPA-Student Affairs Professionals in Higher Education Pillar of the Profession in 2006. He was acknowledged by ACPA–College Student Educators-International as an *Annuit*

Coeptis Senior Professional in 1996, and in 2010 the association honored him with the ACPA *Contribution to Knowledge Award.* In addition, Dr. Strange has over twenty years of experience as a college and university trustee at Saint Meinrad College and School of Theology (IN) and Saint Xavier University (IL).

JAMES H. BANNING is professor emeritus of education at Colorado State University, where he taught courses on campus ecology for the School of Education and environmental psychology for the Department of Psychology. He received his BA from William Jewell College, Liberty, Missouri, in 1960 and his PhD in psychology from the University of Colorado in 1965. Dr. Banning has served in a variety of administrative positions in higher education, including director of the Counseling Center, University of Colorado; program director, Western Interstate Commission for Higher Education; vice chancellor for Student Affairs, University of Missouri–Columbia; and vice president for Student Affairs, Colorado State University. He played a pioneering role in the campus ecology movement and has authored monographs, numerous book chapters, and journal articles on the ecological relationships among students and their campus environment.

Part One

Components and Impacts of Campus Environments

Several critical perspectives have informed educators about the relationship between students and their institutions of higher learning. So named an *unenlightened perspective*, one approach "is built on the premise that not all young people [or returning mature students for that matter] belong in college and that therefore it can be expected that a lot of students won't be able to make it. It follows, therefore, that student failure is evidence of the efficacy of our higher education system" (Banning & Kaiser, 1974, p. 371). The appropriate role for educators holding this perspective, then, is to ease students out of the institution through counseling them toward other opportunities. A second perspective focuses on the concept of *adjustment*; accordingly, "if there are students who can't make it, they should be provided with counseling and other services in order that they might change and be better able to benefit from the educational environment" (p. 371). In other words, the institution's role is to help students solve their adjustment concerns so they can succeed. A third perspective is characterized as *developmental*. This perspective assumes that "college students [of all ages] are in a transition or growth period and that there are certain tasks they must perform in order to reach maturity ... they need to grow up some before they can really benefit from the educational environment" (p. 371). The institution's role in this case is to be appropriately supportive as students reach a point of readiness to benefit from their educational experiences. Although an element of truth is contained in each perspective, according to Banning and Kaiser, "none speaks sharply to the issues of institutions changing, institutions adjusting, or institutions growing up, or more importantly, to the relationship between students and their environment" (p. 371). In response to the limitations of these approaches is the *ecological perspective*, incorporating "the influence of environments on persons and persons on environments" (p. 371). Implicit in this latter perspective is the assumption that institutions themselves bear responsibility for the design and creation of campus environments, arranged appropriately or otherwise for meeting educational purposes.

In a comprehensive review of environmental correlates and determinants of human behavior, Moos (1986) concluded that the "arrangement of environments is perhaps the most powerful technique we have for influencing human behavior. From one point of view, every institution in our society sets up conditions that it hopes will maximize certain types of behavior and certain directions of personal growth" (p. 4). Thus, colleges and universities establish conditions to attract, satisfy, and retain students for purposes of challenging them to develop qualities of the educated person, including a capacity for complex critical reasoning, communication, and leadership; a sense of identity and purpose; an appreciation for differences; and a commitment to lifelong learning. Such goals are the traditional purview of educators, and as Dewey (1933) suggested, they are better served by specificity rather than serendipity: "We never educate directly, but indirectly by means of the environment. Whether we permit chance environments to do the work, or whether we design environments for the purpose makes a great difference" (p. 22). To be more fruitful in our efforts, we concur with Dewey in the assumption that educational settings designed with an understanding of the dynamics and impact of human environments in mind will go further in achieving these ends.

As we approach this topic of the design of effective campus environments, we are persuaded by Moos's (1986, p. 4) distinction between an ideal and an optimum environment:

> There are no clearly defined criteria for an ideal environment that can meet everyone's requirements. But we are much more likely to achieve an optimum environment when critical decisions about constructing and changing the environment are in the hands of people who live and function in it. These decisions are currently in our hands, and to make them wisely we urgently need more reliable information about human environments and their impacts on human beings.

Thus, Part One (Chapters One through Four) of this volume provides an overview of what we believe to be the best information we have on the nature of human environments and their impact on human beings in an educational context.

In the past decade, considerable information on the impact of human environments has emerged in the literature on college students and their experience of higher education (Evans, Forney, Guido, Patton, & Renn, 2010; Levine & Dean, 2012; Pascarella & Terenzini, 2005; Renn & Reason, 2012a). However, what seems missing is an "integrated perspective regarding the human environment" for purposes of creating "conditions to maximize certain intended effects" (Moos, 1986, p. 4). Toward that end our review and synthesis of these materials begins by identifying some of the assumptions and understandings that have shaped our work.

Like Moos (1986), we, too, are guided by the tenets of a social ecological approach, with its emphasis on a "multidisciplinary study of the impacts of physical and social environments on human beings....from the perspective of the individual" (p. 28). This method also "emphasizes individual adaptation, adjustment, and coping, ... maintains a practical applied orientation, [and] has an explicit [humanistic] value orientation ... dedicated to increasing individual freedom of choice in selecting environments" (p. 31). These tenets, we conclude, are consistent with and supportive of the role of educators as they seek to understand and design environments that will maximize student learning.

As educators acquire a more sophisticated understanding of human environments, they will be better positioned to eliminate those features of institutions that are needlessly stressful or inhibiting and ultimately to create those features that will challenge students toward active learning, growth, and development. Whether we want them to or not, or whether we understand them or not, educational environments do exert an impact on students. Our preference is to approach the design of these environments with eyes wide open and intentions clearly informed. This goal will require grounding in a range of behavioral science concepts and models that inform such questions, the purpose we now turn to in this volume.

These first four chapters outline and illustrate core components related to the description and understanding of all human environments. Although we often become insensitive or perhaps even immune to the components and effects of our environments, the experience of a typical day for faculty, administrators, and students alike on any campus will reveal the scope of its effects. These include the sidewalks that encourage us to walk around a building rather than across the rain-soaked muddy pathway to an office, classroom, or residence room; the characteristic styles, conversations, and actions of colleagues, students, and staff within a given department or office; the expectations, routines, and procedures we follow (or ignore) in the execution of our responsibilities and assignments; and, finally, the distinctive values and impressions we seem to intuit from the very air we breathe that help us understand and communicate to others what it's like to be here. These are all exemplars of the components of human environments that serve to prod, bend, and shape the behaviors of those within them. Understanding what to look for and how to identify the components of the environment are the first steps in this overview.

Key components of all human environments include:

- Physical condition, design, and layout
- Collective characteristics of the people who inhabit them
- Organizational structures related to their purposes and goals
- Collective perceptions or social constructions of the context and culture of the setting

Each of four chapters in this part begins with a case scenario alluding to the various environmental features explicated in the chapter. Following the presentation of chapter content, a brief set of suggested discussion questions is included for purposes of exploring key concepts and their application to campus observations, policies, and practices. Thus, in Chapter One, perhaps the most obvious features of any campus environment—its physical characteristics—are addressed. Basic layout and spaces (Griffith, 1994), accessibility and cleanliness, interior color schemes, and even the weather on the day of a campus visit, for example, all shape initial attitudes in subtle yet powerful ways (Stern, 1986; Sturner, 1972; Thelin & Yankovich, 1987). Components of the campus physical environment, natural and synthetic, serve functional and symbolic ends, defining spaces for various activities, functions, and events and sending out nonverbal messages containing a range of possibilities. As places of active learning, colleges and universities contribute to designs that are supportive of student engagement and the experience of community (Chapman, 2006).

Chapter Two recognizes that information about the collective characteristics of environmental inhabitants, whether demographic (e.g., gender, age, ethnicity) or typological (e.g., personalities, learning styles, strengths, activities), is indicative of the dominant features of an environment. A profile of these collective human characteristics reflects the pattern, strength, and character of an environment, according to degrees of differentiation (type homogeneity among inhabitants) and consistency (type similarity) (Holland, 1973).

Highly differentiated and consistent environments (that is, those dominated primarily by a single type) are readily distinguished and clearly focused to those within and without. Such aggregates accent and reinforce their own characteristics over time and exert a powerful influence on the degree to which others are attracted to, satisfied within, and retained by them. Thus, campuses of a particular cultural, ethnic, or age-based group, for example, are more likely to attract, satisfy, and retain individuals who share traits in common with the dominant group. This perspective also suggests that the quality of any student's experience is a function of his or her congruence, or degree of fit, with the dominant aggregate. Those who share similarities with it are predicted to be most attracted to that environment, while those who bear little resemblance are least likely to be reinforced for preferred behaviors, values, attitudes, and expectations, in which case they are at risk for becoming dissatisfied and leaving that environment.

Chapter Three begins with the observation that all environments maintain some degree of organization (formally or otherwise) to meet certain explicit or implied goals. On a typical college campus, most faculty, staff, and students spend a good deal of time every day in purposeful environments such as residence halls, classrooms, department offices, recreation centers, services, and programs. To the extent that these environments are designed to achieve certain ends, getting organized to get things done is a natural conclusion to a number of decisions that must be made with respect to their purposes. Who is in charge? How will decisions about distributing resources be made? By what rules, if any, will the organization function? What must be accomplished and how quickly? How will participants be rewarded for their accomplishments? Answers to such questions generate various arrangements and structures that, in turn, define the organizational dimensions of an environment. Thus, concentrating decision-making power within one or a select few individuals, for example, may define an environment that is highly centralized; in turn, distributing decision-making authority throughout the setting lends itself to creating milieus of varying flexibility or dynamism. These characteristic milieus then influence certain central performances of the environment, such as innovation, efficiency, production, and the morale experienced by participants in the setting.

To complete Part One, Chapter Four focuses on models highlighting the subjective views, experiences, and collective social constructions of participants in an environment. Consensual perceptions, in the form of environmental presses, social climates, and meanings attributed to various cultural artifacts, exert a directional influence on inhabitants' behaviors. Thus, whether individuals are attracted to particular environments, or satisfied and stable within them, is a function of how they perceive and evaluate these environments. In effect, their perceptions are the reality of those environments for them.

These four components—physical, human aggregate, organizational, and socially constructed—comprise the various sources of influence on human behavior in any human environment. In effect, these are the tools of environmental design available to educators as they consider policies and practices that support student learning and success. Recognizing and understanding their dynamics is an important first step in shaping institutions to achieve educational purposes.

1

Physical Environments

The Role of Place and Design

Scenario: The Campus Visit

Eric Carter took a late spring day off work to visit nearby Mountain Pass Community College (MPCC), just fifteen miles away by interstate in the community of Rock City. It had been a while since he had been in a classroom because he took a job in a local factory after graduating from high school ten years before. He was thinking of returning to school, and since his cousin was considering the Wildlife Resource Management program at MPCC, Eric decided to go with him to get more information about the institution. As they neared Rock City, they began to look for signs directing them to the campus. Eric had driven this way many times before but had not had a reason to visit the campus. The first sign indicated that the next three exits would lead to the campus, but he was unsure which exit to use. While discussing where the office might be, they arrived at the second exit and decided to take it. At the top of the exit ramp, the sign indicated that the campus was to the left. After going several miles without any additional clues, they discovered that they were in an area resembling a college campus. On further inspection at the next stoplight, they noticed a faint Mountain Pass Community College sign embedded in a timber-like structure. They also saw a directional sign with the word "Visitor" on it. They appeared to be in luck and faithfully followed the next three visitor signs, assuming that they would end up at an admissions office, a welcome or information center, or at least a visitors' parking lot. But after obeying four directional signs they found themselves at a dead end in front of a campus maintenance building.

After asking a few people for directions, they backtracked and eventually found a visitors' parking lot. Upon examining MPCC's "You Are Here" map, they discovered that the admissions office was in fact nearby. After being confused a bit more by the sign outside the admissions building, they finally entered and took two flights of stairs (finding no elevator) to what appeared to be the admissions office for just the college's nursing program. However, despite the misleading signs at the entrance to the building, they had indeed found the general admissions office, and the friendly and helpful staff inside gave Eric a college catalog and admissions application materials and answered all his questions.

Next on Eric's agenda was a quick, self-guided campus tour. He and his cousin wandered through several buildings just to get a feel for the campus. Although they showed some age, they and the grounds were well maintained. Eric and his cousin peeked into one of several empty classrooms and saw a familiar academic setting—a large, sloped classroom with seats bolted to the floor and an elevated lectern some distance from the first row of students. Despite the familiarity, they thought it appeared a bit incongruous with an institution that touted learning as hands-on and personal. In the Earth Sciences building were several carpeted classrooms and labs with moveable chairs, tables, excellent lighting, and several technical amenities. This was what they were hoping to find: space for smaller classes and more opportunities for student–faculty interaction. The Earth Sciences classrooms seemed to be a better fit for the college's marketing tagline: "A Place for Learning Together."

After a quick tour of the classroom buildings, Eric asked for directions to the campus union. Finding it was relatively simple; it was in the center of campus, with most sidewalks leading to the plaza in front of its entrance and the major student parking lot located out back. The interior steel and plastic had recently been replaced with oak and pine, reflective of MPCC's rolling tree-covered landscape. From a table in a quiet corner of an otherwise bustling food court, Eric and his cousin could see a pleasant lagoon, with geese swimming near the shore. Eric noted that the proximity of the lagoon to the student parking lot offered a welcome sight, especially given the stress sometimes accompanying interstate highway commuting.

After grabbing a quick bite to eat in the food court, Eric and his cousin headed back toward their car, walking past what sounded like a spirited game or rowdy competition in an adjacent arena. They were a bit surprised to learn from an attendant at the entrance that it was actually the campus's spring commencement ceremony, which honored the achievements of graduates from MPCC's twenty six programs and specialties. Eric began to imagine himself among them someday. The campus visit was a bit frustrating at times, but given MPCC's successful job placement reputation, the feel of the campus, and the fact that he could commute, Eric was seriously entertaining the notion that this place might be for him.

Eric Carter's experiences in this scenario are not uncommon to all who visit, study, or work on a college or university campus. This scenario also illustrates just how complex and important the physical layout, design, and spaces of educational institutions and their environs are in terms of how individuals interact with them. Two questions are implicated in this case and form the framework for discussion in this chapter: What is the general nature of the physical environment's influence on human behavior? How do the physical dimensions of any campus environment specifically impact the behavior of participants?

The Campus as Place

Just as Eric Carter in the opening scenario characterized his brief MPCC experience with reference to it, the concept of *place* is an important one in considering the nature of campus environments and how they might influence students' behavior (Chapman, 2006). Drawing from a diverse disciplinary history (Lewicka, 2011) and several philosophical underpinnings, this concept focuses on the "interplay of people and the environment—as a place" (Cresswell, 2004, p. 11). Place is constituted not only by the built environment—buildings, sidewalks, parking lots, natural and designed landscapes—but also by the many people-made objects and artifacts of material culture that adorn the campus and interact with students, faculty, staff, and visitors alike. Thus, "the meaning of place is not inherent in its 'objective' or physical attributes, but rather rises from the interpretive processes that occur in the interplay between people-to-place and person-to-person interactions" (Morrill, Snow, & White, 2005, p. 232).

The concept of place is foundational to the human experience and can serve as a heuristic device for understanding the dynamics of the college campus. Bott (2000) proposed a four-domain descriptive framework for identifying place: setting characteristics, individual/person characteristics, cultural setting characteristics, and functional characteristics. Bott, Banning, Wells, Haas, and Lakey (2006) used this model to develop a series of questions linking these components to the campus environment, including the following: Are the buildings attractive? Is the campus historic? Is there a sense of belonging? Does the campus have personal meaning? Does the campus meet expectations? Is the campus safe? Such probes can guide the assessment of a campus's "sense of place" (Sturner, 1972) and point to ways to improve its design. A sense of place among students has been connected to higher degrees of involvement in the academic life of an institution (Okoli, 2013), issues of "retention, attention, motivation, learning and academic achievement" (Scott-Webber, Strickland, & Kapitula, 2013, p. 1), and alumni interest and giving (Reeve & Kassabaum, 1997).

Colleges and universities, perhaps more than other institutions, are experienced as settings where the sense of place

(Sturner, 1972) leaves lasting impressions on those who participate in them. Annual rituals like Homecoming, for example, confirm that such places cause a great feeling of attachment and are one of the most important spaces for many in our culture to accommodate the transition to young adulthood and other life phases. Colleges and universities by design are memorable places, and students often develop a strong place attachment (Giuliani & Feldman, 1993) to them, to the point that their sense of belonging and identity become deeply entwined in what Proshansky, Fabian, and Kaminoff (1983) coined place identity.

From the view of prospective college students, the sense of place associated with a college or university campus is often among the most important features in creating a critical first impression of an institution (Sturner, 1972; Thelin & Yankovich, 1987). The basic layout of the campus, open spaces and shaded lawns (Eckert, 2013), the accessibility and cleanliness of parking lots, interior color schemes, the shape and design of a residence hall or classroom building, a library or gallery, an impressive fitness center, and even the perceived climate (Knez, 2005) all shape initial attitudes in subtle yet powerful ways (Stern, 1986). In a firsthand study of campus life on twenty-nine different college campuses, Boyer (1987, p. 17) characterized the critical role of such aspects:

> Little wonder that when we asked students what influenced them most during their visit to a campus, about half mentioned "the friendliness of students we met." But it was the buildings, the trees, the walkways, and the well-kept lawns that overwhelmingly won out. The appearance of the campus is, by far, the most influential characteristic during campus visits, and we gained the distinct impression that when it comes to recruiting students, the director of buildings and grounds may be more important than the academic dean.

It is clear that the campus as place is an important factor that influences students' attraction to and satisfaction with a particular institution. What, then, is the nature of that influence, and how does the campus environment shape specific behaviors?

Most introductions to the topic of how physical environments influence behavior begin by noting Winston Churchill's observation that we shape our buildings and then they shape us. While the observation is a simplistic one, it does fit many of our everyday experiences with building designs and spaces and the artifacts we encounter on a college or university campus. Place does matter, and it influences our behavior. For example, once doors and hallways fix the shape of the traffic flow within a campus building, walking behavior within the building is pretty well determined. But we know it has not been entirely determined. Despite many design efforts to direct pedestrian flow through campus or through buildings, it is also a common experience to see someone going the wrong way. In the same way, people on campus often rearrange, change, or remove semifixed elements of interior and exterior furniture (Rapoport, 2005), like bicycle racks, benches, and picnic tables, to meet their own needs, and campus inhabitants are constantly placing, removing, and rearranging the material culture of the campus (e.g., posters, artwork, graffiti, and other symbolic material) for one purpose or another. Whether behavior within an environment is presumed to be caused by it (the position of *architectural determinism*), facilitated by it (an assumption of *possibilism*), or simply made more likely (the conclusion of *probabilism*) (Bell, Greene, Fisher, & Baum, 2001), it is clear that whatever defines the campus environment must be taken into account when understanding the behavior of students. Although features of place lend themselves theoretically to all three positions, the layout, location, and arrangement of space, facilities, and campus artifacts—and the nonverbal messages they convey render some behaviors much more likely and thus more probable than others. A well-planned place is seen as being more active and having greater influence than just making opportunities available and consequently is designed to achieve certain purposes. In the case of institutions of higher education, they are places expressly designed for learning.

Function and Symbol of Place

Whether built or natural, the physical aspect of any campus place offers many possibilities for human response. However, it is the nature of its functional and symbolic influence for some behaviors to be more probable than others. For example, from the opening scenario, an admissions office located on a second floor is *functional* in that its design is capable of allowing necessary activities to be carried out, but its location might also send out *symbolic* messages of other possibilities, perhaps causing some to seriously question the institution's commitment to the users of the service or their needs for convenience and accessibility. Another consideration might be that the institution does not see this function as central to its mission or that it lacks necessary funds to relocate the office. The symbolic view of campus place environments suggests that it can potentially convey all of these messages, depending of course on the meaning people ascribe to them (Gustafson, 2001).

It is this link between function and symbol that leads to an understanding of how campus physical environments and artifacts impact behavior through nonverbal communication (Rapoport, 2005). Such communication incorporates "those messages expressed by other than linguistic means" (Adler & Proctor, 2014, p. 188) and includes cues from the physical environment as well as the material culture of place. Rapoport also concluded, "Environments are more than just inhibiting, facilitating, or even catalytic; they not only remind, they also predict and describe" (1982, p. 77). Each setting "thus communicates, through a whole set of cues, the most appropriate choices to be made: the cues are meant to elicit appropriate emotions, interpretations, behaviors, and transactions by setting up the appropriate situations and contexts" (Rapoport, 1982, pp. 80–81). The research supporting the nonverbal communications link between the physical environment and behavior has long been established. For example, it has been shown that the attractiveness of a room influences positive affect and the energy level of those working in the room (Maslow & Mintz, 1956); low lighting, soft music, and comfortable seats encourage people to spend more time in a restaurant or bar (Sommer, 1978); and the artifacts on the walls of a student room can reflect messages about the student's adjustment to the university (Hansen & Altman, 1976). Even the overall architectural style of a campus can influence students' attributions of individual success, stimulation, and expectations for quality of education, with modern architecture being more favorable in that regard than traditional designs (Bennett & Benton, 2001).

The functional aspects of campus physical environments are designed and built, but the results of designing and building create symbolic nonverbal messages that campus users then read. For example, if the campus decides to make a curb wheelchair accessible by molding some asphalt to the curb instead of installing proper curb cuts, it might be technically functional but may also encode messages of not caring enough to do it correctly, not valuing the user, or just responding minimally to the mobility needs of some. When the student in a wheelchair rolls up to the makeshift curb, the decoded message may reveal that the institution doesn't care about or value the student. On the other hand, if the curb cut is correctly designed and constructed, the encoded and decoded messages may strike a different tone, conveying a sense that the institution cared enough to do it correctly. Either adaptation is functional, but they are quite different in their symbolic effects.

The functionality of the campus physical environment not only affords and constrains certain activities but also communicates important nonverbal messages that are often seen as more truthful than those that are verbal or written (Mehrabian, 1981). In some cases they send ambiguous, if not contradictory, messages, as did the campus entrance welcome sign for Eric Carter in the opening scenario. Similarly, while the campus president may speak about the open posture of the campus in welcoming ethnic minorities, the presence of defamatory graffiti on buildings may suggest just the opposite. Double messages have strong impact, and when a person perceives an inconsistency between the verbal and nonverbal, the latter often becomes most believable (Eckman, 1985). Such was the case with Eric, as he had doubts about MPCC's claim to be a place for learning together after seeing a restrictive physical classroom design. To paraphrase a quote attributed to Sir Kenneth Clark: "If one had to say which was telling the truth about the school, a speech by the principal or the actual school building, classrooms, and material he or she was responsible for providing, one should believe the building" (Anderson, 1971, p. 291). A major function of nonverbal communication is to convey emotion (Adler & Proctor, 2014). If a picture is worth a thousand words, viewing the campus physical environment not only leads to a more truthful perspective but perhaps also to a far more personal one.

Conduits of Nonverbal Communication

Campus places communicate their messages through a variety of mechanisms or conduits: behavior settings, artifacts of material culture, and behavioral traces. A college or university conveys its sense of place intentionally or inadvertently as these mechanisms serve to impress students with a variety of expressed values and tacit images of what it means to be a student on campus or to behave in a certain setting.

Behavior Settings

Behavior settings are the social and physical contexts within which human behavior occurs (Barker, 1968; Wicker, 1984). While the concept has its foundation in ecobehavioral psychology, its linkage to the concept of place is evident (Rapoport, 1994). The college campus is a classic behavior setting, composed of essentially two parts: the human or social aspects of the setting and the inanimate or physical aspects of place. For example, on the college campus, students, faculty, and staff interact within a physical environment including many components such as pathways, parking lots, activity fields, statuary, artwork, and buildings, which all present myriad designs that vary in size, color, and arrangement. It is the transactional (or mutually influential) relationship between these elements in the setting that shapes behavior. Behavior settings can function like nonverbal mnemonic devices (Rapoport, 1982), where messages encoded in the physical component serve to remind participants of what is expected. For example, an athletic field house is a behavior setting, where seating, props, sports teams, cheerleaders, and decor all convey cues that loud and rowdy sports event behaviors are not only appropriate but also expected. The rowdiness Eric observed coming from MPCC's commencement ceremony the day of his visit to campus might prompt consideration of a redesign of the behavior setting or a change to an alternative venue. Institutions experiencing similar concerns often hold their ceremonies in an athletic field house, where students are sometimes seated in the same arrangement as when they attend a sporting event and are most often grouped into departments and colleges, which encourages a competitive team identity. Ceremonial foliage, drapes, and a crested podium are often overshadowed by hoops, scoreboards, time clocks, and bannered reminders from victories past. Such encoded messages, along with the official excitement of the moment, remind students that yelling, cheering, and otherwise rowdy behavior are clued to be appropriate. A change of amenities and artifacts (e.g., classical music, lighting, carpet, and other textured surfaces) can help soften the atmosphere to improve student decorum and send messages about the importance of such events for all involved.

At times behavioral setting components are antagonistic and at other times synomorphic (Wicker, 1984). For instance, physical features often set broad limits on the phenomena that can occur in a setting, making some behaviors more or less likely than others—a concept first labeled by Michelson (1970, p. 25) as intersystems congruence. A classroom of chairs bolted-down in straight rows makes it difficult to form small-group discussions; in contrast, moveable swivel chairs or cushions make the setting more supportive of such interactions, achieving a *synomorphic* relationship. Common sense and experience suggest that when the physical environment of a campus, building, or classroom supports the desired behavior, better outcomes result. From a behavioral setting perspective, campus designs do not merely create functional spaces, moods, or atmospheres; they facilitate certain behaviors (Wicker, 1984).

Social and psychological aspects of behavioral settings also communicate messages to participants in them. A teaching podium placed twenty feet away from the first row of seats sends a distinct message regarding the formal nature of the upcoming classroom experience. Recall that it was this same cue in the opening scenario that raised questions in Eric's mind about the expressed mission of the college. On the other hand, a simple couch located in a secluded cove in the student union signaled the possibility for intimate social interaction. Whether stated or not, all behavioral settings are purposeful places; there must be a confluence of design and activity among participants if they are to be effective.

Artifacts of Material Culture

The concept of place also includes numerous artifacts found on campus that constitute its material culture. These are often objects made or modified by inhabitants of the setting and placed on campus for intended purposes: art, adornments, modifications of the landscape, and furnishings (Prown, 1982), to name a few. Such objects and artifacts give directions, inspire, warn, or accommodate through signs and symbols, artwork or posters, graffiti, and specific physical structures (Banning, Middleton, & Deniston, 2008). In doing so they also often send strong nonverbal messages about campus culture and expectations. Signage on a restroom door indicating "Ladies" gives a different message from one saying "Women" or "Gender-Neutral." An "Admissions Office" sign next to a "School of Nursing" sign at the same entrance sends a confusing message. Many campuses continue to display "Men Working" signs at worksites even though women are involved in the project. While such an implicit message of the invisibility of women would not be supported expressly by any university official, it speaks clearly in this case through the communicative power of a campus artifact.

Campus art also is a source of nonverbal social messages. Older campus buildings often have murals painted by artists whose fame now makes them invaluable, both historically and monetarily. At times these murals are embedded with social messages no longer supported by the campus or society in general. For example, the Kenneth Adam murals depicting assimilation of Native Americans, Mexican Americans as farm laborers, and Anglos as scientists continue to cause controversy after many years at the University of New Mexico's Zimmerman Library (Banning & Luna, 1992; Stockdale, 2011). Campus artworks, particularly statuary, often portray women in passive positions (sitting) and men as more active (standing or in motion), perhaps essentializing gender-based anachronisms inappropriate in a modern world. Sharing visual effect, campus graffiti is also another messaged source of campus culture, especially if its removal should be delayed, potentially sending nonverbal messages about the presumed values of the institution. Racist or homophobic messages visible for months on the side of an academic building may communicate a lack of concern for creating a safe and comfortable environment for all inhabitants.

Last, physical structures themselves can be seen as campus artifacts of nonverbal communication, as illustrated in the opening scenario. The design and placement of a curb cut and the two-story admissions building with no elevator both might convey a lack of concern for students in wheelchairs or students with children in strollers. Likewise, buildings that are hidden or have poorly lit spaces may suggest unaddressed safety concerns. Such examples underscore the point that material culture of place on campus is not just related to function and ambiance but also serves to communicate important campus values and expectations.

Behavioral Traces

Another category of mechanisms conveying nonverbal messages to campus participants is behavioral traces (Zeisel, 2006). Students, faculty, staff, and visitors use campus places in a variety of ways, leaving certain traces from which to infer behavior and identify potential clues and messages. Borrowing from the science of archaeology for gaining a more complete understanding of how people use campus environments, Zeisel (2006) suggested a number of ways to read traces by focusing on: by-products of use, adaptations of use, displays of self, and public messages. Concerning this approach Bechtel and Zeisel (1987) concluded: "Few give a thought ... to the fact that the fossils of tomorrow are the garbage dumps of today" (p. 32). Such is the case with college and university campuses, where many an artifact of earlier history has been uncovered during new construction or renovation projects.

By-products of behavior are often reflected in erosion, leftovers, and missing traces (Zeisel, 2006). Examples of erosion on campus are seen in the worn paths students make as they find the shortest distance from one campus building to the next. Such by-products (paths) can be useful in placing new sidewalks. In fact, on some campuses, sidewalks to new buildings are not constructed until student paths emerge, suggesting patterns of movement that are likely to persist. Leftovers are traces represented by objects not consumed during behavior, with trash and litter being the most common forms. At times these become associated with particular campus groups, such as Greek students on one campus who occupy a sitting wall as their favorite lunch spot. Leftover soda cans and fast-food bags produce a negative image problem there for the fraternity and sorority system. Last, missing traces are apparent where the lack of erosion and leftovers suggest little to no use of expected areas by campus constituents. Some spaces, by virtue of their design, see very little use, and documentation of such missing traces can prove helpful in gaining support for their redesign to better serve campus needs. Missing traces also result from theft or vandalism, such as an iconic clock missing its hands, potentially raising concerns for campus safety.

The concept of adaptations for use refers to where a change has been made to an environment because of failure of the design to serve its original purpose (Zeisel, 2006). Many of the adaptive traces include objects moved to separate elements once connected or to join elements once separated, for example, chaining down outdoor furniture on campus to prevent theft or adapting the corridors of residence halls for recreation because of limited alternate spaces on campus. Larger-scale adaptations would include renovations, expansions, and other changes or improvements. The addition of better lighting, for example, may follow an increase in campus crime; converting an open space to a parking lot could signify an increase in commuter student enrollment; an attempt by students to adapt any space for an unintended purpose might be the first clue that a redesign or renovation effort is needed.

Displays of self, such as the positioning of Greek letters on fraternity and sorority houses, illustrate how the physical environment is used to convey messages about individual and group ownership (Zeisel, 2006). Such displays are important for individualizing and personalizing spaces. Huge signs are often found in residence hall windows marking a particular floor, wing, or learning community, and no one can enter a campus without noticing T-shirts displaying messages of self and group, from student organizations to academic majors, from attendance at rock concerts to spring break location. Again, such traces not only increase understanding of the social environment on campus but also convey an entire social environment to others. Many academic buildings also illustrate how props are used symbolically as displays of self: a world globe on top of an international studies building, an oil derrick on the roof of a petroleum engineering building, and cannons in front of an ROTC building. Such symbols not only serve as displays in themselves but also send public messages about the values and interests of various campus units, the focus of the next category of traces.

Public messages include official, unofficial, and illegitimate signs on campus (Zeisel, 2006); often problematic are their design, location, and degree of clarity. Eric's experiences while visiting MPCC in the opening scenario once again are familiar testaments to the confusion ambiguous signage can create. Such problems often lead to the posting of additional signs or a redundancy of messages (Rapoport, 1982), usually a signal that the intended messages are not being communicated accurately. In addition to the more formal signs are artifacts of campus graffiti, which can signal creativity or local issues or can lend insight into prevailing attitudes on issues of diversity and social justice. Collectively, these concepts of behavior settings, material culture, and behavioral traces offer useful tools for the campus observer. Understanding their power as conduits of communication can assist in the improvement of campus environments and the creation of a powerful sense of place.

Places of Learning

Colleges and universities have always been places of learning, although the manner in which they have evolved over the past fifty years has resulted in renewed discussions about their capacity to sustain their stated mission and fundamental purpose. Following World War II and continuing through the 1960s and 1970s, the American college campus went through a period of great expansion unlike any other time in its history (Bonner, 1976). Large public universities were becoming even larger, numerous branch campuses were being established, and community colleges were beginning to take root in untold numbers of locations to accommodate growing enrollments and the desire for convenient access to learning at the postsecondary level. The physical infrastructure of higher education was rapidly infused with new facilities, including residence halls, classroom buildings, science labs, sports arenas, student unions, and recreation centers, all in an effort to create campuses with a sense of place among students as the preferred setting for their learning experience. Concurrent to this, new areas of research on student development and campus ecology also began to infiltrate the academy, eventually altering the conversation about the purposes and practices of higher education. Questions about good teaching evolved into concerns about student learning, and probes into the outcomes of it all led to new areas of research in the service of student engagement and learning.

In the meantime, structures and facilities designed and built at one time, with one set of assumptions, forty years later found themselves obsolete and in disrepair, no longer able to serve purposes grounded in new understandings and expectations. Over the past ten years especially, American higher education has undergone a resurgence of campus renovation and new construction, and the conversation has once again changed to a new question: How do we design and build facilities in our institutions that support the core mission of student engagement and learning? This current period of renewal has become an era of rich discussion about educational purposes and practices to fundamentally reshape our thinking about spaces and their importance in facilitating student learning. In a rare opportunity to build a college from scratch, Troyer (2005) reported on the processes engaged in while constructing a new campus: "Before campus and classroom design could begin, administrators needed to identify the college's 'learning signature'—the values and beliefs about how learning would be facilitated at the institution" (p. 6). Being places of learning, this is where discussions must begin for postsecondary institutions.

Colleges and universities are first and foremost places of learning, and the relationship between their designs and intended outcomes is well documented (Chapman, 2006; Chism & Bickford, 2002). As social places, postsecondary institutions place a premium on the interaction of constituents to effect new insights and understandings. Such is the nature of the learning enterprise. Thornburg (2001) likened this to the anthropological experience of the campfire or watering hole, where group discussion facilitated by a leader replaced the individual work of the cave (or perhaps the tribal smoke signals of early distance learners). The consequential importance of physical design in shaping the outcomes of student learning is considerable (Banning & Cunard, 1986), and American higher education over the last several decades has struggled with the results of too many ineffective designs from the past. As one review suggested, "Faculty and students alike have become so accustomed to meeting in spaces that are sterile in appearance, unable to accommodate different instructional approaches, and uncomfortable for supporting adult bodies that most have taken this condition as a fact of college life" (Chism & Bickford, 2002, p. 1). Consequently, in the mix of numerous institutional projects to renovate or build new campus learning spaces, formal and informal, recent research has begun to articulate key findings and propose guidelines for improving their design (Oblinger, 2006).

Following this line of inquiry, Strange (2014) proposed a typology of learning spaces that can be used to assess campus-wide options for supporting the engagement and learning of students during the college experience. Reflecting a hierarchy of campus design (Strange & Banning, 2001; see Part Two of the present volume), ten kinds of campus spaces are suggested for supporting the inclusion, security, engagement, and community experience of students. For purposes of inclusion and safety, campuses need spaces that are *welcoming* (i.e., creating a sense of belonging and security for newcomers and visitors) and *inclusive* (i.e., affirming identities and supporting expressions of self and others). To support student engagement, institutions must offer spaces that are *functional* (i.e., supporting key working tasks and activities), *sociopetal* (i.e., encouraging open and spontaneous human interaction and encounters), *flexible* (i.e., adapting to multiple purposes and participant imprint), *esthetic* (i.e., inspiring a creative sensibility and uplifting the human spirit), *reflective* (i.e., encouraging quiet individual imagining and meaning making), and *regenerative* (i.e., restoring energy and motivation for persisting). In addition, spaces needed to achieve community are *distinctive* (i.e., creating unique and memorable impressions), and *sustainable* (i.e., supporting human experience through right proportion, scale, and resource). Such spaces form a palette of learning textures from which to draw and apply as plans are put into place and resources permit. Spaces addressing inclusion and security must be top priority; without them, opportunities for engagement are diminished, and so on. Ultimately, each type of space exerts a cumulative effect as those designed to promote inclusion, security, and engagement are instrumental in effecting the ultimate experience of community—the prototype powerful learning environment.

Other researchers have focused on specific types of teaching and learning facilities in their analyses. For example, Kopec (2012) addressed the challenges of academic building design, noting the importance of student ease in finding classrooms (supporting wayfinding), where the sunlight enters the building, how the design of halls and corridors can influence social interactions, how the flexibility of furniture can accommodate different types of learning, how students can experience a sense of ownership and feel attached to the learning space, and how issues of privacy and crowding impact their learning. In addition, the author outlined the importance of ambient conditions, including color, noise, lighting, and temperature. Connections between space quality and learning are also addressed, from a planning perspective, in a report issued by the Learning Spaces Collaboratory (Narum,

2013); this document provides assistance to institutions for assessing campus learning facilities to enhance their potential as "spaces for becoming" (p. 20). Further evidence that implementing quality learning places makes a difference is presented in Scott-Webber, Strickland, and Kapitula (2013), where the use of an active learning postoccupancy evaluation tool measured the effects of intentionally designed classroom interventions. Accordingly, classroom layout increased student perceptions of their engagement, ability to achieve a higher grade, and increased motivation for attendance.

In a synthesis of extant research on the topic, Painter et al. (2013), under the aegis of the Society for College and University Planning (SCUP), issued a report on learning space design, describing both its current state and future directions. Based on a review of empirical data, cases, anecdotal studies, and conceptual analyses, the authors categorized three groups of campus learning spaces: *formal learning spaces* (e.g., classrooms, laboratories); *informal spaces* (e.g., libraries, group study spaces, gathering areas); and *campus as a whole* (e.g., buildings, layout, natural settings) (p. 6). Within each category, they further delineated a taxonomy of spatial design. Among *formal learning spaces* are the following:

1. *Traditional classrooms*—"flat floor plan, forward-facing desks and chairs, podium at front, clearly visible division of a front and back of the classroom" (p. 8).
2. *Lecture halls*—"large-capacity auditorium with tiered seating plan, podium at front, clearly visible division of a front and back of the classroom" (p. 8).
3. *Technology-infused classrooms*—"similar to the layout of the traditional classroom, but includes computers at the lecture podium, overhead digital projectors, projection screens, and/or video and Internet viewing capabilities" (p. 8).

4. *Laboratory*—"spaces equipped with formal/traditional, often fixed lab equipment for use in experimentation, creation, and design that is associated with specific, discipline-based course content" (p. 9).
5. *Active learning classroom*—modified in-the-round space with "moveable furniture, accessible outlets, ports, computers, mobile whiteboards, projectors, video, Internet, and/or other accessories" to accommodate "diverse pedagogies, to ease the transition between teaching modes, and deliberately engage students in a more interactive learning environment" (p. 9).

Their review of outcome data on these designs found that active learning classrooms, more so than the other designs, yielded higher grades, more discussion, greater movement of instructors while consulting with individuals and groups, and more frequent use of marker boards; such rooms were better accepted by urban students and those in the first or second year of college. Compatible and flexible furniture served to accommodate different learning strategies within the same class session. Similarly, the technology-infused designs promoted greater class participation, an increased sense of responsibility for completing assignments, and a greater desire among students to work collaboratively. Addition of "swivel desks" increased the interactive quality of another classroom, allowing students to know one another better, to ask questions, and to participate in discussions (Henshaw, Edwards, & Bagley, 2011). The authors concluded that formal spaces best facilitated learning through flexible designs that encouraged interaction among students and faculty alike, supported varied pedagogies and strategies, and were equipped with complementary technology. Overall, "classroom design has an impact on teaching methods, instructor behaviors, and student activities" (Painter et al., 2013, p. 11), an observation that is consistent with what others have concluded: "Different classroom types are linked causally to the observed differences in instructor and student behavior" (Brooks, 2012, p. 1).

Recognizing that "a considerable portion of students' learning happens outside of formal spaces," also referred to as *incidental learning* (Marsick & Watkins, 2001), Painter et al. (2013) focused on informal learning spaces as well, evaluating the potential for libraries, social gathering spaces, and corridors to contribute to such ends. Regarding libraries, again in addition to comfort, convenience, and technology, design parameters students rated highest were space flexibility to accommodate varied learning tasks and the availability of resources and staff support. Other features, such as windows, art exhibits, and color, attracted students as well, along with the presence of other people and appropriate services. Quoting from one emeritus librarian, the authors suggested that mission-focused library design "insists, as its point of departure, that students are before all else learners and that library space design should be primarily concerned not with services but with learning" (Bennett, 2007, p. 18).

In an analysis of academic library design, Cunningham and Tabur (2012) constructed the problem as one of hierarchical design; they proposed a four-tiered model that constitutes the ideal learning space (Figure 1.1).

> [The] most basic characteristic is access and linkages at the bottom of the pyramid. Once this attribute meets the primary pragmatic needs of students, they will then look to see if the space also meets their ascending needs of varied learning and social activities. A learning space which not only has these attributes, but also possesses the fourth and highest level attribute of comfort and feel will distinguish itself as an ideal learning space. (p. 1)

A response to Cunningham and Tabur's (2012) challenge to create "transcendent learning space" (p. 5) is perhaps found

Figure 1.1. Hierarchy of Learning Space Attributes

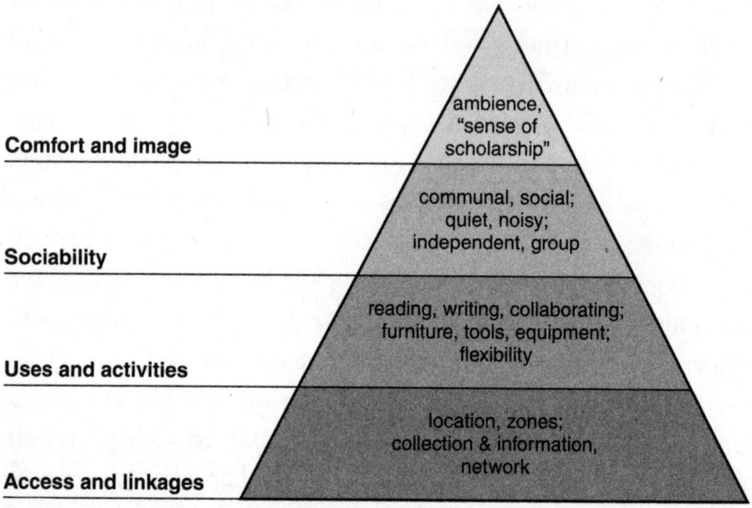

Source: Cunningham, H., & Tabur, S. (2012). Learning space attributes: Reflections on academic library design and its use. *Journal of Learning Spaces*, 1(2). Retrieved from http://libjournal.uncg.edu/index.php/jls/article/view/392/283

best on any number of campuses today in the development of modern learning commons (McMullen, 2008), facilities designed to support relationships in the service of learning, whether "student-to-student, student-to-faculty, student-to-staff, student-to-equipment, or student-to-information" (Lippincott & Greenwell, 2011, p. 1).

Another informal source of learning can be found among social gathering spaces, which include areas of campus that "accommodate large groups of individuals interacting informally for academic, social, and personal purposes" (Cunningham & Tabur, 2012, p. 14) or combination thereof; such spaces are often descriptive of food-service areas, student unions, and outdoor patios and cafes. A recent survey of student life facility trends (Treanor Architects, 2011) indicated that plans for such spaces are on the rise in many institutions, for purposes of strengthening a sense of community, supporting teaching and learning, and attracting and retaining students. Although the research is limited, there is evidence that social learning spaces are effective in the levels of engagement, peer-to-peer interactions, and collaboration they promote, albeit at times at the expense of individual study (Matthews, 2010; Matthews, Adams, & Gannaway, 2009; Matthews, Andrews, & Adams, 2011). In moments of focused collaboration, intermittent exchange, serendipitous encounter, and ambient sociality in such spaces (Crook & Mitchell, 2012), students pursue group work activity, socializing, individual relaxing or reading, interaction with staff, and discussion of career goals (Randall & Wilson, 2009; Wilson & Randall, 2012). Beginning with entryways and proceeding through, the physical designs of such facilities offer an array of possible and probable influences. For example, the proxemics associated with seating arrangements in a student union lounge can either promote or inhibit social interaction. Messages of material artifacts can signal a sense of belonging (or rejection), a feeling of being welcomed (or ignored), a sense of safety (or risk), and a sense of role, worth, and value (Banning, Middleton, & Deniston, 2008), enhancing or detracting from students' ability to cope with college stress. Consider, for example, the contrasts between a flyer advertising an upcoming gay, lesbian, bisexual, and transgendered awareness week and a hostile homophobic graffiti found in a campus restroom; a student wheelchair user anticipating the excitement of an on-campus event but who cannot find an accessible entrance to the hosting facility; and a resolution of commitment to campus diversity but posters that never feature any race other than Caucasian. Processes of student growth and development are inevitably hindered by such undeserved stress.

Another significant social space with potential for enhancing learning is found where many students live: residence halls. In her seminal work on the questions and dreams of young adults, Parks (2000), citing John Henry Newman on the "power of the social environment to train, mold, and enlarge the mind," noted that if

Newman "had to choose between a school without residence hall life and one with only the life of the residence hall, he would choose the latter, where 'the conversation of all is a series of lectures to each' (Newman, 1982, p. 110)" (Parks, 2000, p. 95). Lawless (2012) posted what she described as "rudimentary design ideas for creating academic residential spaces that benefit both the physical and social well-being of the student."

- Small individual living spaces to foster involvement and interaction.
- Overall, low- to mid-rise buildings (five or fewer floors) with no more than 500 residents total to foster community oriented traffic and interaction patterns.
- Multiple, small social and study spaces to increase incidental social opportunities and increased sense of secondary, neighborhood-like personal space.
- Use of hybrid style spaces, for example a suite designed with ten to twelve rooms opening onto common living, dining, and kitchen facilities.
- Space to complement the academic programming, for example, flexible rooms for formal study space, social activity, or informal learning opportunities
- Flexible opportunities for customization by residents, for example adaptable furnishings, paintable surfaces, bulletin or whiteboard walls and doors. (Retrieved from: http://www.treanorarchitects.com/news/sector/treanor-architects/2012–01–30/residence-hall-design-success-student-learning/)

Supplementary to social spaces are also those found by students themselves, sometimes outside offices or along corridors, where they often spend a few moments, either alone or with others, connecting online or reviewing assignments prior to their next class or appointment. As potential in between learning spaces, they need to be welcoming with appropriate aesthetics and seating comfort and access to power outlets.

Another type of informal learning space is identified in the concept of a *third place* (Oldenburg, 1989); these are typically coffee shops and bookstores adjacent to many institutions. A third place is a "setting beyond home and work (the 'first' and 'second' places respectively) in which people relax in good company and do so on a regular basis" (p. 2). Furthermore, they function as spaces that bring people together and introduce them to each other and the community. They serve as a source for new friends and a place to plan activities and have fun and to engage in important conversation. Oldenburg (1989, p. xxiii) underscored the role of place in these functions: "An individual can have many friends and engage them often only if there is a place he or she can visit daily and which plays hosts to their meetings." Much of the value of such spaces in students' lives is that they encourage informal learning through discussion and the formation of student communities (Oldenburg, 1997; Stantasiero, 2002). When asked to identify such a place, 80 percent of students in one recent study (Banning, Clemons, McKelfresh, & Gibbs, 2010) had no problem locating and describing one, where most visited at least once a week or more for socializing and conversation, eating and drinking, and reading and studying. For the students of Bowling Green State University (OH), that place—a coffee-shop-used-bookstore-music-venue on South Main Street—has been known affectionately among them for twenty-five years as Grounds (an abbreviated form of its commercial name, *Grounds for Thought*). In spite of new student reports of frequently or occasionally feeling lonely or homesick and worried about meeting new people (Keup & Stolzenberg, 2004), they also express disappointment with how campuses address social life (Miller, Bender, & Schuh, 2005), perhaps reflecting the limited availability of third-place spaces on campus. Students need third places to talk with friends away from the complexities of the classroom and their campus experiences.

Complementary to third places are those spaces where students go to rest, relax, unwind, recuperate, and feel safe (Banning et al., 2010). So named *restorative places* (Staats, 2012), they offer relief from the stresses of everyday life and might include nature, the home, the workplace, museums, and religious settings. According to Kaplan, Kaplan, and Ryan (1998), such places must be identifiable, away from any source of stress, and hold fascination for the individual so one can engage in thinking, wondering, figuring out things, and feeling congruent with where one wants to be. Arguably, college students encounter many stresses (Vye, Scholljegerdes, & Welch, 2007) as they sort through a full range of psychosocial concerns (Chickering & Reisser, 1993) and respond to the challenges of life and learning. Locating a secret escape on or off campus is an important task for finding one's way through the college experience. A related study (Banning et al., 2010) found that 45 percent of a sampled group of students could identify their restorative place on campus, usually in buildings or a setting with designed water features, gardens, and park areas, where they often read or studied alone. The 55 percent who named off-campus restorative sites identified various hiking trails, lakes, wooded areas, and mountains. One of five students indicated seeking out a restorative place every day, while 67 percent did so at least once a week.

Last, even campus walkways, a current popular feature in institutional master plans (Kenney, Dumont, & Kenney, 2005), can contribute to the mix of campus learning outcomes through the message-bearing pedestrian experiences of safety, functionality, pleasure, and institutional culture. Such was the case with the incidental learning Eric encountered in the opening scenario as he explored Mountain Pass Community College. A campus walking tour, depending on its features and amenities, might convey an immediate sense of security or threat. For example, emergency phones, adequate lighting, and signage to regulate bicycle and skateboard traffic suggest one thing; lack of step railings, damaged benches, and worn landscaping suggest another message. Issues of convenience and accessibility are also apparent in the functional experience of a campus. Efficient and barrier-free pedestrian routes improve wayfinding and convey a sense of good design, while sitting walls, benches, flowers, and weather protective features can make for an overall pleasant experience. Finally, in the course of finding one's way, encounters with artifacts of material culture tacitly instruct pedestrians further about what is important and what is valued in the institution.

In summary, campus facilities that support formal and informal learning do so primarily through their capacity to connect peers to one another and to respected mentors and resources. However, in the end, it must be recognized that to support whole student learning, access to a balance of both private quiet spaces and socially interactive spaces is required. Ultimately the impact of these spaces is realized in their capacity for developing "social networks with peers that can lead to greater engagement in active and collaborative learning and that facilitates the sharing of knowledge to meet academic challenges" (Matthews, Adams, & Gannaway, 2009, as cited in Painter et al., 2013 p. 18). Institutional leaders intent on strengthening their commitment to student learning would be wise to consult the work of Felix and Brown (2011) and Felix (2011), which proposed a learning space performance rating system (http://www.educause.edu/eli/initiatives/learning-space-rating-system) for campus planners as they consider options in building and renovation. Focusing on both spatial and institutional characteristics, their system attempts to:

- [Create] a common set of measurable criteria to guide the planning, design, and support of learning spaces.

- [Encourage] the design of learning spaces that promote active learning and student engagement
- [Enable] institutions to standardize design and support across campus
- [Facilitate] interinstitutional sharing of best practices in learning space design and comparison with peer institutions
- [Measure] institutional progress toward strategic active learning goals (Felix & Brown, 2011)

Connecting Through Sense of Place

The study of the concept of place draws widely from a multidisciplinary base to include contributions from "environmental psychology, sociology, community psychology, human geography, cultural anthropology, gerontology, demography, urban studies, leisure sciences and tourism, forestry, architecture and planning, and economics" (Lewicka, 2011, p. 207). From these related and disparate fields has come a rich deposit of constructs and tools that lend themselves to further understanding how a sense of place evolves within an institution and how participants connect to it. They include wayfinding, placemaking and placemarking, public space, servicescape, atmospherics, and postoccupancy evaluation. Collectively, application of these concepts can improve the design of campus space, the ease with which constituents connect with it, and ultimately the quality of sense of place experienced by those who use it.

Wayfinding

The evening before opening day classes in most institutions, the campus is filled with map-and-flashlight-toting (or cell-phone-app-viewing) students who are out exploring, giving special attention to the buildings and rooms where their first scheduled classes are to meet the next day. No student wants to appear lost, and the prospect of not knowing where to go at the very least is unsettling. The solution, as students quickly intuit, is to acquire "the knowledge or understanding of self in relation to [one's] surroundings (built or natural)" (Devlin, 2012, p. 42), or in other words, to find one's way around campus.

Passini (2002) noted that wayfinding involves two important aspects: the organization of space and circulation and the environmental communications provided by signs and graphics. It is through the location of buildings, walkways, paths, signs, symbols, supplemented by current you-are-here maps or apps and clear building identifications, that a campus earns the distinction of being user friendly and provides enjoyable wayfinding, in particular for visitors.

Wayfinding and comfort go hand in hand in the navigation of campus space. The best designed colleges and universities facilitate this through legible environments, that is, those with open and distinctive landmarks and a landscape through which one could safely wander but not become lost. The ease with which one succeeds at this is a function of previous experiences and immediate cues provided in the setting about how to plan and carry out movement. Eric's limited exposure to a college campus prior to visiting MPCC added to the puzzlement he encountered in misplaced signs and erroneous directions once he arrived. The consequences of such experiences for individuals are immediate.

> Most people find that wayfinding difficulties and disorientation are highly stressful even in benign cases when the user of a setting is merely confused or delayed. Total disorientation and the sensation of being lost can be a frightening experience and can lead to quite severe emotional reactions including anxiety and insecurity. Self-esteem and assessments of competence may also be affected. (Passini, 2002, p. 96)

Failure to attend to concerns of campus wayfinding also exerts a negative functional impact on the institution that "is measurable in terms of efficiency and monetary value" (Arthur & Passini, 1992, p. 11).

Campuses intent on strengthening the mechanics of wayfinding should pay heed to the kinds of questions newcomers and visitors often bring with them as they move through the campus environment. Where is the student union? Where is the entrance to this building? Is there an elevator? Where are the campus direction signs? Is there a you-are-here map available? Can someone explain this information? Why is it so complicated to find that office? And in today's digital world the expected question is: Does this college have an app for that?

As institutions seek to make their environments more inviting and hospitable to all users, and ultimately to implement a more positive sense of place about them, wayfinding must be given serious consideration.

Placemaking and Placemarking

Two institutional strategies that can add to the quality of sense of place on campus are placemaking and placemarking. *Placemaking* is about the creation, transformation, maintenance, and renovation of places we inhabit (Schneekloth & Shibley, 1995). A major focus today in college and university master planning is how campus designs contribute to the achievement of institutional mission. Justification for various projects often includes reference to strengthening placemaking and thus a sense of place. As Dober (1992) articulated in a comprehensive approach to campus design, the principal components of any institution are its "buildings, landscapes, and circulation systems" (p. 4). These components come together in an institutional metaphor that guides the "positioning and arrangement of campus land uses and pedestrian and vehicular routes, the location of buildings and functional open spaces ... the definition of edges, and the interface between campus and environs" (p. 4). Placemarking, on the other hand, focuses on "certain physical attributes which give a campus a visual uniqueness appropriately its own" (Dober, 1992, p. 5), including landmarks, style, materials, and landscapes. The combination of these elements leads to a distinct and memorable sense of place on campus. As activities, "placemaking resembles town planning, producing the larger picture of the future, while placemarking involves the specifics of campus architecture, landscape architecture, and site engineering" (Dober, 1992, pp. 229–231). Thus, an institution committed to educational purposes and student engagement can enhance its sense of place for students by focusing placemaking and placemarking efforts on fulfilling its planning metaphor as a community of learning.

Placebuilding

Another important aspect of sense of place on the college and university campus is how it is connected to other places (Cronon, 1992; Cresswell, 2004), and in particular to the community in which it resides. "Do the patterns of open space and building that are conventionally associated with 'campus' have a place within neighborhoods that the institution influences? Conversely, should the apparatus of the city [or community] have something to say about how campus spaces are formed?" (Lyndon, 2005, p. 3). Institutions engage in place building for purposes of situating themselves as one entity within a larger environment. Thomas (2004) and Thomas and Cross (2007) conceptualized four such possibilities. *Exploitive* institutions view themselves as independent agents, with little to no obligation to the places in which they are located; the larger community is thus exploited as a resource for their use to fulfill organizational needs. *Contingent* institutions consider themselves part of, but having no specific responsibility to, the larger community; they look to what the community can do for them and in turn agree to not disturb or question the norms of the community. *Contributive* institutions see themselves as contributing in some way to the well-being of the larger community, often times through fundraising efforts. *Transformational* institutions see themselves as interdependent change agents within the larger community, who are trying to improve the conditions of both through various partnerships.

As both a strategy for strengthening the sense of place within a college or university, the place-building framework can serve to inform a variety of common campus concerns, such as issues of town–gown relationships and the interrelationships of intrainstitutional subunits. For example, Kuk, Thomas, and Banning (2008) conceptualized student organizations and their connection to the broader institution through this scheme, and Kuk, Banning, and Thomas (2009) explored how the model could be used to understand and promote the civic engagement efforts of student organizations.

Public Spaces

The notion of public space (Gehl & Svarre, 2013) also contributes to the mix of ideas informing the creation of a sense of place on campus. Public spaces, which include both physical features and the activities that ensue in them, frame the pedestrian experience in a college or university and are often the first to be encountered by visitors and potential enrollees; they also serve as the in between space of the college experience. How an institution approaches public space on campus can either detract from or affirm a sense of place among participants. In related research on new housing developments, Francis, Giles-Corti, Wood, and Knuiman (2012) found that public space quality is a correlate of sense of community among residents. Sucher (1995) suggested that, in terms of public space, good design is "how well it fosters and encourages communication" (p. 166). Thus, campuses that affirm a sense of place about them feature good wayfinding, sufficient seating, generous use of green spaces, settings for games and activities, outlets for food and other vendors, limited impact of parking lots and vehicular traffic, and opportunities to enjoy the sunlight and benefit from the incidental learning that occurs when people come together. Banning (2002) called for increased attention to how student learning and development could be fostered by designing campus environments that were safe for walking, that were attractive for resting and enjoying the moment, and that would encourage social discourse.

Kenney, Dumont, and Kenney (2005) also emphasized the learning potential of public spaces on campus as they relate to the mission of higher education: "Places set aside for automobiles are almost never a part of the learning campus. But beautiful outdoor spaces framed by buildings often are. So are noisy, bustling, crowded public places—cafes, coffee shops, public computer terminals, perhaps even the mail room" (pp. 40–41). The authors further identified key design principles for increasing students' opportunities for engagement and learning on campus:

- A pedestrian campus environment reinforced by appropriate closeness of buildings (density) and by juxtaposition of activities that complement one another (mixed use).
- Indoor and outdoor social spaces scattered throughout the overall framework of the campus (not just in the campus center), such as lounges in the residence halls, meeting spaces in the lobbies of buildings, and outdoor sitting areas.
- Informal settings that provide opportunities for interaction, including adding cafes, coffee shops, and bistros in various places on campus. Providing food in multiple locations is clearly a draw both for faculty and for students.
- Integration into the wider community to take advantage of community-based learning resources, and to contribute to (and learn to be a responsible part of) the larger community.

- Access to technology and digital communication, including opportunities to socialize online and in person while online.
- Places and opportunities to participate in co-curricular activities. (pp. 40–41)

In addition, the authors stressed the importance of building layout and open public spaces in a campus master plan, calling for careful consideration of the density of their placement: "Putting buildings and uses in close proximity is a key factor for a thriving community. This proximity improves the chances that people will cross paths with other people, thus increasing the likelihood for spontaneous interaction and exchange of ideas, which are fundamental to collegiality and to interdisciplinary communication" (p. 111). They concluded, "When a place promotes interaction through compactness appropriate to its size, location, and culture, then the benefits of density may be realized even in a small, rural setting" (p. 105). The effectiveness of a campus in doing so may depend largely on its layout, as implicated in the distinction between sociofugal and sociopetal spaces (Osmond, 1957)—two major systems for patterning space: "Sociofugal space (gridlike) tends to keep people apart and suppress communication while sociopetal space (radial) does just the opposite. It brings people together and stimulates interaction as routes merge and overlap" (Howard, 2008). Thus, like other spaces in the institution, those that are public offer an important asset for achieving the educational purposes of a college or university. Focusing more intentionally on their use can only strengthen students' experiences of a sense of place in them.

Servicescape and Atmospherics of Place

Two concepts from the literature on marketing and retailing, servicescape and atmospherics, offer additional tools for shaping the quality of sense of place at an institution. Whether understood in terms of the increasing number of retail opportunities sponsored by many campuses or as general strategies for presentation of the campus to consumers, such ideas emphasize the importance of the service environs on campus and the service experience of those who encounter them. From the very first contact with an institution, whether as a visitor or potential student and parent, the interplay of these dynamics creates an immediate and significant impression that feeds into the shaping of a sense of place about a college or university. The physical environment and material culture of an admissions office, a university union, a bookstore, an advising center, and a financial aid office, for example, constitute much of the servicescape encountered in the early stages of the college experience. The ambient conditions of temperature, humidity, air quality, smells, sounds, light, and comfort (Ford & Heaton, 2000)—and the quality of service itself—often determine how a consumer is likely to proceed. An uncomfortable waiting area or limited lighting could send an individual back to the parking lot, but pleasant human scale surroundings can go a long way in making a necessary delay more acceptable. The focus of servicescape is to enhance the sense of hospitality felt and the quality of guest or consumer experience (Ezeh & Harris, 2007). Atmospherics also figure into the mix of creating a sense of place by focusing on the transactional experience in the setting (Thang & Tan, 2003). One employee misstep can lead to a bad impression of the whole; likewise, one above-and-beyond effort can result in a positive story told time and again. The lesson of these two concepts is that paying attention to the details of enacting the institutional mission through allocation and display of campus spaces may be as important as what is espoused.

Postoccupancy Evaluation

Finally, a sense of place is a quality that is never finalized in any setting but rather an objective that must be nurtured and maintained continuously. While one group of individuals might experience a campus at one point, another at a different time might recall something quite different about the setting. Thus, just as the characteristics of places evolve, so, too, do the needs of individuals who engage in them. Postoccupancy evaluation, in its narrowest application, is the process of reevaluating building performance (Gabr & Al-Sallal, 2003). Typically, a building is evaluated regarding its systems performance (e.g., heat, air, ventilation), along with its functionality in relation to its occupants and intended uses. The evaluation is carried out after the building has had sufficient use for the appropriate assessments to be made. Such an analysis has led more than one campus administrator to conclude, "I'd like to tear it down," as was the sentiment at the University of California at Berkeley where the overpowering Evans Hall, once characterized as a fortress or prison, never fulfilled its purpose (Keller, 2007). But a broader interpretation of this process makes it useful in other campus applications, such as evaluating campus use patterns, effects of material culture, pedestrian experiences, engagement with natural environments, and interactions with other facilities. Postoccupancy evaluation has a long history of methods and procedures (Mallory-Hill, Preiser, & Watson, 2012; Preiser, 1989), and if these can be extended to the broader notion of sense of place and include users from present, past, and prospective students and current faculty, staff, and visitors (Sanoff, 2000), then such methods can enhance the future of campus placemaking and sense of community (Schneekloth & Shibley, 1995). Monitoring and soliciting participant impressions and experiences in a setting is an ongoing effort at any institution aspiring to a strong sense of place, and postoccupancy evaluation is one of a number of institutional tools effective for achieving such ends.

Gordon Gee, an eight-time college president at five different institutions, once commented, "In accepting the significance of how decisions regarding bricks and mortar affect not only individual programs but also our ability as an institution to sustain our mission, we begin to fulfill our highest potential" (as cited in

Kenney, Dumont, & Kenney, 2005, p. viii). Placemaking on the college and university campus must be a mission-driven process involving all participants and stakeholders, and to nurture a sense of place about an institution requires both intention and good design. Whether built or natural, components of the campus physical environment figure prominently in the process and must be considered a critical asset that warrants the attention and full support of institutional decision-makers.

In a seminal piece on the sense of place and the college campus, Sturner (1972) charted an agenda for institutional design that continues to play out among campus planners today, and perhaps even more so, as interest in student learning has recaptured the academy's attention at a time when campus construction, renovation, and renewal are once again rising to the top of the higher education agenda. What was done poorly in the past can be corrected; what has been imagined for the future can find form and function once again. Sturner (1972) articulated six precepts of an environmental code to guide this process and to be essential for supporting student engagement and learning:

1. "The university is a total environment, a system of exploratory activities occurring in various forms of order and disorder, which take place in a particular physical setting" (p. 98).
2. "The physical environment, that which houses the formal learning component, simultaneously reflects and shapes, is both a response to and a cause of, the values and practices of an educational institution" (p. 98).
3. "The design and construction of the physical aspects of the university should complement and strengthen the mission of the university to stimulate students in the effective use of learning opportunities. The physical environment should facilitate the process

by which men and women seek to understand themselves and others through experiential and vicarious encounters with the extensions of man and nature" (p. 99).

4. "The physical environment of the campus should be integrated into an organic habitat or 'village' which reflects and instills a tactile sense of place" (p. 99).
5. "The physical environment of a given campus should not only mirror and support the learning process in general, but it also should reflect the distinctive values and aspirations of those who actually live at and use a particular college or university" (p. 100).
6. "Campuses cannot be planned, designed, and constructed for the inhabitants by others. They must be formed by, for, and of the students, faculty, and staff. This essential role of the user in shaping [one's] own habitat can be guaranteed only by inclusion of students, faculty, and staff in the decision-making processes that affect the design and construction of buildings, transportation systems, landscaping, and decorations." (pp. 100–101)

Contained in the composite of these tenets is a yet relevant prescription for any postsecondary institution intent on creating a sense of place for supporting student learning and success. Keeping in mind these tenets and the concept of place that underlies them, this chapter surveyed the impact of the campus physical environment as the first component of our framework for understanding how the designs of colleges and universities exert their influence on students, especially as they shape opportunities for their learning, growth, and development. We now turn our attention in the next chapter to the aggregate impact of those who come to occupy our campuses.

Questions for Discussion

1. What are the signature buildings on your campus, and what messages do they convey about your institution?
2. If you were to map out a tour of your campus, where would you lead prospective students and why? What would you say about the natural environment of your campus?
3. Where are the sociopetal spaces on your campus that promote student–faculty interaction?
4. If you were to design a new facility on your campus, what would it be, and what purposes would it serve?
5. What recommendations would you offer for renovating a current space on your campus and for what purposes?

2

Aggregate Environments:

The Impact of Human Characteristics

Consider the following scene at Midwestern University as a group of students discuss adjustments to college life during a biweekly First Year Seminar meeting. Led by a faculty moderator, an orientation staff member, and one senior student, group members are focusing on some of the experiences they encountered during their first month on campus.

Scenario: They're Not Like Me

"So, how is everything going in your accounting program, Sarah?" asked the faculty moderator.

"Not so well, Dr. Cummings," she replied. "I'm not so sure that being in the accounting department, and taking accounting courses, is a good fit for me. I can do that stuff, but I don't really enjoy it all that much. I'm hoping to meet with my faculty advisor next week to talk about it. Maybe I should think about another major, but I'm not sure."

Phil, a declared theater arts major, was anxious to say how thrilled he was to become acquainted with so many other students who shared his interests. "I always felt out of place with most of my friends in high school. None of them were all that involved. Here it seems like everybody wants to get in on the act. It's great!"

Mike, a transfer social work major from a nearby small private college, had an experience similar to Phil's, but for somewhat different reasons. "I've already met a lot of different kinds of people at this university," Mike said, "and I have so many more choices. I don't feel like I have to be like everybody else anymore." He went on to say how all the students seemed so much alike at his previous institution and how difficult it was to be different from them. "It seemed like I was always in a fishbowl, with everyone watching, and no place to get away."

"Hey man, I know what you mean," said Felix, a Latino student who was seriously questioning whether he was going to stay for the remainder of the semester. In fact, two of his friends from high school had already left. Felix was doing fine in his classwork as a biology major, but it was becoming increasingly difficult for him on a day-to-day basis to feel like he belonged at the university. "When I walk down the sidewalk, in between classes, all I see are White faces. Nobody looks like someone I should know. It's weird." He continued by saying how he couldn't wait to get home the following weekend to a place that looked and felt familiar.

Jill, a student who was an undecided major and whose parents both graduated from Midwestern University, acknowledged how uneasy she felt during the first few weeks of school until she became involved in a sorority. "This school is really big compared with my high school, and I wasn't really sure what it was going to be like to make friends here. But I'm really comfortable in my sorority now. The friends I met remind me a lot of some of my friends back home. We have a lot in common," she said enthusiastically.

"Well, it sounds like some of you have really found your spot, and some might be questioning whether this is the best place for you," said Carolyn, an orientation staff member.

"You got that right!" responded Felix.

"What do you think might make the difference for all of you this semester?" asked Greg, the senior in the group.

"I know I'll feel a lot better when I find a major I like," said Sarah.

"I think it probably has a lot to do with the people you hang out with and the friends you make, too," said Phil.

"Yeah," agreed Jill, "somehow, being with friends who like the same things you do makes it a lot easier."

"As long as you have a chance to meet others, too, though," Mike reminded the group. "We can't all be alike!"

Although these incidents may reflect aspects that are truly unique to each student in the group, collectively their experiences share a common dynamic basic to understanding the human aggregate component of environments presented in this chapter. That is, environments are transmitted through people, and the dominant features of any given environment are partially a function of the collective characteristics of the individuals who inhabit it (Holland, 1973). For the students in this opening scenario, the experience of Midwestern University the first few weeks on campus was greatly influenced by the collective composition of people with whom they interacted in residence halls, classes, academic departments, student groups, and campus organizations. For Phil, Mike, and Jill, they found a source of congruence and satisfaction in their association with others; for Sarah and Felix, disparities of interests or personal-cultural characteristics caused them to question whether they even belonged at Midwestern.

Achieving an early sense of belonging at an institution is pivotal for any student, a point underscored in the conclusion to a recent ten-year study (Chambliss & Takacs, 2014, p. 155) of the student experience at one liberal arts college in the Northeast:

> Relationships are central to a successful college experience. They are the necessary precondition, the daily motivator, and the most valuable outcome … Relationships shape in detail students' experience: What courses they take or majors they declare; whether they play a sport or join an extracurricular activity; whether they gain skills, grow ethically, or learn whatever is offered in various programs. Relationships are important because they raise or suppress the motivation to learn; a good college fosters the relationships that lead to motivation.

Thus, in the larger picture of student learning, the dynamics of human aggregates explored in this chapter figure prominently in supporting student success.

Environments as People

Moos (1986) noted, "The character of an environment is implicitly dependent on the typical characteristics of its members" (p. 286). Such human characteristics influence the degree to which people are attracted to, satisfied within, and retained by those environments. Thus, academic departments, depending on the nature of their work and as reflected in the collective characteristics of present members, will attract, satisfy, and retain students and faculty of certain types. Sarah's concern in the opening scenario reflected the fact that she found few similarities with, and therefore little enjoyment from, the characteristics of faculty and students in the accounting department. In like manner, as implicated in Felix's assessment, campuses dominated by one cultural, ethnic, or age-based group are inherently challenging and therefore are less likely to attract, satisfy, or retain individuals who do not share traits with the dominant group. Likewise, but with different results, is the case of Jill, who found that a student organization focusing on special interests and traditions (a sorority) enhanced her satisfaction by contributing to a sense of fit between her and the campus. What these vignettes suggest is that any information about individuals in an environment collectively informs the aggregate components of an environment. From each of the theoretical perspectives reviewed in this chapter, information about the collective characteristics of environmental inhabitants, whether demographic (e.g., gender, age, or race-ethnicity) or psychological (e.g., personality types, interests, styles, strengths), is predictive of the dominant features of the environment. We now turn to a consideration of a sampling of human aggregate models found in the literature on college students and their campuses.

Students of a Feather

A number of researchers have examined differences attributed to various human aggregates on college and university campuses. Employing what Astin (1993) called a "taxonomic or typological language that implicitly sorts students into a variety of discrete categories or boxes" (p. 36), a variety of models have emerged from this line of inquiry. Among the first to do so were Clark and Trow (1966), who applied the concept of student subcultures to understand the influence of peer groups on campus. In their pioneering work, the researchers described four "broad patterns of student orientation toward college [or student subcultures], which tend to give meaning to the informed relations among students" (Walsh, 1973, p. 41): academics, nonconformists, collegiates, and vocational students. Collegiates, for example, strongly identify with the institution and place a premium on campus social life, extracurricular activities, athletics, living group functions, and intimate friendships. Could Indiana University, for example, sustain its rich tradition of residence life, campus activities, Greek letter organizations, and intercollegiate athletics without a significant collegiate student subculture? In contrast, nonconformists seemed to "value and reward individualistic styles, concern for personal identity and self-awareness, and, frequently, contempt for organized society" (Walsh, 1973, p. 42). Where would Evergreen State University or Oberlin College be without such a student subculture? The point of Clark and Trow's analysis is that the character of an institution is partially a function of the dominance of one or more extant student subcultures. As moderators of peer influence, student subcultures on any campus can play an important role, for good or otherwise, in introducing students to and maintaining their engagement in the learning process. Whatever their nature, it is critical to understand their collective influence on the overall campus environment.

Focusing on similar dynamics, other researchers have since examined the aggregate influences of student vocational interests (Holland, 1973), personality types (Myers, 1980), learning and adaptive styles (Kolb, 1984), personal strengths (Clifton, 1997; Clifton & Harter, 2003), and empirically derived student engagement types (Astin, 1993; Kuh, Hu, & Vesper, 2000).

These lines of research are summarized with relevant illustrations and examples grounded in the postsecondary context. Rather than a comprehensive review, these summaries merely introduce the key concepts of each approach as it illustrates the basic dynamics of the human aggregate component of campus environments.

Vocational Interests

According to Holland (1973), "We can characterize people by their resemblance to each of six personality types: realistic, investigative, artistic, social, enterprising, and conventional" (p. 2). Thus, individuals' interests, activities, and behaviors can be assumed to be a direct reflection of their personalities that, in turn, shape the development of interests and the degree of attraction to various experiences. A description of each of these six types contains a characteristic set of preferences, activities, competencies, values, and interests (Exhibit 2.1).

Exhibit 2.1. Holland Vocational Interest-Personality Types

Realistic—prefers activities that entail the explicit, ordered, or systematic manipulation of objects, tools, machines, animals; averse to educational or therapeutic activities; perceives self as having mechanical and athletic ability and lacking ability in human relations; values concrete things or tangible personal characteristics—money, power, status.

Investigative—prefers activities that entail the observational, symbolic, systematic, and creative investigation of physical, biological, and cultural phenomena to understand and control such phenomena; averse to persuasive, social, and repetitive activities; sees self as scholarly, intellectually self-confident, and having mathematical and scientific ability but lacking in leadership ability.

Artistic—prefers ambiguous, free, unsystematized activities that entail the manipulation of physical, verbal, or human materials to create art forms or products; averse to explicit, systematic, and ordered activities; shows self to be complicated, disorderly, emotional, feminine, idealistic, imaginative, impractical, impulsive, independent, introspective, intuitive, nonconforming, and original.

Social—prefers activities that entail the manipulation of others to inform, train, develop, cure, or enlighten; averse to explicit, ordered, systematic activities involving materials, tools, or machines; perceives self as liking to help others, understanding of others, having teaching ability, and lacking mechanical and scientific skills.

Enterprising—prefers activities that entail the manipulation of others to attain organizational goals or economic gain; exhibit behavioral tendencies that lead to an acquisition of leadership, interpersonal, and persuasive competencies, and to a deficit in scientific competencies.

Conventional—prefers the explicit, ordered, systematic manipulation of data, such as keeping records, filing materials, reproducing materials, organizing written and numerical data according to a prescribed plan, operating business machines and data processing machines to attain organizational or economic goals.

Source: Holland (1973, pp. 14–17)

Extending his typology into a model of human environments, Holland (1973) concluded that information about the collective personalities in an environment is the key to understanding its dominant features. Assessment of various interests, activities, and behaviors represented among the participants of any given environment constitutes an adequate measure of that environment. Holland then built a framework for understanding various human aggregates with reference to each of the vocational interest personality types. Thus, social environments encourage and reinforce those behaviors, attitudes, skills, and interests most compatible with characteristics of social personalities; enterprising environments reinforce enterprising characteristics, and so on. The six templates of personality patterns described in Holland's typology become frames for understanding the collective features of human environments. Sarah, in the opening scenario, knew that something was amiss with her participation in the accounting program, but she lacked a formal understanding of how her interests seemed to vary significantly from those of the dominant Conventional type in her department.

Personality Types

One of the more widely disseminated and persistent models in the literature on personality differences has been the work of Isabel Myers and Katherine Briggs (Myers, 1980; Myers & McCaulley, 1985), which is based on Jung's (1923/1971) theory of psychological type. Similar to other typologies, this model employs the assumption that "much seemingly random variation in behavior is actually quite orderly, being due to basic differences in the way individuals prefer to use their perception and judgment" (Myers & McCaulley, p. 1). According to the authors, "Perception involves all the ways of becoming aware of things, people, happenings, or ideas. Judgment involves all the ways of coming to conclusions about what has been perceived.... [People] differ correspondingly in their reactions, interests, values, motivations, and skills" (p. 1).

Through application of the Myers-Briggs Type Indicator (MBTI) (Myers & McCaulley, 1985), individual differences are described in terms of four dichotomous personality dimensions: extraversion (E) or introversion (I); sensing (S) or intuition (N); thinking (T) or feeling (F); and judgment (J) or perception (P). The extraversion–introversion (EI) dimension, for example, assesses whether an individual prefers to direct mental activities (i.e., perceiving and judging) toward the external world of people and objects, as extraverts do, or toward the inner world of concepts and ideas, as do introverts. The various combinations of these dimensions yield sixteen different personality types, each with a unique set of preferred attitudes, processes, and styles of dealing with the world. Thus, in terms of learning, an extraverted, intuitive, thinking, and perceiving (ENTP) student might be drawn to an open discussion of the theory behind a phenomenon, while an introverted, sensing, feeling, judger (ISFJ) might be more inclined toward reflecting on the details and impact of its applications. One can imagine a much different experience, say, of an introverted judging student versus an extraverted perceiving one in a small, open-ended, discussion-based seminar; the lack of structure and closure for one might be the perfect opportunity for the other. A classroom dominated by one type or another could well set the tone for how it is likely to proceed and succeed.

The personality differences defined in this model have been shown to be useful in understanding peoples' occupational interests, interrelationships, and learning styles (Myers, 1980). Others have also applied the Myers-Briggs model extensively to campus issues of retention, the design of residential environments, student involvement, advising and counseling, career planning, and effective teaching (Provost & Anchors, 1987). Although not without its critics and detractors (Pittenger, 1993, 2005), the Myers-Briggs typology, if not empirically definitive, does offer a conceptual framework that seems to make intuitive sense in sorting through differences of personality and preferences. Patterns of personality differences are apparent to most, and having a language to express those differences is perhaps the real contribution of such theories.

Learning Styles

Although a model meant initially for understanding the learning cycle, Kolb's (1984) theory of experiential learning, identified in the most recent iteration as the experiential learning theory (ELT), (Kolb & Kolb, 2012) is helpful in examining the aggregate effects of academic environments in particular, such as academic departments, majors, and classrooms. Kolb and Kolb (2012) described two axes related to the learning process: a vertical continuum from the concrete (CE) to the abstract (AC) (grasping dimension), intersected by a horizontal continuum from the active (AE) to the passive (RO) (transforming dimension). Some individuals prefer concrete experience as a learning mode, whereas others prefer abstract conceptualization; some prefer to actively experiment, whereas others would rather simply reflect on the situation. Some also exhibit simultaneous preferences for two or more of these modes. The four modes (i.e., experiencing, reflecting, thinking, and acting) manifest themselves in predictable orientations toward learning as well as reflect associated differences in values and approaches to a variety of tasks. In combination, they yield nine learning styles that are at once characteristic, but also somewhat fluid, across various situations and contexts: experiencing, diverging, reflecting, assimilating, thinking, converging, acting, accommodating, and balancing (Kolb & Kolb, 2005, 2012). Each style exhibits a range of strengths and preferences when it comes to learning (Exhibit 2.2).

Exhibit 2.2. Kolb Learning Styles

Experiencing—[emphasizes] feeling (CE), while balancing acting (AE) and reflecting (RO). Their greatest strengths reside in their ability to deeply involve themselves in concrete experiences while being equally comfortable in the outer world of action and the inner world of reflection. They are particularly adept in relationships with people. They learn by actively involving themselves in new and challenging situations and by stepping back and reflecting on their experiences from differing points of view. They love hands-on activities, but also learn by carefully observing the world around them. Informal learning situations, working in groups, role-playing, brainstorming, or fieldwork may appeal to them. Because they place the least emphasis on Abstract Conceptualization they sometimes are disorganized, lacking plans and theories to guide them.

Reflecting—[emphasizes] reflection (RO) while balancing feeling (CE) and thinking (AC). The learning strengths of this style are the capacity for deep reflection informed by the ability to be both feeling oriented and conceptual. They learn by combining the abilities of creative idea generation and putting ideas into concise, logical form. They feel equally at home in reflection on experiencing and thinking. As a result, they have a rich and intuitive understanding of matters of importance to them. They enjoy exploring "why" things are the way they are, but also thrive in uncovering "what" makes the world turn. They thrive in learning environments rich in discussions, interactions, and through readings that provide them with a deeper understanding of themselves and the world around them. Because of their low emphasis on Active Experimentation they have trouble in putting plans into action, spending much time buried in thought. Because action is short-circuited in the learning cycle, their thoughts are about their feelings rather than direct actions. This imbalanced cycle lacks the rejuvenation provided by testing ideas in action.

Thinking—[emphasizes] thinking (AC) while balancing reflecting (RO) and acting (AE). They are deep thinkers who are able to inductively develop a particular concept or idea and deductively evaluate its validity and practicality by testing them in the real world. They can draw both on the rich inner world of reflection and abstraction and outer world of action. They thrive on creating conceptual models that can be applied or generalized to other situations. Because they place little emphasis on feeling in their style, they value being logical and unemotional. They may be uncomfortable with personal relationships and prefer working alone. They learn best in a well-structured learning environment in which they can design or conduct scientific experiments, or manipulate data.

Acting—[emphasizes] acting (AE) while balancing feeling (CE) and thinking (AC). They combine the ability to find solutions to questions or problems based on their technical analysis with attention to the needs of people and sources of information in concrete situations. They are equally comfortable in functioning in a practical world that can make use of their feelings and actions, as well as in a subjective world that requires their thinking abilities. As a result, they excel in identifying and integrating tasks and people's needs. Their low emphasis on reflection can sometimes be a problem when they become overcommitted to their idea of how things should be done. In formal learning situations, they learn best through real-life projects, field trips, and hands-on experiments.

Diverging—[they] learn primarily through feeling (CE) and reflecting (RO). They are best at viewing concrete situations and exploring them from many different points of view. Their approach to situations is observing rather than taking action. People with this style enjoy situations that call for generating a wide range of feelings and ideas, such as brainstorming sessions. They are imaginative, sensitive to feelings, have broad cultural interests, and like to gather information. In formal learning situations, they like to receive personalized attention and feedback. They prefer working in groups to gather information and listening with an open mind.

Assimilating—[they] learn primarily through thinking (AC) and reflecting (RO). They are best at understanding a wide range of information and putting it into concise, logical form. They are less focused on people and more interested in abstract ideas and concepts. Generally, they find it more important that a theory have elegance and logical soundness than practical value. Because they place less emphasis on feeling and acting in their style, they may prefer to work alone. They do not make quick decisions but think things through. In formal learning situations, they may prefer lectures, readings, exploring analytical models, and having time to think things through.

Converging—[emphasizes] thinking (AC) and acting (AE) in learning situations. People with this style are best at finding practical uses for ideas and theories. They like to solve problems and make decisions based on finding logical solutions to issues or problems. They prefer dealing with technical tasks and problems rather than with social and interpersonal issues. Because they place less emphasis on feeling and reflection in their learning style, they can be uncomfortable in ambiguous situations and interpersonal issues. In formal learning situations, they may prefer to experiment with ideas and engage in simulations, laboratory assignments, and practical applications.

Accommodating—[they] learn primarily through acting (AE) and feeling (CE). They have the ability to learn from "hands-on" experience and function well in ambiguous and uncertain situations. They enjoy achieving goals and involving themselves in new and challenging experiences. Their tendency may be to act on intuitive "gut" feelings rather than on logical analysis. In solving problems, individuals with an Accommodating learning style rely more heavily on people for information than on their own technical analysis. Because they place less emphasis on reflection and thinking in their approach to learning they can sometimes be disorganized and act before thinking. In formal learning situations, people with this learning style prefer to work with others to get assignments done, to set goals, to do field work, and to test out different approaches for completing a project.

Balancing— [they] balance the extremes of the dialectics of action/reflection and concrete/abstract by finding a middle ground between them. Their central position on the four learning modes allows them to see many different perspectives on issues and bridge differences between people with different styles. They are often creative, but also experience difficulty in making decisions. They are able to change their learning style to meet the learning demands of the task they face. In a team they often adapt to fill in the missing style needed to get the task done. In formal learning environments they can change their learning style to meet the learning demands of the task they face.

Source: With kind permission of Springer Science+Business Media.

The implications of these differences are many, and, as the ELT model suggests, the various preferences and strengths identified in each style translate into additional variance in personality type, educational specialization, career and job preferences, and general adaptive competencies. One can imagine how a particular class, dominated by certain styles, can be swayed in its motives and interests with respect to both the material engaged and the methods pursued. Such a connection also raises certain questions about student satisfaction and instructor evaluations. When both are in alignment with preferred styles, one would expect a more positive result; a mismatch of approach and style could lead to a less than positive outcome, suggesting that individual differences are clearly important to student success and should be accommodated in the teaching process.

The connection of these learning style differences to various professional groups is also interesting. As Kolb (1984) observed, "The social professions—education, nursing, social work, and agricultural extension—comprise people who are heavily or primarily accommodative in their learning style. Professions with a technical or scientific base—accounting, engineering, medicine, and, to a lesser degree, management—have people with primarily convergent learning styles" (pp. 88–89). Such patterned relationships suggest that the human environments characteristic of various academic specialties and professional fields, much like the vocational interest patterns identified by Holland (1973), select and reinforce certain learning orientations and styles over others.

Talents and Strengths

A relatively new approach emerging from the field of positive psychology (Seligman & Csikszentmihalyi, 2000) is the strengths approach (Clifton & Harter, 2003), focusing on the "identification of positive personal and interpersonal characteristics, along with their integration into one's view of self, resulting in behavioral changes" (Louis, 2012, p. 2). Under the aegis of the Gallup Organization, this approach, through application of the *Clifton StrengthsFinder* (Louis, 2012), identifies individuals' inherent talents or traits used as their basis for "interacting with others, processing information, or navigating an environment" (Louis, p. 3). Such talents, or "naturally recurring patterns of thought, feeling, or behavior that can be productively applied" (Hodges & Clifton, 2004, p. 57), are clustered into thirty-four different talent themes, which in turn are used to identify an individual's signature themes (Clifton & Anderson, 2002). The top-five most dominant themes for a given individual ultimately lead to the development of personal strengths with additional experiences, knowledge, and skill. For example, the arranger theme identifies individuals who "can organize, but [who] also have a flexibility that complements this ability. They like to figure out how all the pieces and resources can be arranged for maximum productivity" (Gallup, 2008, p. 9). Combined with four additional themes—communication, deliberative, includer, and self-assurance—this may be the signature theme profile of a student leader who confidently guides an organization toward its goals while engaging others in the process. Such individuals are often found leading, for example, student activities groups, political organizations, and Greek letter societies on campus. Another example might be found in a student member of the Social Work Club, whose signature theme profile includes combinations of belief, empathy, harmony, positivity, and restorative and whose involvement in the group reinforces her predispositions toward helping others. Over time she develops skills of problem-solving, articulating value commitments, and expressing concern for others. In pursuing these experiences, these students exercise their talents, develop cumulative strengths that others notice, and continue to learn about the types of situations they are capable of and enjoy handling, having experienced a synergy of skills and opportunities along the way. The logic of this model is to identify, develop, and capitalize on individuals' strengths rather than spend inordinate time and energy shoring up their deficits. In doing so, opportunities for individuals to receive positive feedback motivates them to become engaged, to learn more, and to succeed. Although not a panacea, this approach can offer a wide variety of descriptors (talent themes) capable of capturing the diversity of students represented on our campuses and informing them in the myriad choices they make about where and how to invest their time and apply their strengths during the college experience.

Applications of the strengths or talent development approach to date on college campuses are considerable. Braskamp (2008) reviewed a number of such campus-based uses, ranging from singular program interventions to systemic change initiatives to campus culture. Among notable practices highlighted were those in student leadership development at Texas Christian University, career counseling and advising at Lee University (TN), residence life at Southern Methodist University, and the Freshman Year Experience at the University of Nebraska College of Business Administration. Further attention was given to colleges attempting to build a talent development culture on campus, including Greenville College (IL) and Tompkins Cortland Community College (NY). Similar to the previous illustrated models of interests, types, and styles, the strengths approach again offers another tool for examining how collective aggregate dynamics can favor one difference over another, reinforcing some while resisting others.

Engagement Types

Another line of inquiry has focused on how students use their time on campus as a measure of involvement or engagement. Grounded in the foundational work of Astin (1968), this research continues to analyze the collective activities of college students as a measurable source for understanding the impact of a particular campus environment. Accordingly, the extent to which a campus environment influences intellectual or academic interests, for example, would be reflected in collective observable behavioral differences among students, such as the frequency of their formal and informal discussions, in and outside of the classroom, and the number of faculty–student interactions. This line of reasoning has informed the development of several empirically grounded student typologies (Hu & Li, 2011), two of the more notable examples being those of Astin (1993) and Kuh, Hu, and Vesper (2000).

Astin (1993) identified a typology of college students, derived from self-reported student responses to the Cooperative Institutional Research Program's (CIRP) national freshman survey. According to the data, seven student types demonstrated substantial concurrent and predictive validity: scholars, social activists, artists, hedonists, leaders, status strivers, and uncommitted students. Each type can be differentiated from the others by characteristic behaviors, attitudes, expectations, values, and self-concept (Exhibit 2.3). These seven student types are also useful in describing the attributes of aggregates of students on campus. For instance, a predominance of scholars would likely create an institutional emphasis on activities and interests of an academic nature. In contrast, social activists and artists would create a collective environmental influence toward social action and involvement.

Exhibit 2.3. CIRP Freshman Survey Typology of Students

Scholar—high degree of academic and intellectual self-esteem, high expectations for academic success in college, aspirations for high-level academic degrees, and a significant disinclination toward careers in business and social work.

Social Activist—emphasis on participating in community action programs, helping others who are in difficulty, influencing social values, and influencing the political structure; propensity for discussion of political/social issues, participation in campus protests, attending racial/cultural workshops, and participating in volunteer work.

Artists—from relatively well-educated families, include a higher proportion of women (65%) than any other type; substantially more likely to major in fine arts, music, speech, theater, journalism, and English and to pursue careers in the arts (music, writing, theater), interior design, and architecture.

Hedonists—have poorer high school grades, report a greater frequency of poor study habits, and are more often bored in class; prefer careers that are professional or vocational in character (e.g., business, nursing, health technology, and secretarial studies); propensity for lower career aspirations; likely to spend more time partying while in college, less time attending religious services, but more likely to participate in campus protests, spend a lot of time socializing with other students, and get relatively poor grades.

Leaders—disproportionately concentrated in private colleges and universities, and underrepresented in the community colleges; excelled in speech and debate in high school, frequently studied with other students, and were far more likely to have been elected president of some student organization and to have won varsity letters in sports.

Status Strivers—committed to being successful in their own business, having administrative responsibility for the work of others, being very well-off financially, obtaining recognition from colleagues for contributions in their special field, and becoming an authority in their field; strongly materialistic values reflected in their inclination toward college majors and careers in accounting and business and toward partying, watching television, and joining fraternities or sororities.

Uncommitted Students—more likely to be undecided about either their major or their career choice; associated with participation in study abroad programs, enrollment in foreign language courses, and hours spent discussing political or social issues.

Source: Astin (1993, pp. 38–44)

Employing similar techniques, Kuh, Hu, and Vesper (2000) identified ten proportionate types of undergraduates from 51,155 student responses to the College Student Experience Questionnaire (CSEQ) across 128 institutions: individualist (7.4 percent), grind (15.0 percent), disengaged (18.2 percent), intellectual (5.4 percent), scientist (8.8 percent), socializer (10.2 percent), artist (7.2 percent), recreator (10.3 percent), collegiate (9.8 percent), and conventional (7.7 percent). Each student type was distinguished from the others by its relative emphasis on certain kinds of activities and experiences encountered and preferred during the college years. For example, disengaged students (the largest single proportion in the sample) "scored below average on all the activity factors as well as sum of effort and were especially low on academic activities and socializing with peers"; they were "more likely to be men and to attend public universities"; they also "studied fewer hours per week, reported lower grades … [and] had the lowest reported gains on all outcomes measures" (p. 237). In contrast, grind students were distinguished by their "high level of academic effort" and "doing very little else in college but work on academic tasks"; they tended to enroll in comprehensive colleges and universities, and "were more likely to be women, first generation college attenders, older, and from a lower [socioeconomic] SES background" (p. 238). Different from either of these two groups, though, were the intellectuals, who were "engaged across the board at an above average level" and "were more likely to be upper division students, humanities majors, and attending small colleges" (p. 238).

These ten student types were also differentiated by gender, year in school, and major field of study. Among male respondents, the three largest proportions of types found were disengaged (22.9 percent), recreator (18.9 percent), and scientist (11.8 percent) students. For females, the largest proportions were found among grind (19.5 percent), disengaged (15.2 percent), and socializer (13.5 percent) students. First-year students exhibited mostly the disengaged (20.9 percent), grind (15.8 percent), and socializer (11.3 percent) types, whereas seniors reflected students who were grind (15.5 percent), disengaged (14.4 percent), and collegiate (13.3 percent) patterns. When examining differences across academic fields, students in the humanities identified in the largest proportion as artist (29.2 percent), science and math majors scientist (30.0 percent), social sciences collegiate (15.5 percent), applied students disengaged (20.8 percent), and the largest single proportion of undecideds were also disengaged (28.3 percent). While all types were distributed across all demographics, the aforementioned patterns lend some validity to one of the themes explored in this chapter, that is, that differing students can be identified by a range of distinctive interests and activities and that such characteristics are related to their pathways through the college experience. In fact, such a premise served to generate a typology of four-year institutions, each exerting a different overall press toward certain forms of engagement and reflecting the aggregate profile of each campus's graduating seniors (Pike & Kuh, 2005) (Exhibit 2.4).

Exhibit 2.4. Types of Engaging Institutions

Diverse, but Interpersonally Fragmented. Students at these colleges have numerous experiences with diversity and tend to use technology, but do not view the institution as supporting their academic or social needs nor are their peers viewed as supportive or encouraging. All and all, not a very easy place to live and learn it seems.

Homogeneous and Interpersonally Cohesive. Students at these colleges have relatively few experiences with diversity, but view the institution and their peers as supportive. These institutions are the mirror image of the first engagement type.

Intellectually Stimulating. Students at these colleges are engaged in a variety of academic activities and have a great deal of interaction with faculty inside and outside the classroom. They also tend to engage in higher-order thinking and work with their peers on academic matters (i.e., collaborative learning).

Interpersonally Supportive. Students attending these institutions report high frequency of diversity experiences and view their peers and the campus as supportive of their efforts. Students also have a reasonable amount of contact with faculty members inside and outside the classroom.

High-Tech, Low-Touch. Information technology rules at these universities to the point of muting other types of interactions. There is a sense of stark individualism as little collaboration occurs, academic challenge is low, and the interpersonal environment is not a distinguishing feature of the campus.

Academically Challenging and Supportive. Faculty set high expectations and emphasize higher-order thinking in traditional ways. Little active and collaborative learning is required. At the same time, students support one another and view the campus as supportive. A generally friendly and congenial place to be an undergraduate interested in learning.

Collaborative. Peers rely on and are generally supportive of one another for learning, mediated somewhat by technology. Although there are few opportunities for experiences with diversity, students have a reasonable amount of contact with faculty, who along with other dimensions of the campus climate, are viewed as supportive.

Source: With kind permission of Springer Science+Business Media

With these descriptors as anchor points, one can imagine how such features can shape the student experience, for good or otherwise, as these varying dynamics effect differing interpersonal environments from one institution to another. Thus, large research universities are predictably different from small liberal arts colleges in the tone they create, in terms of student support, due largely to their respective aggregates in combination with other design factors.

Building on this work, Zhao, Gonyea, and Kuh (2003) and Hu and McCormick (2012) extended their analyses to employ responses from the National Survey of Student Engagement (NSSE) and corroborative data from the Wabash National Study of Liberal Arts Education (WNSLAE) to identify eight so-named student types: maximizer, grind, academic, collegiate, vocational, conventional, unconventional, and disengaged. Again, understanding these various type groups as a basis for assessing students can yield useful information about an institution's undergraduate culture and how such collective characteristics among students exert various peer influences relative to the institution's goals. Most recently, Hu and McCormick (2012) published a typology of first-year students from a diverse group of four-year institutions included in the 2006 cohort of the Wabash National Study of the Liberal Arts. They identified seven student types representing different engagement patterns relative to the five student-level NSSE outcome benchmarks: academic challenge, active and collaborative learning, student-faculty interaction, enriching educational experiences, and supportive campus environment. Although these benchmarks have since been refined further (McCormick, Gonyea, & Kinzie, 2013), the five referenced in this study approximate what is current. The seven first-year student-type proportions included the following: academics (12 percent), unconventionals (17 percent), disengaged (13 percent), collegiates (17 percent), maximizers (10 percent), grinds (15 percent), and conventionals (15 percent). The distribution of these types by demographic is

Table 2.1. Demographic Groups by Student Engagement Types

Engagement Type	Men %	Women %	White %	Black %	Hispanic %	Asian %
Academics (12%)	10.2	13.9	12.3	17.5	10.9	10.1
Unconventionals (17%)	13.8	19.8	17.3	11.9	25.0	15.4
Disengaged (13%)	12.8	13.6	12.5	19.8	10.1	18.0
Collegiates (17%)	13.5	19.7	18.6	11.1	9.4	13.8
Maximizers (10%)	16.4	5.9	9.4	15.9	14.8	10.1
Grinds (15%)	10.1	17.9	14.6	7.9	14.8	18.6
Conventionals (15%)	13.6	16.0	15.3	15.1	14.8	13.3

(From: Hu & McCormick, 2012, p. 748, Table 2).

presented in Table 2.1. Interesting patterns were related to these identifiers, with larger proportions of maximizers found among men and, in contrast, larger proportions of unconventionals, collegiates, and grinds found among women. Among White students, the largest proportions were collegiates, unconventionals, and conventionals, while Blacks identified mostly with academics, disengaged, and maximizers. Hispanic students were found in the largest proportion among unconventionals, and Asians identified primarily as Disengaged and Grinds. These data suggest that certain demographic characteristics are systematically related to how students experience college, when it comes to the kinds of learning-related activities in which they engage. To the extent that some types are more dominant on one campus versus another bears import for the kinds of engagement the peer culture at that institution is likely to reinforce over time. It's especially important to understand such differences when recruiting and engaging underrepresented students.

A Synthesis of Concepts

Several key concepts emerge in common from these models of human environments. First, all of these theories are reductionist in their approach to assessing human environments in that they attribute campus environment differences partially to the collective effects of members' personalities, styles, preferences, strengths, and types of engagement. Therefore, an environment dominated by a particular type is presumed to reflect and reinforce the primary characteristics of that type. For example, an environment dominated by Holland (1973) Social types (e.g., a learning community of education majors) would stimulate people to engage in social activities, would foster their social competencies, and would encourage them to see themselves as liking to help others, to be understanding of others, to be cooperative and sociable, and to see the world in flexible ways. This Social environment would in turn reward people for the display of social values, leading to various secondary effects such as participants becoming "more susceptible to social, humanitarian, and religious influences, more attracted to social occupations and roles in which they can express themselves in social activities, and more apt to cope with others by being friendly, helpful, [and] cooperative" (Holland, pp. 31–32). Similarly, in the parlance of Myers-Briggs types, a human work environment dominated by judging and sensing types (perhaps a campus registrar or bursar's office) would place a premium on things being organized, systematic, and foreseeable (Myers, 1980). Further, a student organization focusing on entrepreneurship is likely to attract students with competition among their signature themes, and a residence hall wing with a preponderance of disengaged students will likely face significant challenges of inertia when it comes to getting students involved on campus.

From each of these perspectives, information about the collective characteristics of environmental inhabitants is presumed to be predictive of the dominant features of that setting. Therefore, an amalgamation of the characteristics of inhabitants constitutes an assessment of environmental characteristics, which can then be understood further in terms of their degrees of differentiation and consistency.

Environmental Differentiation and Consistency

The pattern, strength, and character of any human aggregate are a function of its degree of differentiation (i.e., the degree of type homogeneity among inhabitants) and consistency (i.e., the similarity of type among inhabitants). According to Holland (1973), the originator of these constructs, "the percentage difference between the most and least common personality types in a given environment equals the degree of differentiation of that environment" (p. 34). For example, a human environment composed of 75 percent realistic types, 10 percent investigative types, and 15 percent conventional types would exhibit a higher degree of differentiation than an aggregate with 35 percent realistic types, 30 percent investigative types, and 35 percent conventional types. It would seem that such a principle would also apply to differences of demographic and behavioral patterns. Thus, a highly differentiated, or focused, environment is dominated by a single type (e.g., a socializer), while an undifferentiated environment is more diffuse, being characterized by a variety of different types (e.g., an even distribution of social activists, leaders, artists, hedonists, and status strivers). Consequently, highly differentiated environments are very clear and readily distinguishable to those within them as well as to those outside them, precisely because the dominance of a single type consistently encourages certain behaviors, values, attitudes, and expectations while discouraging those that are dissimilar. This would also be the case with environments dominated by any given demographic profile (e.g., women or Latino/a students). The effect appears to be that differentiated or highly focused environments actively reinforce or accentuate their own characteristics over time, by exerting a press toward conformity, while undifferentiated environments "stimulate a broad range of behavior and provide ambiguous guidance" (Holland, 1973, p. 34), being more flexible and open to a variety of inputs and influences. Until a particular type becomes dominant, a wider range of behaviors, values, attitudes, and expectations will be accommodated and encouraged, contributing further to the environment's variegated image. Thus, undifferentiated human environments, by definition, are probably more difficult to understand and characterize, mostly because of their lack of clear focus.

The degree of consistency among types, that is, their similarity, also adds to the dynamics of human aggregates. For example, Holland (1973) presented his six personality-occupational interest types in a hexagonal arrangement that defined the degree of similarity between any two types (Figure 2.1). Beginning at the top of the figure and moving clockwise, realistic types are followed in order by investigative, artistic, social, enterprising, and conventional types. Those adjacent on the hexagon, for example, social and enterprising types, are presumed to share greater similarity than types that are opposite, such as artistic and conventional types. Astin's (1993) typology illustrates this point as well; status strivers might be thought of as dissimilar to and inconsistent with social activists. In Myers-Briggs terminology, an ENTP (extraverted, intuitive, thinking, and perceiving) can be said to

Figure 2.1. Holland Personality Vocational Interest Types

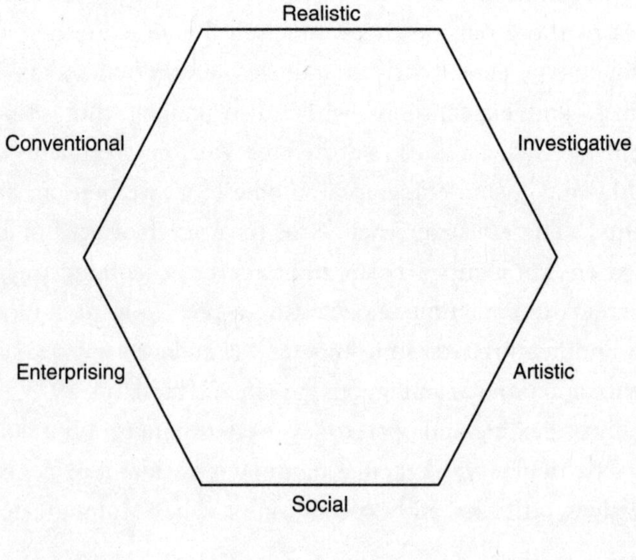

have greater similarity with an ENFP (extraverted, intuitive, feeling, perceiving) than with an ISFJ (introverted, sensing, feeling, judging) because of their shared orientations toward extraversion, intuition, and perception. Finally, Kolb's learning style model, the Gallup Strengths approach, and the various typologies of student engagement might also offer similar examples. For instance, Kolb's assimilators prefer the same emphasis on abstract concepts as convergers yet differ on their preference for reflective over active modes of learning. From the point of strengths, individuals who are talented in the achiever theme would most likely share greater consistency with those talented in competition rather than harmony. Differences of engagement also imply varying degrees of type consistency, for example, with collegiate students sharing more commonalities with socializers than with grinds.

Highly consistent environments contain individuals of similar types, and inconsistent environments are made up of individuals who are divergent types. Thus, according to Holland (1973), "Consistent environments provide similar rewards and demands; inconsistent environments provide divergent rewards and demands" (p. 34). In summary, human environments most easily distinguished are those dominated by a particular type (highly differentiated) and those most similar (highly consistent). An implicit goal in these conceptions is the achievement of person–environment congruence or resolving the challenge of fitting in.

Person–Environment Congruence

A person is said to be congruent with an environment if his or her type is the same or nearly the same as the dominant type within that setting. For example, an artistic type is more likely to experience person–environment congruence within a theater arts department, and a social-enterprising type is most congruent with a social fraternity comprised mainly of business majors. Dissimilarity with the environment's dominant characteristic results in person–environment incongruence and personal discomfort.

The degree of person–environment congruence is thought to be predictive of an individual's attraction to and satisfaction or stability within an environment. Grounded in the sociological principle of *homophily* (McPherson, Smith-Lovin, & Cook, 2001) or the patterned relationship between association and similarity, individuals who share much in common with the aggregate component of an environment are presumed to be most attracted to that environment. Once inside, the person is likely to be encouraged for exactly those behaviors, values, attitudes, and expectations that attracted him or her to that environment in the first place, thus reinforcing person–environment similarities. Consequently, all things being equal, the likelihood of remaining in that environment is increased in such circumstances. Conversely, since people are presumed to prefer and be satisfied with a state of congruence rather than incongruence, a person is not likely to be attracted to an environment that bears little resemblance to his or her own characteristics. If placed inside an incompatible environment, there is less chance of being reinforced for preferred behaviors, values, attitudes, and expectations, and the likelihood of leaving that environment is increased significantly. Congruent person–environment combinations allow individuals to exercise their strengths, "but of equal importance, [they also allow them] to avoid the activities [they] dislike, the demands for competencies [they] lack, the tasks and self-images [they] do not value, and the situations in which [their] personality traits are not encouraged" (Holland, 1973, p. 38). Thus, perhaps the most important question to be addressed, much like Sarah's inquiry in the opening scenario to this chapter, is whether or not a person seems to fit within any particular environment. Evidence of a high degree of person–environment congruence is usually apparent in higher satisfaction, a desire to persist, and ultimately greater retention (Smart, Feldman, & Ethington, 2000).

Since person–environment congruence is thought to contribute to satisfaction and stability through selective reinforcement, by implication, lack of congruence must lead to dissatisfaction and instability, a condition that is likely to be resolved in one of three ways: by seeking a new and congruent environment, by remaking the present environment, or by adapting behavior to the dominant characteristics of the present environment. The option an individual is likely to exercise depends on the degrees of differentiation and consistency characterizing the environment as well as the individual. A highly differentiated and consistent environment is thought to be resistant to change in that its strongest tendency is to reinforce itself. The same can be said about an individual whose characteristic profile is highly focused (differentiated) and consistent. Therefore, when a highly focused individual is placed in a highly focused but incongruent environment, that individual is most likely to leave and seek a new, more congruent environment, as may eventually be the case with Felix, the Latino student in the opening scenario who expressed concerns about seeing only White faces while in between classes. However, as Holland (1973) hypothesized, "Persons with undifferentiated and inconsistent personality patterns tend to adapt to incongruence by changing their own behavior and personality pattern to achieve greater congruence with their environment" (p. 42). The option of remaking the environment is most likely to be selected by a differentiated and consistent individual who finds himself or herself in an unfocused or undifferentiated environment. Thus, the arranger may quickly structure the student organization that lacks purpose and direction.

These hypotheses underscore the importance of aggregate characteristics for influencing members' behaviors, that is, whether they are likely to adapt to, leave, or try to change an environment. While such formulations were derived specifically from the study of vocational-interest behavior, Holland concluded that they appear, as well, to be "applicable to other phenomena, to educational and social behavior" (Holland, 1973, p. 42). It seems reasonable, then, to expect, for example, that Kuh, Hu, and

Vesper's (2000) Intellectuals would be more congruent in some institutional cultures than others and that the closer a student would resemble that type the less likely adaptation would occur in a culture dominated, say, by a different type (e.g., a recreator), and likewise with the other models of human environments presented here. Collectively they illustrate the potential power of homogeneous groupings on campus and the importance of person-environment congruence as a source of attraction to the institution and satisfaction and stability once within.

In summary, the human aggregate models and concepts examined in this chapter offer useful descriptive and prescriptive tools for identifying and constructing, to educational advantage, the patterns campus environments acquire as a result of the various types of people who participate in them. Development of personal identity is a major life task associated with the college experience (Chickering & Reisser, 1993), and these various aggregate models, in particular, have much potential for informing the design of educational environments, from residential settings (e.g., living learning centers and theme houses) and freshman interest groups to student organizations and special student services. Furthermore, these concepts (as discussed in subsequent chapters) can help in unraveling the significant challenges of diversifying institutional profiles and in responding more successfully to the needs of underrepresented students.

Questions for Discussion

1. What do enrollment demographics of your institution say about the dominant aggregate on your campus?
2. Using Pike and Kuh's (2005) typology, how would you characterize the type of engaging institution your college or university represents? What contributes to that conclusion?

3. What learning styles might be favored or disadvantaged in what academic majors on your campus?
4. How would you describe the strengths and talents of two differing students who seemed to be most effective leaders on your campus?
5. What subgroup of students at your institution are challenged by the greatest degree of incongruence on your campus? Why?

3

Organizational Environments:

How Institutional Goals Are Achieved

Consider the following scene as Fran, a junior earth sciences major, returns to campus following a summer term away to discover that a few things have changed since the time she was elected to a leadership position for an undergraduate student organization.

Scenario: "That's Not How We Do Things!"

"But that's not what we're about!" said Fran in frustration with the university's new procedures for registering student activities. As the newly elected chair of an undergraduate women's environmental advocacy group, Students for a Healthy Environment (SHE), Fran had just returned to campus following a summer internship with the Department of Interior in Alaska to discover that the system for organizing and funding campus organizations had changed drastically since the previous semester.

"If we have to do all these forms and go through this review process each time, we'll never be able to complete the programs we planned for this semester. What was wrong with the way we used to do things around here?" Apparently, the new director of campus organizations and activities had restructured her administrative unit to reflect a new emphasis on efficiency and accountability in the allocation of student fees. Implementation of new application materials and forms, as well as an additional and time-consuming review process, placed more responsibility on student leaders to submit plans and proposals one semester in advance. "I have nothing against being responsible for what we do," Fran reasoned with the new director, "but this really discourages us from suggesting ideas if we have to complete all those materials and wait that long before we get approval."

Fran's experiences with her introductory sociology course weren't all that good either that semester. She was finally able to get into a class that she deferred her first year due to scheduling conflicts. "You wouldn't believe it—265 of us in a room with 225 seats; you can hardly see the board!" she exclaimed to her advisor. "What the professor has to say is really interesting, but we never have time to discuss any of her ideas or what we read about that week in one of our books. Most of the students standing in the back leave before the end of the class period."

Back in Williams Hall, though, Fran was at home. One of the five residential learning communities available to students on campus, it was a place where her leadership skills were frequently challenged as a floor convener, whose responsibility it was to coordinate the agenda and activities of the community team members on each of the floors in her wing of the building.

"My hands are going to be full this semester," she commented to her advisor, "with all the goals we've set for getting people involved." Fran looked forward to and enjoyed these kinds of opportunities, finding them to be a good fit for her skills and interests in planning and organization. Communication and problem-solving were also two areas she enjoyed but had not had much experience with prior to assuming her current responsibilities in Williams. "Around there, everybody gets a chance to make a difference; it just wouldn't work if people weren't involved," she said.

The surprise, frustration, challenge, and excitement in Fran's observations upon returning to her college betray the effects of components not accounted for in the environment thus far in our analysis. In all settings are found varying degrees of organizational structure and process that evolve for purposes of achieving specific goals. *Getting organized* is a common practice in colleges and universities that shapes and influences the behavior of staff in administrative units, faculty in academic departments and classrooms, and students in residence halls, student groups, and campus services. Whether in the form of expectations for greater efficiencies—as with the new registration procedures imposed upon Fran's student group—the economies of scale in her large sociology class, or the complexity of roles and responsibilities available in her residence hall, decisions about the goals to be achieved and the resources to be allocated to them result in organizational infrastructures that significantly shape and influence the behavior of individuals in their environments. Developing a language for identifying and assessing the effects of these organizational dimensions is the purpose of this chapter.

The Nature of Organized Environments

The notion that human environments, such as schools, workplaces, hospitals, clubs, and churches, are often characterized by planned, systematic, and organized structures that affect their functioning is an idea perhaps first explored systematically in the work of the German sociologist Max Weber (1947). Weber articulated a series of observations and propositions about modern bureaucracies that formed much of the groundwork for understanding how organizations function (at least from a conventional-bureaucratic perspective). Organizations, unlike other social groupings (e.g., friendship circles), are "deliberately constructed and reconstructed to seek specific goals" (Parsons, 1960, cited in Etzioni, 1964, p. 3).

As organizations, colleges and universities seek to educate students (typically measured, for example, by numbers of courses offered, students graduated, or test scores increased), to construct and disseminate knowledge (as indicated by research grants and faculty publications), and to serve the community (reflected in consultation with and participation in professional and related groups). Etzioni (1964, p. 3) framed his discussion of organizations by reference to three key characteristics:

> Organizations are characterized by: (1) divisions of labor, power, and communication responsibilities, divisions which are not random or traditionally patterned, but deliberately planned to enhance the realization of specific goals; (2) the presence of one or more power centers which control the concerted efforts of the organization and direct them toward its goals; these power centers also must review continuously the organization's performance and re-pattern its structure, where necessary, to increase its efficiency; (3) substitution of personnel, i.e., unsatisfactory persons can be removed and others assigned their tasks. The organization can also recombine its personnel through transfer and promotion.

Thus, colleges and universities exhibit such characteristics as academic departments are organized, and units and offices report to deans and administrators about assigned responsibilities and allocated resources (division of labor); administrators, staff, and faculty plan, guide, and implement policies, programs, and practices designed to meet institutional goals (distribution of power); and procedures for peer and administrative review provide for the evaluation of personnel and their promotion or dismissal when appropriate. On a typical college campus most students spend a good deal of time in implicitly or explicitly purposeful environments. For Fran in the opening scenario, these environments included the student organization she led, the sociology class she attended, and the residence hall where she lived. These environments are all designed to achieve certain ends, and their success is often gauged by the extent to which they do so or, in other words, by their effectiveness.

The tendency to get organized to get things done is a common one, and in accomplishing such a task a number of decisions must be made along the way. Who is in charge? How should decisions about distributing resources be made? By what rules, if any, will the organization function? What must be accomplished and how fast? The decisions made with respect to these questions create a variety of organizational structures or systems in an environment that, in turn, affects an environment's overall design and functioning as well as an individual's attraction to, experience of, and satisfaction within a given environment.

Colleges and universities have drawn the attention of numerous researchers intent on understanding how they work; after all, countless lives and limited resources are at stake in their functioning effectively. Perhaps two of the best-known proponents in this line of inquiry are found in Birnbaum (1988) and Bolman and Deal (2011), each offering a model of interpretive frames for examining the organizational features of an institution. Birnbaum described four cognitive frames that can "help us to order the world and decide what action to take" in an organization: bureaucratic, collegial, political, and anarchical. Frames are interpretive in that they serve to make meaning of what is going on in the setting (Exhibit 3.1). For example, the task of determining an organization's goals is a matter of assembly from a bureaucratic perspective, consensus-building from a collegial view, negotiation through a political lens, and emergence from an anarchical frame. Each of these positions suggests a different way of exercising ones leadership role in the setting, ranging from issuing mandates to enabling creativity. These frames on average approximate what one would expect to experience respectively at a public two-year community college (bureaucratic), a liberal arts college (collegial), a regional state university (political), and a flagship research university (anarchical).

Exhibit 3.1. Organizational Archetypes—Selected Examples

Bureaucratic	Collegial	Political	Anarchical
Focus on aligning goals of various bureaucratic units	Agreed-upon goals	Contested goals	Amiguous goals
Chain-of-command decision making	Consensus-based decision making	Bargaining and negotiation	Unclear decision making processes
Top-down leadership	Distributed leadership, but with more power among certain groups	Conflict and confrontation between bottom-up and top-down leadership	Leadership emerging anywhere
Operate by directives	Operate by agreed-upon values	Operate based negotiated agreements	Operations based more on individual decision making and professional values
Change occurs by mandates	Change occurs through dialogue and conversation	Change occurs when competing interests clash	Change occurs on the margins of the organization, based on the work of innovative individuals

Source: Birnbaum, 1988. Used with permission.

Similarly, Bolman and Deal (2011) suggest a four-frame model as well (Exhibit 3.2): structural, human resource, political, and symbolic. Like Birnbaum, the authors contend that managers and policymakers use various images of an organization "to gather information, make judgments, and determine how best to get things done" (p. 11). Thus, an administrator from a structural perspective will create rules, clarify goals, assemble units, and align resources with tasks to achieve organizational ends. In contrast, from a political lens, an administrator will mediate conflicts, advocate for certain directions, and consolidate a power base to support a particular agenda. Whether to build, empower, advocate, or inspire is a function of one's perspectives on the organized environment. Manning (2013), in a recent review of core organizational concepts

Exhibit 3.2. Overview of the Four-Frame Model

	Structural	Human Resource	Political	Symbolic
Metaphor for organization	Factory or machine	Family	Jungle	Carnival, temple, theater
Central Concepts	Rules, roles goals, policies technology, environment	Needs, skills, relationships	Power, conflict, competition, organizational politics	Culture, meaning, metaphor, ritual, ceremony, stories, heroes
Image of leadership	Social Architecture	Empowerment	Advocacy	Inspiration
Basic leadership challenge	Attune structure to task, technology, environment	Align organizational and human needs	Develop agenda and power base	Create faith, beauty, meaning

Source: Bolman and Deal (2008). Used with permission.

in higher education, addresses similarly the anarchical, collegial, political, cultural, and bureaucratic perspectives while contributing three additional perspectives to the mix of motives and processes in organizational settings: quantum science, feminist, and spiritual. Each frame contains within it different assumptions about reality and meaning making, uses of power, and foundational sources and mechanisms for decision-making, the exercise of leadership and communication, and perceptions of coworkers. Thus, leaders from a quantum perspective are not distinguished from followers, function collaboratively from a feminist frame, and rotate transformationally from a spiritual lens. While decisions may be made in each case, their motive and process differs accordingly.

Anatomy of Organized Environments

Regardless of which frames are used to interpret one's experience in them, organizations can be thought of as purposeful environments. In that sense, all environments have certain aims—some expressed and some implied. Whether an organized environment is defined by a clearly stated mission, complete with targeted goals and objectives, or just a consensual tacit understanding about its overall purpose, decisions about where the organization is going and what and how various resources should be expended must be made.

Some of the more revealing moments in organized environments (whether tightly or loosely arranged) come when resources are cut, boundaries of authority are ignored, or someone proposes the development of a new program or practice. Such moments in an organization (not infrequent in colleges and universities) always seem to stimulate discussions about organizational purposes, processes, and traditions as well as the inevitable questions about whether it can afford to implement new initiatives yet alone maintain current ones. This backdrop of collective purposes, decision-making, and resource allocation gives rise to the organizational infrastructure of any purposeful environment such as a college or university, a classroom, a residence hall, an academic department, or a student activities group.

Organized infrastructures take on many different forms depending on what aspects are examined in the environment (Kuh, 1996). For example, a conventional, rational-bureaucratic view (e.g., structural lens) may focus on a description of the formal functions, responsibilities, and reporting lines of the infrastructure; other conventional perspectives, such as the collegial and political views, might focus respectively on mechanisms of representation and persuasion or power and conflict resolution. From postconventional perspectives, including organized anarchy, organizational culture, quantum science, feminist, spiritual, and learning organizations, the infrastructure may be recognized as points of disjuncture, informal channels of communication, the influence of consensual values, traditions, history, and various tensions of fluidity and structure. What ultimately comprises the organizational infrastructure of an environment, though, is a function of the kinds of common concerns often raised by participants and illustrated in the following questions: How shall we divide up the work? How will decisions be made? By what rules, if any, will we function? How shall members be rewarded for their work? How much should we be expected to do? Will we continue to do what we've always done? How much should it cost to do what we do? How do members feel about their involvement and work?

Each of these questions presents an opportunity to consider options that, in turn, will result in certain structures being imposed upon the environment; those structures create the organizational components of an environment and in turn influence the behavior of participants within it. Consideration of each structure is important for understanding the nature of intentional systems and how organizational aspects shape the character of human environments and the experience of those within them. Seven of these structural features overviewed here are complexity, centralization, formalization, stratification, production, routinization, and efficiency. Varying emphases on these organizational components lend themselves to the creation of different characteristic environments, from fixed to fluid, ultimately affecting participant morale and the extent to which environmental goals are achieved.

Complexity

Questions about the division of work and responsibilities in a setting can lead to numerous options of environmental design. Should assignment of duties be fixed or rotated? Should some individuals assume responsibility for certain functional specialties or certain whole projects? Who should work with whom? Which arrangements more clearly communicate organizational purposes, goals, and functions? What sort of preparation, credentials, or ongoing training, if any, are required to complete these assignments?

Such questions have to do with the degree of structural and task complexity present in an environment. Structural complexity (horizontal and vertical) concerns the number of occupational subunits and specialties present; task complexity refers to the intensity and extensity of knowledge and expertise (or degree of professionalization) required in them (Hage & Aiken, 1970). Obviously, colleges and universities are characterized by high degrees of complexity, where a variety of highly credentialed professionals conduct the business of postsecondary education. Many different departmental subunits require a variety of specialties dedicated to meeting the needs of campus constituents. Departments of natural sciences require advanced training and preparation of appropriate personnel to meet the goals, for example, of teaching chemistry and biology courses. Career planning and placement offices require the services of trained counselors and advisors who can effectively assist students in sorting through the maze of academic and occupational interests, skills, and choices. In the context of various campus subenvironments, complexity might be apparent for example in the number of discussion groups created in a classroom or the number of specialized task groups in student organizations or residence hall governments.

How many units and subunits are needed to best serve the purposes of the organization, and how should they be arranged? This is the fundamental concern of organizational complexity. This dimension is also evident in "the degree to which members of an organization attempt to gain greater knowledge about their respective work activities and the overall activities of their organization" (Hage & Aiken, 1970, p. 18). Colleges and universities are organizations that generally place a good deal of emphasis on staff development and continued learning. Often, decisions have to be made in complicated contexts that require judgment and knowledge of many aspects. In that sense, educational institutions and their various subunits are typically high in structural and task complexity, an inherent quality of professional work environments.

Centralization

Concerns about decision-making in an environment also lead to various design options. Who has the power to make decisions for others in the organization? What kinds of decisions require greater participation? Should we decide by consensus or majority vote? Who decides which way to go when there are competing interests? How do we respond to equally compelling choices? Such questions are concerned with the use of power in an organization, that is, its degree of centralization.

> Organizational centralization refers to the way in which power is distributed in a setting. Power is the "capacity of one social position to set the conditions under which other social positions must perform, that is, the capacity of one social position to determine the actions of other social positions. . . ." Every organization needs to make decisions about the allocation of its funds, the

> promotion of its personnel, and the initiation of new programs. Responsibilities for these decisions must be allocated to some jobs; this helps ensure coordination of many different occupations. (Hage & Aiken, 1970, p. 19)

Thus, colleges must decide what courses will be offered and when they will be scheduled; the number, type, and due dates of assignments for individual classes; and how various budgets will be allocated, spent, and accounted for. Organizations vary widely in how such decisions are made. Those in which few individuals share this power are said to be highly centralized (or autocratic and authoritarian); organizations where many share formal power with respect to such decisions (as might be the case, for example, under an egalitarian collegial or feminist model) are described as having a low degree of centralization or are said to be decentralized. In the context of a classroom setting, for example, a high degree of centralization might be evident when an instructor makes all decisions about the course syllabus, such as assigned readings and papers, and relies principally on lecture methods of presentation. In contrast, a seminar format where students and instructor work collaboratively to create the syllabus around emerging student interests and learning styles, where assignments are individualized, where grading practices are negotiated, and where an open discussion format is preferred might be described as a decentralized learning environment. Likewise, a student organization or a residence hall association might exhibit similar characteristics depending upon how decisions are made about various programs and resources. Highly centralized organizations simply have fewer participants making various decisions.

Formalization

The focus on rules and regulations goes hand in hand with a discussion of power and centralization in an organization. Power is often formalized and distributed through established rules. Some rules are very explicit and can be found in formal written handbooks, manuals, and other related documents. Other rules or guidelines are more implicit, general in scope, and at times only verbally communicated in passing or conveyed symbolically (such as those imbedded in organizational culture). What sort of rules will guide the organization? How specific will they need to be? What concerns will the rules address? How will members know the rules? How will they be enforced? Will there be any exceptions to them? What are the consequences of rule infractions? All of these concerns reflect issues of the degree of formalization present in any organized environment.

From some perspectives, getting organized often means generating a set of guidelines and procedures for operating, thereby establishing an organization's degree of formalization. More specifically, formalization refers to the importance of rules and regulations (whether formally written or customarily understood) in an organization (Hage & Aiken, 1970). Three aspects are contained in this concept: the number of rules (highly formalized organizations are characterized by many rules), the specificity of established rules (highly formalized units establish rules that are explicit and specific in nature), and the extent to which such rules are enforced (highly formalized organizations place greater emphasis on rule enforcement).

Especially from a bureaucratic perspective, rules are thought to provide guidelines for efficient functioning and lend a certain degree of predictability to organizational efforts. Thus, for example, course catalogs and registration materials codify when and where classes will meet. Proper forms communicate correct steps one must follow for reimbursement of expenses. Evidence for the degree of formalization in various campus environments might be reflected in the nature of student codes, administrative manuals and job descriptions, college catalogs, course syllabi, organizational constitutions and bylaws, or customary understandings of how things are done. High degrees of formalization are associated with organizational rigidity and inflexibility (a common limitation of the rational-bureaucratic model). Low degrees of formalization lend themselves to organizational fluidity and flexibility. Recall in the opening scenario that the increase in formalization instituted by the new director of campus organizations and activities was what Fran found most challenging upon her return to school. Nevertheless, frustrations over concerns like, how can we ever get anything done around here?, are frequently met by the establishment of rules or guidelines.

Stratification

Rewards are important in any organization, usually as motivators, and they often reveal conditions of status, position, and favor. Whose work is given greater priority and esteem? Are there differing levels of remuneration associated with differing functions? What are the perks of power and position in the organization and how are they used? How do individuals lower in the organizational structure gain access to those higher (in the case of a hierarchical bureaucratic arrangement)? Are rewards used to maintain the status quo or to encourage change? These are all questions about the degree of stratification in an organization, that is, the differential distribution of its rewards (Hage & Aiken, 1970).

Highly stratified systems have many different levels of status, delineated by differential rewards (such as income, esteem, and prestige). Those at higher status levels receive higher recognition and rewards (such as parking spaces) than those at lower status levels. Stratification is also a reflection of the degree of mobility members have in moving from lower to higher status levels in the organization. Highly stratified systems often tend to preserve current status distinctions to maintain current reward structures; they also tend to restrict mobility of members, where opportunities to move up are few. While the application of power and rules exert a conforming influence on an organized system, stratification tends to be more divisive since reward structures are usually cast into a competitive framework. Merit systems and productivity bonuses are often sources of contention among participants, despite claims of objectivity asserted in their implementation.

The relevance of this stratification concept can be further understood in applying it to the various organized systems that affect students' campus experiences. For example, classrooms might appear to be highly stratified where distances between students and instructor are maintained by the insistent use of formal titles and the exercise of formal academic authority. Likewise, high stratification might be apparent in a student organization where rewards (such as access to office space and equipment, titles, and campus recognition) are differentially and exclusively distributed to leaders of the group. So, too, an emphasis on stratification might be evident in a residence life system where head residents and resident assistants are distinguished significantly from others by higher status and appreciably better living arrangements. Other analogous reflections of stratification in a college setting are typically associated with factors such as class level (seniors have greater claim on campus than first-year students), academic major (students in so-called hard sciences might be perceived by peers to possess greater intellectual acuity than students in education), or status (athletes may have access to preferential course schedules and special living arrangements on campus). Organizationally, environments characterized by high degrees of stratification tend to divide members, and those who share disproportionately in the accrued rewards of such a system more often have a vested interest in maintaining the status quo.

Production

The value of any organization is often assessed by what it does, most frequently in terms of what it produces (especially from the perspective of a rational-bureaucratic model). To justify any organized unit that does little, particularly in times of diminishing resources, is to ask the impossible. Since organizations are purposeful systems, success is more times than not measured in terms of how many this and thats have been achieved, produced, or discovered in reference to whatever index seems appropriate to those who must make such decisions. A fair year is doing about the same as last year, a good year is exceeding last year's output, and a great year means doubling projected goals. Trouble ensues when the year ends in something less. So academic departments must produce graduates, faculty must publish papers, and staff must offer more programs to more people. Such issues relate to the relative emphasis on quantity versus quality of an organization's products or services, that is, its level of production (Hage & Aiken, 1970).

All organizations need to produce, for reasons of justifying their existence, for maintaining current resources or attracting additional ones, and for creating a sense of accomplishment among members who contribute to the organization's goals. When quantity of production is high, or at least sufficient, it is presumed that the organization is functioning well. A unit that is on target implies success. However, any drop in quantity of production usually signals the need for reexamination and evaluation. As organized systems, colleges are also often driven by production mandates, whether from student consumers, who request certain classes to be held more frequently, or from boards of trustees, who look at the number of graduates placed from various programs as an indicator of fulfilling institutional mission. Student credit hours, program enrollments, fulltime equivalent faculty, retention rates, proportion of ethnically diverse students, degree completions, placement goals, students served, advisee contact appointments, hours devoted to teaching, research activities, public or professional service commitments, research dollars generated, manuscripts published, programs sponsored, term papers assigned, and books read are all very familiar indicators of production in an academic setting. Annual reports teem with such data, with the assumption often being that an increase from year to year on any of these measures is indicative of organizational improvement or success. Further, especially as budgets fall short, such measures are invoked and examined for purposes of reallocating resources to units that are perceived to have a greater need—ironically units that are already most productive.

How much to produce, though, is often a trade-off with the quality of production. Increasing enrollments and class sizes can stimulate student credit hour production. Such strategies, often seen to be more efficient by raising the students-to-faculty ratio, capitalize on economies of scale (albeit false ones). Allowing 100 students in a classroom increases production fourfold compared with restricting enrollment to sections of 25. A higher number of students admitted to a program usually results in a higher number of graduates from the program. However, questions about the quality of student experiences resulting from such strategies must figure in any formula of institutional success. Does having more students in a particular classroom affect the quality of intellectual engagement known to contribute to the development of critical reasoning abilities? Will students have fewer opportunities to communicate in the form of written papers and essays in such a setting? Will there be sufficient time for the instructor to give quality feedback to all students enrolled in the class? In terms of overall program enrollment, how will the quality of advising and student–faculty contacts be affected by a significant enrollment increase? Will the expectations for learning outcomes change? Answers to such questions have implications for not only the productivity of various institutional environments but also certainly their ability to meet educational goals.

Routinization

Price (1972) defined this structural feature as "the degree to which role performance in a social system is repetitive" (p. 150). A certain macro level of institutional routine is built into the cycle of the academic year. Class registration and welcoming events commence each fall semester. Course drops and adds must be accomplished and tuition bills finalized by certain dates. Midterm grades are issued and final exams are scheduled with course grades due shortly thereafter. In between, fall break and Thanksgiving holidays offer time away from the academic grind, and winter break gives the chance to reunite with family and friends, absent the usual deadlines and pressures of term paper assignments and projects. Winter and spring term set in motion another rhythmic experience, as class requirements are front-loaded for completion prior to spring break and the headlong march to spring commencement ensues. Beginnings and ends follow a fixed calendar in most colleges and universities, offering a predictable experience of ebb and flow as each year passes.

At the micro level, routine also characterizes some roles more than others in the academy. The distribution of financial aid entails the timely review of stacks of completed Free Application for Federal Student Aid (FAFSA) forms and responses to repeated questions and concerns. Accommodating major changes involves seemingly endless iterations of curriculum requirements and acquisition of appropriate signatures. In contrast, the academic department chair might find the ordinarily planned day interrupted by unexpected events and demands that require immediate attention, and the typical day of a director of services for any designated student group (e.g., adult learners, international students) may be full of surprises as the unpredictability and complexity of students' lives unfold. Routine can be both a comfort and constraint for professionals, depending on their own characteristics and expectations. For some, checking off the same list of tasks lends a sense of stability and accomplishment to their work; for others it becomes of metric of banality and boredom. Regardless, it is often a mechanism for productivity that some count on and others resist. When people are into the routine of things, smooth functioning is presumed; when one falls out of the routine, renewed efforts are required to get back on track. Routinization, when combined with an emphasis on productivity, becomes a tool for maximizing organizational efficiencies, the focus of the next structural component here.

Efficiency

Concerns about what and how many an organization produces are usually accompanied by questions of cost. Are we getting our money's worth? Can more be produced for the same overall cost? Can we save with less? How do we cut back? What is the bottom line? These are all concerns about organizational efficiency and reflect the relative emphasis on cost reduction of an organization's products or services (Hage & Aiken, 1970).

Similar to the aforementioned assumptions about productivity, maximum efficiency is presumed to reflect a smooth functioning system. From a rationalist perspective, if the highest production levels are being realized from the fewest resources, then why tinker with a system that works so well? Like other complex organizations, colleges and universities emphasize the efficient use of resources by a variety of institutional strategies. For example, restricting access to copying machines, raising minimum quotas for course enrollments, and assigning lower-salaried graduate teaching assistants to large introductory sections all have the effect of lowering the overall cost of production. Ensuring full occupancy rates in residence halls, usually by overbooking 10 to 15 percent and eliminating common space, and keeping classrooms full also reduce the cost of physical plant investments.

Although cost reduction is a necessary goal in any organized system, it is particularly difficult to measure and evaluate in the context of an academic setting. Colleges and universities are in the business of creating new ideas and programs responsive to changing conditions and needs. New ideas and programs are inherently risky, inasmuch as they may or may not succeed. Failures are detrimental to the efficient use of resources because productivity is interrupted and resources are apparently misplaced or squandered. In that respect, should a different standard of efficiency apply to an educational institution where the mission itself often challenges conventional standards of productivity and resource use? What is an efficient number of resources to produce: A graduate of a program? A publication in a professional journal? A grade of B in a particular course? What is the cost of a new idea? Clear and reasonable benchmarks are notoriously absent in such discussions.

Furthermore, without a clear and succinct definition of the goals of an organized system, demonstration of their accomplishment is problematic. What exactly are the goals of a college or university? Is there agreement on such matters? Whose point of view counts? Does a graduate of a teacher education program who uses transferable skills to pursue a career in a different field or chooses to become a full-time parent count as a failure or success in the larger scheme? Does the cost of a publication fluctuate with the salary of the faculty member who produces it? Answers to such questions are inherently messy and value laden and serve to complicate discussions about efficiency in higher education. Unfortunately, vague and elusive outcomes of the college experience (such as development of personal autonomy, tolerance for ambiguity, exercise of critical judgment) are often reduced to convenient measures that may or may not capture the totality of such goals. That immediately raises questions about what is or is not an efficient use of resources, to which satisfactory answers simply may not exist. Nonetheless, like all other organized systems, colleges and universities are held accountable and must address concerns of efficiency, however challenging they may be.

Morale

Somewhere in the mix of these organizational concerns lies a fundamental question about the satisfaction of the members and participants in an organized system. Are members excited about their assignments and work? Do they respond positively to those with whom they work? Is there a general feeling of goodwill and satisfaction among participants? While not an organizational structure in itself, morale, or satisfaction, is a summary measure of many aspects associated with participating in an organized system. All things being equal, it is also often a reflection of the rate of turnover in the system. Higher morale is usually associated with lower turnover, and higher turnover often reflects lower morale. For example, high student absenteeism in a particular class, or lack of student involvement in a particular student organization, among other aspects, might be indicative of general dissatisfaction with the organizational features of those systems.

At the institutional level, attrition or dropout rates provide a measure of turnover, and an increase on such indicators warrants serious concern on the part of campus administrators to identify sources of student dissatisfaction and low morale. Human organizations, if they are to survive, must "maintain a minimal level of morale and loyalty" (Hage & Aiken, 1970, p. 27) among their members. Failure to do so may lead to other difficulties (such as lower efficiency, violations of rules, subterfuge, and a general lowering of productivity). These consequences may ultimately undermine the purposes and goals of the organized system, as members cease to fulfill their roles and eventually withdraw from the system. This may be the impending fate of some students in the opening scenario as they grow tired of the anonymous atmosphere in Fran's large sociology section. As learners in a purposeful classroom environment, the lack of opportunity to engage in discussion of the topics may continue to challenge their morale to the point that some simply withdraw from the setting and get notes from somebody else. The timeless adage that satisfied people are productive and productive people are satisfied makes the connection clear to the importance of morale among participants in any environment. Whether high morale results in higher productivity or high production yields greater satisfaction is arguable. Nonetheless, both claims underscore the need to consider the affective experience of participants in an environment as both cause and consequence of their involvement.

Dynamics of Organized Environments

The previously discussed models, structures, and characteristics combine to create certain environmental milieus, readily described in varying degrees of organizational flexibility. Hage and Aiken (1970) posited that organized systems could be characterized generally along a continuum from dynamic to static. At one end are dynamic environments that are flexible in design and respond easily to change; at the other end are static environments, which tend to be more rigid in design and therefore resist change. This distinction is used to summarize the points made thus far with regard to the general dynamics of various organizational designs (Exhibit 3.3). The extent to which any environment—whether

Exhibit 3.3. A Synthesis of Organizational Models

Mechanistic ←——————→ **Organic**
Static, Fixed — **Dynamic, Flexible**

Structural/ Bureaucratic

Higher Structural Complexity
Lower Task Complexity

Political

Lower Structural Complexity
Higher Task Complexity

(Higher)
Centralization
Formalization
Stratification
Production
Routinization
Efficiency

Collegial/ Human Relations

Symbolic/ Anarchical
Quantum Science
Feminist
Spiritual

(Lower)
Centralization
Formalization
Stratification
Production
Routinization
Efficiency

Stability ←——————→ **Change**

Systems → Power → Relationships → Influence

a classroom, a department office, a student organization, or a residence hall—is likely to exhibit dynamic or static organizational characteristics can be understood with reference to the aforementioned components and features. Predictions of participant morale within them depend on the characteristics of the individuals involved.

Of particular importance is an understanding of how these organizational structures contribute to the nature of dynamic systems most often associated with successful educational experiences. Adapting Hage and Aiken (1970), structural arrangements of dynamically organized environments combine a higher degree of task complexity with lower centralization, formalization, stratification, efficiency, routinization, and a relative emphasis on the quality (in contrast to quantity) of their products or services. Through the organizational frames covered already, these are the designs of collegial/human relations, symbolic/anarchical, quantum science, feminist, and spiritual models, where leaders more often focus on the quality of relationships in the setting while supporting change and attempting to influence directions. In the context of a classroom environment, higher task complexity may be apparent in multiple perspectives on topics and in the nature of self-directed assignments and learning tasks. The degrees of centralization and formalization (two aspects that often work hand in hand) may be lowered by a more facilitative approach, engaging students actively in the planning and determination of the course syllabus and encouraging them to pursue a variety of creative options for completing course goals (e.g., collaborative projects, independent assignments, or multiple and hybrid formats). This, of course, is a very labor-intensive process for instructors and students alike. That is, evaluating essay exams and other unique learning products, such as Web pages and performances, requires much greater time and effort on the part of the instructor than evaluating machine-scored, multiple-choice exams, therefore lowering the degree of efficiency in the setting. However, such environments are highly conducive to change and innovation, the essence of powerful educational systems responsive to individual needs (Strange, 1983).

Static environments, on the other hand, tend to discourage change and innovation and are characterized by lower degrees of task complexity, higher centralization, formalization, stratification, efficiency, and a relative emphasis on the quantity of their products or services. Applying this template again to a classroom setting, it becomes apparent how such an arrangement might discourage creativity and innovation, and therefore active learning. A course syllabus where only the instructor has input exacts little investment from students with respect to their learning interests and goals; class assignments that are highly structured and explicitly and rigidly formatted are less likely to be responsive to individual learning styles and needs; insistence on formal titles and status diminishes the kind of personalized atmosphere supportive of the risk-taking inherent to learning new ideas; and an overemphasis on efficiency (e.g., "We just don't have time to explore that") and quantity of readings and assignments (at the expense of quality) tends to invoke a just get it done attitude among students as the course unfolds. A key point in this analysis is that powerful developmental environments, whether in the classroom, student organization meeting, or residence hall association, are those that exhibit characteristics of dynamic organizations, where individual differences are appreciated, participation is expected, interactions are personal rather than functional, and risk-taking is encouraged (Exhibit 3.4).

The degree to which any organized environment is static or dynamic can also potentially affect the morale of participants in the setting, depending on individual differences. For example, consider the case of a more static classroom environment (rational-bureaucratic and political), where the instructor makes all the decisions about the timing and content of what is taught (higher centralization), where assignments are governed by highly

Exhibit 3.4. Static Organizations Versus Developmental Environments

Static Organizations	Developmental Environments
• Uniformity, simplification, and routinization of procedures	• Appreciation for the unique and creative
• Minimize conflict and variance	• Encourage complexity, diversity, and controversy
• Centralize substantive decisions	• Maximize responsibility of participants in making decisions (role-taking)
• Clear stratification of authority and responsibility	• Encourage personalism and community by minimizing status and power
• Formalize and specify regulations for accurate accountability	• Minimize formality to create levels of ambiguity and flexibility in response to individual need
• Maximize achievement per unit of time and resource	• Maximize time and resource per unit of achievement
• Interactions based on functional responsibilities	• Interactions based on personal modeling and mentoring
• Minimize risk-taking to maximize efficient use of resources	• Encourage opportunities for risk taking to maximize educational effectiveness

Source: Strange, C. C. (1983). Human development theory and administrative practice in student affairs: Ships passing in the daylight? *NASPA Journal* 21(1): 2-8. Reprinted by permission of NASPA--Student Affairs Administrators in Higher Education (http://www.naspa.org).

specific and inflexible rules (higher formalization), where few questions or comments are encouraged for fear of wasting time (higher emphasis on production and efficiency), and where lectures prevail and quizzes assess simple recall of information (higher routinization and lower task complexity). Such a classroom environment may be comforting to some students, who, for example, hold assumptions of a prereflective level of cognitive reasoning

(King & Kitchener, 1994), which supports the acquisition of answers in the midst of certainty. On the other hand, it may also be very boring and unchallenging to students with a different set of assumptions about what it means to learn, such as those of a more relativistic (Perry, 1970) or reflective judgment orientation (King & Kitchener, 1994), who pursue reasoned probabilities within an uncertain world. Various personality styles may also respond differently to this same environment. Sensing and judging Myers-Briggs types (Myers, 1980), with their emphasis on specificity and closure, or conventional and realistic Holland types (Holland, 1973), whose orientation is toward order and organization in their environment, might enjoy the routine and standardization of such a class, but the consequent high structure may frustrate intuitive perceivers and artistic or social types, who share many different and opposing preferences. As another example, student organizations structured around a hierarchical model of constitutionally based roles and powers (rational-bureaucratic in style) may be less attractive to female students socialized in a relational ethic of care and connectedness (Forrest, Hotalling, & Kuk, 1986; Gilligan, 1982), preferring a more heterarchical, fluid, and more informal arrangement (collegial in style).

A similar person-environment dynamic may apply to understanding attraction and satisfaction of students in a residence hall setting. The overall degree of organizational structure in the hall, as is reflected in the manner in which goals are set, rules implemented and enforced, policies decided, and resources expended, may or may not be compatible with the characteristics of students living there. For example, residents who are limited in their knowledge of organizational leadership and participation or who are simply inexperienced may not be ready to assume the responsibilities of an intentional democratic community (Crookston, 1974). A more highly structured and static organizational environment may be appropriate in such cases. On the other hand, a more advanced student group, whose talents and styles have been tested in a variety of settings, may become disinterested and turned off by a highly structured system that allows for little student input and involvement. It is therefore critical for residence life professionals, along with faculty and other student affairs administrators, to have an accurate understanding of the developmental characteristics of students as a source of information for encouraging an appropriate organizational environment (Strange, 1983, 1994, 2010, 2014).

Organizational Performances

We conclude this discussion of the organizational features of human environments with reference to what Hage (1980) argued are the essential four performances of organizational functioning: innovation, efficiency, quantity of production, and morale.

These indicators are "central to any theory involving how well an organization is doing ... [and] are necessary for the survival of [any] organization. If all the workers [e.g., staff, faculty, students] quit or costs skyrocket; if there is never any product [service] change or worst of all, there is no production [service] whatsoever, then the organization presumably ceases to exist" (Hage, 1980, p. 35). Although the language of his comments (e.g., "production") may reflect a presumed focus on business-like organizations, the importance of Hage's four performances is also relevant to the context of educational institutions. Obviously, colleges or universities could not exist if low morale led to high attrition among students, faculty, and staff. Turnover is unsettling to any organization and it contributes further to a sense among those remaining that perhaps something is wrong. From the human relations tradition in organizational research comes the importance of member morale and satisfaction in understanding organizational functioning. Satisfied members tend to remain productive in the organization longer; dissatisfied members are at risk for becoming unproductive or just dropping out.

Innovation, too, is an important performance criterion for colleges and universities. As dynamic institutions, colleges must be responsive to societal conditions, reflecting changes in programs and curricula to continue to attract a sufficient student enrollment base. The foundation of any institution of higher learning must support the creation and implementation of new ideas and practices for purposes of expanding our understanding of the world around us and for improving its functioning. In that sense, colleges and universities, in addition to their role as transmitters of culture, are institutions dedicated to innovation. Resistance to change and innovation threatens the very ethos of any organization committed to new knowledge and learning.

Educational institutions must also be productive. Programs must be offered, courses must be taught, students must graduate, grants must be procured, research must be conducted, and manuscripts must be published. Annual reports typically highlight increases on various measures (students served, graduates placed, student credit hours generated) over the previous year and bemoan any decreases (e.g., that enrollments are down). Finally, as important as all of our institutional goals are, they can be accomplished only with finite resources. Fiduciary responsibility and striving for efficiency is a mandate of both public and private trust for colleges and universities, as the competition for support increases and pressures for accountability persist, both from sources that fund them and consumers that use them. Indeed, being responsive to change, being productive and efficient, and supporting the morale of members is a useful template for successful performance in any organizational subunit of a college or university, whether a classroom, an administrative office, a service center, a student organization, or a residence hall.

Challenges of Organizational Size

Whether or not an organization is able to maintain a dynamic or static quality and how well an organization functions with respect to the above performances have much to do with (among other factors) organizational size. As size increases, an organization develops a different set of characteristics that distinguishes it from smaller, human-scale systems. These characteristics, in turn, have certain effects on organizational performances, including the morale of members.

Among key organizational issues that challenge and shape collegiate environments today are those related to organizational size. Size of institutions has become a concern only relatively recently in the history of American higher education. Since World War II, and especially during the decade of the 1960s, when the higher education community responded to unusual demands for access and opportunity, colleges and universities grew rapidly, fed by an infusion of federal dollars and promises of an economy of scale. Institutional growth became the order of the day. Classrooms grew larger, new high-rise residence halls were built, and faculty and staff were hired in unprecedented numbers to accommodate quickly expanding enrollments. By the end of the decade, large campuses of over 10,000 students enrolled the majority of college students. This expansion, both in the number and size of postsecondary institutions, resulted in tremendous strides forward in the higher education community. New populations were served (Cross, 1971), campus-based research continued to fulfill its promise of unraveling the secrets of the universe, and graduates emerged with the key to the Information Age (Toffler, 1970), ready to participate as members of a society on the verge of great things. At the same time, though, American higher education also began to reveal itself as increasingly impersonal, bureaucratic, and indifferent to the many and varied needs of individual students, features principally related to its new expanded size. Boyer (1987, p. 145) found this issue to be related to institutional mission:

> Class size, like so many other aspects of teaching and learning, varies from one type of institution to another. Twenty-nine percent of the students at research universities report that "most" or "all" of their classes have

> more than one hundred students enrolled; at liberal arts colleges only 1 percent of the students report having most or all classes of this size. At the other end, only 5 percent of students at research universities said they had no classes larger than one hundred students. At liberal arts colleges, it was 80 percent.

Boyer went on to conclude that "one important way to measure a college's commitment to undergraduate education it to look at class size in general education" (p. 145).

Because of this increased reliance on an economy of scale for efficient use of resources, larger institutions are typically *overmanned* settings (Wicker, 1973), where too many people compete for too few opportunities for meaningful involvement and achievement. In his seminal work on student development and the college experience, Chickering (1969) first identified this as a condition of redundancy. Generally speaking, larger institutions tend to be overmanned and redundant, and smaller institutions tend to be undermanned; that is, there are more opportunities for meaningful achievement than there are people to assume them.

The issue of institutional size is a particularly crucial organizational concern in higher education, with no easy solution. Blau (1973, pp. 99–100), in his classic study of academic organizations, identified the dilemma institutions face in that respect:

> The ability of a university or college to recruit good faculty and good students and to attain and maintain a high academic reputation depends on conditions that in turn depend to a considerable extent on the large scope of the academic enterprise. High academic standing requires specialized academic pursuits in a large number of diverse fields, which simply cannot be developed in a small college. It also requires competing with other

> institutions for the best faculty and the best students, and the financial resources for doing so can rarely be mobilized by a small academic institution. Once a top reputation has been achieved, it attracts financial contributions, outstanding students, and great scientists and scholars, helping to sustain the elite standing of the academic institution, and at the same time fostering further growth.

The other side of the coin, Blau (1973) recognized, is imprinted with the deleterious effects large size invariably brings to education and that "endanger the quality of academic work. It [large size] inevitably makes the academic institution more impersonal and engenders bureaucratic developments in it, both of which reduce its attraction for the best students and faculty members" (p. 100). The trade-off, then, for an economy of scale in higher education is the challenge educators face in supporting conditions known to be related to a powerful educational experience, such as a sense of community, opportunities for involvement and creativity—in effect, those that contribute to an economy of learning (Strange & Hannah, 1994, March). Overall, as institutional size increases, such conditions are simply more difficult to create and maintain.

Organizational size also has implications for how people function and evaluate their experiences in a system. In a discussion of organizational environment factors related to size, Moos (1986) drew attention to one empirical conclusion: "As group size increase[s], morale and attitudes become less positive, and absenteeism is more frequent" (p. 410). He went on to suggest that these forces might have particular negative effects on "marginal individuals in large schools (i.e., schools with relatively overmanned settings) [who] have a much lower sense of obligation to the school than do non marginal students" (p. 408). Banning (1989, p. 59) concurred in his analysis of the impact of college environments on first-year students.

> The ratio of persons per setting is critical to what happens to the people within the setting. In the undermanned setting [see Wicker, 1973], people more frequently serve in responsible positions, engage in actions that are challenging, perform activities that are important to the setting, engage in a wide range of activities, see themselves as important and responsible for the setting, and work hard to maintain the function of the setting.

The college campus offers numerous illustrations of the organizational dynamics highlighted in these observations. Fighting the bureaucracy becomes a rallying cry for all too many students attempting to negotiate the barriers inevitable in the organized systems of a large flagship university. Endless long lines, numbers instead of names, and forms in triplicate all take their toll on the human spirit at a time in students' lives when questions of identity and purpose (Chickering & Reisser, 1993) demand, and are better served by, a higher degree of individualization, personalism, and support (Widick, Knefelkamp, & Parker, 1975). Even the expressed goals of the academy—the development of intellect and reason—are jeopardized by the limitations of size. As Fran inquired with frustration in the opening scenario, what are the chances of any individual student posing a question, offering a comment, exchanging a point of view, or writing a position statement, in a classroom with 200 students? What are the chances of any individual student assuming a position of responsibility in a residence hall where 900 students compete for only six available governance committee vacancies? The implications of this conclusion on organizational size are clear and consistent: Bigger is not better when it comes to education and learning.

Asking how many are enough is certainly justifiable in this context. There are no hard and fast rules, but clues might be found in the research on human scale development or design and the work on social networking. The Human Scale Development (H-SD) model emerged from the field of economics to focus on the problem of human well-being (Max-Neef, 1989). Although a thorough presentation of this model is beyond the scope of the present chapter, suffice it to note that the authors construct the problem as a function of different types of satisfiers (i.e., being, having, doing, and interacting) satisfying within a given context presumed axiological human needs (i.e., subsistence, protection, affection, understanding, participation, idleness, creation, identity, and freedom). In that respect, human scale development and design theory seeks to identify and create environments and systems that are humanly fulfilling. In essence, institutions of higher learning share that same purpose and can benefit greatly from such a human scale template. Beyond such a qualitative endpoint is the practical concern for where one draws the line on institutional size, whether overall or within any given campus subgroup. Here the work of the British anthropologist Robin Dunbar is instructive. According to Dunbar (1992), the number of people with whom one can maintain stable social relationships, in which an individual knows who each person is and how each person relates to every other person, is approximately 150 (i.e., Dunbar's number). It is no secret that large institutions tend to have higher attrition rates than smaller ones. Perhaps the greatest challenge to many enrollment-driven institutions is to compensate for problems of overmanning with the intentional development of smaller subenvironments, such as cluster colleges (Blau, 1973), residential learning communities, student organizations, and class discussion sections. Beginning with the principles of Human Scale Development, combined with an eye on the limits of Dunbar's number, may be a good place to start.

This chapter began with the recognition that many features of human environments reflect the mix of organizational structures that emerge in social systems for purposes of meeting specific goals.

Dimensions of complexity, centralization, formalization, stratification, production, routinization, and efficiency contribute to varying degrees of flexibility or rigidity in the environment. The resultant degree of environmental dynamism then, in turn, affects the organizational performances of innovation, efficiency, production, and participant morale, as mediated by the impact of organizational size. Finally, to be more responsive to students' individual learning needs, educational environments must be flexible, encourage innovation, and engage students as meaningful participants within the boundaries of human scale design.

Questions for Discussion

1. What organizational frames best describe the immediate environment of your office or department?
2. What organizational structure is emphasized most in your institutional work environment?
3. If you were to change (increase or decrease) a particular organizational structure in your work environment, what would it be, how would you do so, and why?
4. How does institutional size (small or large) impact the organizational performances of your college or university?
5. How is student success enhanced or inhibited by the overall organizational dynamics of your setting?

4

Socially Constructed Environments:

Different Views Through Different Eyes

Scenario: There's Something About This Place

Returning from the first year convocation ceremony where the president, several faculty members, key administrators, and the student body president explained some of the history and traditions of Adams College, Clare, a first semester social work major, was impressed with what she heard and experienced that day.

"There's something about this place; it just feels really neat to me," she said in a phone conversation with her parents that evening. "They're really serious about hitting the books early here. But I get a sense that they really care about how we do, too." Earlier that day, Clare was introduced to her faculty co-investigator, Dr. Williams, in the social sciences division where they spent some time going over the curriculum and discussing the Adams program with a small group of other related majors.

"It was really interesting to hear about the service learning projects we can get involved with; they even have you over for dinner twice a semester to talk about how things are going!" she continued, amazed and excited.

Adams College had always considered the social sciences to be among its strengths, and through recent grants from the National Institute of Health and the Ford Foundation it had established an innovative, collaborative research program where interdisciplinary teams of students and faculty pursued various projects relevant to regional concerns.

"They asked me to join a project looking at some of the effects of underemployment on family well-being here," Clare explained. "We even have a faculty member from philosophy and one from sociology on our team." Clare had worked on a few small projects before in high school with one of her teachers. "But nothing like this!" she exclaimed. "It seems like they really emphasize working together as a team here, and getting out and doing things, not just reading about things." Pictures of past teams and descriptions of the projects they completed lined the entry hallway in the Fischer Building where several of Clare's classes were held.

"It's exactly how I thought it would be, from the first day I spent here last March," she said, acknowledging her first impressions of the challenging but very supportive atmosphere she felt while participating in a campus visit weekend at Adams. "I'm really looking forward to the end-of-the-year banquet they have to celebrate what each team accomplishes!"

Out-of-class life also evoked distinct impressions at Adams College. Clare's orientation team became a key involvement group for her, once matriculation got under way. "They really encourage us to join a student organization on campus and get involved. The first week I was here, someone asked me to become part of a committee whose job it was to talk to other first year students about leadership opportunities. I was amazed at all the things you get to do in these groups."

Special value seems to be placed on serving the needs of the community adjacent to Adams, too. Clare remembered reading in a welcoming letter from the chair of the social sciences department that "understanding of the world must be balanced with action to improve it."

"It seems like everyone spends some of their time each week volunteering for something; I need to think about that myself, once I get all my schedule worked out," she thought.

For almost a decade, Adams College had offered a developmental transcript system, whereby students are encouraged to identify, evaluate, and record their various campus involvement experiences with the guidance of a senior student peer advisor and an emeritus faculty mentor. At the completion of the degree, this transcript becomes part of the student's official academic record, complete with the college's seal and motto: In Omnia Experientia Eruditio (In Every Experience There Is Learning). Clare's final note, after only one week at Adams, was, "This place is so cool!"

Clare's early experiences at Adam's College in this scenario are less about the formal materials she was given to read as part of her orientation than they are about the general impressions and intuited understandings communicated to her through conversations with current students; stories she heard; and artifacts, symbols, and rituals she observed and participated in. She expected to work hard as a new student and, at the same time, she anticipated a strong, positive atmosphere of caring and support in the process. What came through clearly were the values Adams College espoused as well as the manner in which they were enacted. Emphases on academically challenging work, interdisciplinary teams, personalized relationships with faculty, holistic learning, leadership opportunities beyond the classroom, and the need to serve others all merged to create a distinctive campus ethos that proved attractive and very satisfying to Clare, as she came to understand quickly that she had found a special place. She had always dreamed of college being like this. The notion that environments exert their influence on students' expectations, attitudes, and behaviors through the mediated and subjective perceptions or collective social constructions of those who participate in them is the touchstone for this fourth perspective on human environments.

Socially constructed models of the environment recognize that a consensus of individuals who perceive and characterize their environment constitutes a measure of environmental press, climate, or culture in a setting. These perceived characteristics of the environment and their cultural expressions, in turn, exert a directional influence on behavior (Moos, 1986). For example, inferred from the perspective of Clare, the press, social climate, and cultural artifacts at Adams College are directed toward, among other ends, achievement in the social sciences and a supportive atmosphere that encourages faculty–student collaboration in research and learning. A consensus of similar perspectives from other participants would suggest that such characteristics pervade the campus environment at Adams. Thus, developing an understanding of any environment entails asking participants what they see, understand, and feel about the place.

Seeing Is Believing

Differing from the physical, human aggregate, and organizational components and models discussed in the previous three chapters, constructed approaches focus on the collective subjective views and experiences of participant observers, assuming that environments are understood best through the perceptions of the individuals within them. Although characteristics of an environment can be measured independently as being, for example, 70° Fahrenheit (a physical fact), it may seem warm to one person and cool to another, leading one individual to put on a sweater and another to take one off. Likewise, identically composed human aggregates may seem friendly to one person, but "overbearing" to another. Similarly a higher degree of formalization (many explicit rules), a feature of the organizational environment, may be reassuring to one participant, it may be overly restrictive to another, with obvious consequences for their respective satisfaction in the setting.

At the core of these various perceptual approaches to human environments is the notion that examining collective personal perspectives of an environment (from inside participants as well as from outside observers) is critical to understanding how people are likely to react to those environments. Whether individuals are attracted to a particular environment or are satisfied and stable within that environment is partially a function of how they perceive, evaluate, and construct the environment. In effect, their perceptions are the reality of that environment for them. In that sense, these approaches espouse a phenomenological orientation to human environments, inasmuch as they explore what participants see in the environment as a basis for understanding and predicting their behavior. These models of constructed environments share conceptual roots with the early work of Murray (1938), Pace and Stern (1958), and Stern (1970) on the interaction between individual needs and environmental presses. Extensions of this idea are apparent in the subsequent social climate frameworks developed by Rudolph Moos (1974, 1979) and the renewed interest in the dynamics of campus culture (Kuh, 1993; Tierney, 1993) as a tool for describing and understanding institutional environments.

Environmental Press

The foundational constructs of environmental press were first articulated within the context of postsecondary education by Murray (1938), Pace and Stern (1958), and Stern (1970). Pace and Stern (1958), in their pioneering investigations of varying institutional characteristics, defined *press* as "the characteristic demands or features of the environment as perceived by those who live in the particular environment" (Walsh, 1973, p. 114). Either participants in or observers of an environment therefore can infer measurement of an environmental "press" from consensual self-reports of activities. For example, if 75 percent of a representative sample of students on a given campus (such as Adams College in the opening scenario) report that students frequently spend time volunteering in the local community, a significant press toward altruism and service might be inferred, perhaps a reputation concurred with by those outsiders who observe also what goes on there. The various identified presses in an environment may or may not correspond to participants' needs, that is, those "organizational tendencies that seem to give unity and direction to a person's behavior" (Stern, 1970, p. 6). For example, an academic achievement need might be inferred from an individual's self report of a high level of studying and engagement in additional intellectual activities, such as Mortar Board or an honors student organization. General correspondence (or congruence) between individual need and environmental press is presumed to be growth producing. Such a match would be apparent in the case of a student who, like Clare in the opening scenario, has a high need for achievement, affiliation, and involvement and finds herself in an opportunity-rich environment, like Adams College, that encourages and allows her to do so. Significant dissonance between need and press is presumed growth inhibiting, usually contributing to dissatisfaction and turnover.

This need-press line of inquiry resulted in original development of the College Characteristics Index (CCI) (Saunders, 1969), a measure of environmental press within a framework of eleven factors capable of differentiating among college environments: aspiration level; intellectual climate; student dignity; academic climate; academic achievement; self-expression; group life; academic organization; social form; play-work; and vocational climate. Grouped thematically, these factors yield a profile of the general intellectual and nonintellectual climate of an institution. For example, a limited emphasis on play-work and vocational climate—in combination with a significant press toward aspiration level, intellectual climate, student dignity, academic climate, academic achievement, and self-expression—may result in an overall higher intellectual climate image for an institution. Such features were picked-up on by Clare as she learned about the Adams College experience in the beginning scenario. An institution's overall nonintellectual climate might also be apparent in its relative press toward self-expression, group life, academic organization, social form, play-work, and vocational climate.

Related to this approach is the College and University Environment Scale (CUES) (Pace, 1969), which yields participant descriptions of an institution in reference to seven distinctive presses: scholarship, awareness, community, propriety, practicality, campus morale, and quality of teaching (faculty–student relationships). Again, the logic of this method is to exact participants' collective impressions and experiences. The extent to which participants intuit these features constitutes the environmental press of a college or university and can be used to distinguish fundamental differences between institutional types. Thus, a consensus among students at a two-year community college might emphasize a press toward vocational climate or practicality, consistent with the educational mission of such an institution. In contrast, a small, selective private liberal arts college, like Adams, might be recognized for its competitive press toward academic achievement, community, and quality of teaching. Regardless of whether these same thematic features noted in these assessments remain current, it seems clear that to increase their marketability and retention many of today's campuses of all types are placing considerable emphasis, for example, on community, propriety, campus morale, and quality of teaching (faculty-student relationships), especially during campus orientation programs and first-year experiences. Nonetheless, assessing participant impressions through these or other frameworks can yield valuable information for how an institution is succeeding in its mission. Indeed, such an approach continues to serve as the methodological foundation for both the College Student Experience Questionnaire (CSEQ) assessment (Pace & Kuh, 1998) and the National Surveys of Student Engagement (NSSE) (Kuh, 2003), which continue to inform the higher education community about the functioning of various kinds of institutions.

Social Climate

Consistent with the assumptions of the environmental press models discussed previously, Moos (1979, 1986) and his colleagues at Stanford University developed a *social climate* model, describing the nature and effects of various "environmental personalities" as perceived by participants. According to Moos, social climate is composed of three social-environmental domains, each with a respective set of dimensions contributing to that particular domain: *relationship dimensions*, reflecting "the extent to which people are involved in the setting ... support and help one another, and ... express themselves freely and openly" (Moos, 1979, p. 14); *personal growth and development dimensions*, measuring the "basic goals of the setting ... areas in which personal development and self-enhancement tend to occur" (Moos, 1979, p. 16); and *system maintenance and change dimensions*, assessing "the extent to which the environment is orderly and clear in its expectations, maintains control, and responds to change" (Moos, 1979, p. 16). These three domains guide the understanding and assessment of key aspects of any social climate, and they manifest themselves in specific ways depending on the type of environment being examined. For example, using this three-domain model, Moos (1979) identified ten aspects important to understanding the impact of campus residential living environments (see Exhibit 4.1). Classrooms, another significant environment in students' lives, can also be understood in terms of this framework (Exhibit 4.2).

To complete this picture of the various interactive social climates that affect students' lives, Moos's (1994) model also provides descriptions of the social climate dimensions of social or task-group environments, helpful for understanding students' experiences as participants in various campus groups and organizations; work environments, important for examining the experiences of many students who hold jobs either on or off campus; and family environments, a basic set of relationships that students, traditional and nontraditional alike, bring with them as a pretext for the college experience (Exhibit 4.3).

Exhibit 4.1. University Residence Environment Scale (URES) Dimensions and Subscales

Relationship Dimensions:

Involvement—degree of commitment to the house and residents [and] amount of interaction and feeling of friendship.

Emotional Support—manifest concern for others in the house, [the extent of] efforts to aid one another with academic and personal problems, [and] emphasis on open and honest communication.

Personal Growth and Development Dimensions:

Independence—emphasis on freedom and self-reliance versus socially proper and conformist behavior.

Traditional Social Orientation—stress on dating, going to parties, and other traditional heterosexual interactions.

Competition—degree to which a wide variety of activities, such as dating and grades, are cast into a competitive framework.

Academic Achievement—prominence of strictly classroom and academic accomplishments and concerns.

Intellectuality—emphasis on cultural, artistic, and other intellectual activities.

System Maintenance and System Change Dimensions:

Order and Organization—amount of formal structure, neatness, and organization (rules, schedules, established procedures).

Student Influence—extent to which student residents formulate and enforce rules and control use of the money, selection of staff, roommates, and the like.

Innovation—organizational and individual spontaneity of behaviors and ideas [and] number and variety of new activities.

Source: Moos (1979, p. 29).

Exhibit 4.2. Classroom Environment Scale (CES) Dimensions and Subscales

Relationship Dimensions:

Involvement—extent to which students have attentive interest in class activities and participate in discussions [as well as] the extent to which students do work on their own and enjoy the class.

Affiliation—level of friendship students feel for each other; the extent to which they help each other with homework, get to know each other easily, and enjoy working together.

Teacher Support—amount of help, concern, and friendship the teacher directs toward the students [and the] extent to which the teacher talks openly with students, trusts them, and is interested in their ideas.

Personal Growth and Development Dimensions:

Task Orientation—extent to which it is important to complete the activities that have been planned [and the] emphasis the teacher places on staying on the subject matter.

Competition—emphasis placed on students competing with each other for grades and recognition [as well as] the difficulty of achieving good grades.

System Maintenance and Change Dimensions:

Order and Organization—emphasis on students behaving in an orderly and polite manner and on the overall organization of assignments and classroom activities [and the] degree to which students tend to remain calm and quiet.

Rule Clarity—emphasis on establishing and following a clear set of rules, and on students knowing what the consequences will be if they do not follow them [as well as] the extent to which the teacher is consistent in dealing with students who break rules.

Teacher Control—how strict the teacher is in enforcing the rules, and the severity of the punishment for rule infractions [in addition to] the number of rules and the ease of students getting in trouble.

Innovation—how much students contribute to planning classroom activities, and the amount of unusual and varying activities and assignments planned by the teacher [and the] extent to which the teacher attempts to use new techniques and encourages creative thinking in the students.

Source: Moos, R. H., & Trickett, E. J. (1974). *Classroom environment scale: Manual.* Palo Alto, CA: Consulting Psychologists Press. p. 3.

Exhibit 4.3. Social Climate Dimensions and Subscales Across Environments

	Relationships	Personal Growth and Development	System Maintenance and Change
Residence Organization Environments	Involvement Emotional Support	Independence Traditional/Social Orientation Competition Academic Achievement Intellectuality	Order and Innovation Student Influence
Classroom Organization Environments	Involvement Affiliation Teacher Support	Task Orientation Competition	Order and Rule Clarity Teacher Control Innovation
Group Environments	Cohesion Leader Support Expressiveness	Independence Task-Orientation Self-Discovery Anger and Aggression	Leader Control Innovation
Work Environments	Involvement Coworker Cohesion Supervisor Support	Autonomy Task-Orientation Work Pressure	Clarity Control Innovation Physical Comfort
Family Environments	Cohesiveness Expressiveness Conflict	Independence Achievement Orientation Intellectual-Cultural Orientation Active-Recreational Orientation Moral-Religious Emphasis	Organization Control

Source: Adapted from Moos (1974). *The social climate scales: An overview*. Palo Alto, CA: Consulting Psychologists Press.

As illustrated further, specific dimensions vary according to the type of environment assessed. For example, relationship dimensions of social task groups include degrees of cohesion, leader support, and expressiveness; for work environments they include involvement, peer cohesion, and supervisor support; and for family environments, cohesiveness and expressiveness. Each of these social climate dimensions differs in strength along a continuum, from low to high, depending upon the characteristics attributed to the setting by participants in them. Also, the particular combination of dimensions in any given environment may create a special focus or orientation in that setting. For example, using data from the URES, Moos (1979) identified six characteristic environments or personalities he attributed to various campus living groups:

1. Relationship-oriented living environments or units characterized by a supportive relationship orientation that strongly values emotional support and involvement, with some stress on dating and cultural pursuits but little emphasis on engaging in new and different activities.
2. Traditionally socially oriented living environments, units that "give priority to dating, going to parties, and other traditional heterosexual interactions, as well as to aspects of formal structure and organization, such as rules, schedules, established procedures, and neatness" (p. 55).
3. Supportive achievement-oriented living environments, those that place "their highest emphasis on the relationship dimensions of involvement and emotional support and on the personal growth dimension of academic achievement ... [in a] noncompetitive context ... [but with] very little focus on independence" (p. 56).

4. Competition-oriented living environments, where there is "high stress on competition [with] very little involvement or emotional support" (pp. 56–57).
5. Independence-oriented living environments that "encourage a wide diversity of student behaviors without specific social sanction and do not value socially proper or conformist behavior" (p. 57).
6. Intellectually oriented living environments, relatively rare units consisting "primarily of theme houses and living-learning and cooperative units composed largely of students in the humanities and social sciences" (p. 58) and emphasizing intellectuality and independence.

Likewise, varying emphases on certain aspects in classrooms, social task groups, work settings, and family environments may create a combined characteristic effect toward one orientation or another. For example, one classroom may be very innovation oriented, while another is control oriented; one work environment might be very competitive and another oriented toward supportive relationships; one family's social climate may express itself in a strong supportive achievement orientation while another emphasizes independence.

These various environmental orientations have been found to be a function of differing aggregate and physical configurations as well, at least in the context of living environments. For example, Moos (1979) found that predominantly male units tend to be more competition oriented, female units more traditionally socially oriented, and coed units independence and intellectually oriented. Furthermore, supportive achievement and relationship-oriented units tend to be almost exclusively female and coed. Living units composed of a greater proportion of single rooms tend to be more oriented toward competition and less toward supportive achievement, independence, intellectuality, or relationships. Thus, variations in the differing features of students' perceived environments yield constructed milieus that, in turn, further influence students' attraction, satisfaction, and stability within those environments.

Finally, perhaps the value of this social climate approach to evaluating socially constructed features of environments is that it offers integrated models particular to various contexts and settings on campus. In doing so it suggests ways various components of the environment cohere to have an overall effect on students.

Campus Culture

Another framework for assessing institutional environments from a perceptual or constructed approach is found in the literature on organizational and campus culture. Researchers such as Chaffee and Tierney (1988), Horowitz (1984, 1987), Kuh and Whitt (1988), Moffatt (1989), Kuh, Schuh, Whitt and Associates (1991), Matthews (1997), Magolda (2000; 2001), Kuh, Kinzie, Schuh, Whitt, and Associates (2005), and Thornton and Jaeger (2007) have all drawn attention to applications of this approach to understanding colleges and universities. Culture, with roots in anthropology, sociology, and social psychology, is inherently a perceptual construct, in that the culture of any environment reflects the assumptions, beliefs, and values inhabitants construct to interpret and understand the meaning of events and actions in the setting. Schein (1992) referred to culture as "a pattern of basic assumptions—invented, discovered, or developed by a given group as it learns to cope with its problems of external adaptation and internal integration—that has worked well enough to be considered valid and, therefore, to be taught to new members as the correct way to perceive, think, and feel in relation to those problems" (p. 9). In their introduction to the concept of campus culture, Kuh and Hall (1993) defined it as the "confluence of institutional history, campus traditions, and the values and assumptions that shape the character of a given college or university" (pp. 1–2). Culture, then, is essentially "a social construction" (Chaffee & Tierney, p. 10), reflected in traditions, stories, ceremonies, history, myths, heroines and heroes, interactions among members, policies and practices, symbols, and mission and philosophy. It was precisely these aspects of Adams College that most powerfully impressed Clare in the opening scenario of this chapter.

Drawing on the work of others (Dyer, 1986; Lundberg, 1985; Schein, 1985), Kuh and Hall (1993) described four levels of culture—artifacts, perspectives, values, and assumptions. Cultural artifacts include those tangible aspects (physical, verbal, and behavioral) "the meaning and functions of which may be known [only] by members" (Kuh & Hall, p. 4). Virtually all campuses have some distinctive physical artifacts, usually buildings, landscape features, or various other physical attributes, which mark points of interest on a typical admissions or orientation tour. A historical quadrangle, a state-of-the-art recreation center, a well-manicured green space, a Founders' Hall, a majestic library, a bell tower, or a technologically advanced classroom building can all serve to convey to members and nonmembers alike some of the core values that shape an institution's culture and the historical roots from which they came. Verbal artifacts include language, stories, and myths. Language often incorporates terms of endearment (Kuh et al., 1991) associated with specific institutions, as well as slang terms typical of traditional college-age cultures and subcultures (Hancock, 1990). Stories about significant campus leaders, personalities, and even mythical figures convey key moments of institutional history and offer personal models of emulation consistent with institutional values and assumptions. Behavioral artifacts might include a host of celebratory activities and events (such as orientation and convocation) that serve to connect members with the institution, acknowledge their participation in institutional subcultures and groups (e.g., sorority and fraternity initiation), or send them on their way following completion of their institutional experience (e.g., commencement). Various campus rituals, another form of behavioral artifact, also serve to connect the past to the present (Masland, 1985), as happens annually, for example, when anniversary classes are remembered at homecoming or alumni week.

Perspectives, or "the socially shared rules and norms applicable to a given context" (Kuh & Hall, 1993, p. 6), constitute a second level of institutional culture. As "social conventions manifested through behavior," perspectives define the "way things are done" and "determine what is 'acceptable behavior' for students, faculty, staff and others in various institutional settings. They are relatively easy to determine and the members of various groups who adhere to perspectives are usually aware of them" (p. 6). Thus, students quickly become aware of appropriate campus customs, attire, and ideologies associated with, for example, Earlham College (Krehbiel & Strange, 1991), where consensus is the way decisions are made; Iowa State University (Schuh, 1991), where participation in departmental clubs and organizations is the norm from the first day on campus; or University of Louisville (Strange, 1991), where a history of social consciousness and causes contributes an air of political liberalism to many campus discussions. Members of the campus community and subcommunities come to recognize certain perspectives as typical of those who reflect and construct institutional culture.

Values, a third level of institutional culture, are more abstract than perspectives and reflect the "espoused as well as the enacted ideals of an institution or group, and serve as the basis on which members of a culture or subculture judge situations, acts, objects and people" (Kuh & Hall, 1993, p. 6). College catalogs, convocation speeches, campus philosophy and mission statements, and core planning documents are important sources for understanding institutional values in their espoused forms. At Earlham College, an institution built on Quaker principles and practices, specific institutional documents underscore the importance of shared governance and responsibility as its principal operating value, which is conveyed to each new member upon entering the college (Krehbiel & Strange, 1991).

Assumptions comprise the fourth and deepest level of institutional culture and are implicit, abstract axioms or "tacit beliefs that members use to define their role, their relationship to others, and the nature of the organization in which they live" (Kuh & Hall, 1993, p. 7). Schein (1992, pp. 95–96) suggested that various other artifacts of organizational culture—such as organizational missions, primary tasks and goals, and the means chosen to achieve and measure goals—all reflect these fundamental assumptions:

1. *The nature of reality and truth*: The shared assumptions that define what is real and what is not, what is a fact in the physical realm and the social realm, how truth is ultimately to be determined, and whether truth is revealed or discovered.
2. *The nature of time*: The shared assumptions that define the basic concept of time in the group, how time is defined and measured, how many kinds of time there are, and the importance of time in the culture.
3. *The nature of space*: The shared assumptions about space and its distribution, how space is allocated and owned, the symbolic meaning of space around the person, the role of space in defining aspects of relationships such as degree of intimacy or definitions of privacy.
4. *The nature of human nature*: The shared assumptions that define what it means to be human and what human attributes are considered intrinsic or ultimate. Is human nature good, evil, or neutral? Are human beings perfectible or not?

5. *The nature of human activity*: The shared assumptions that define what is the right thing for human beings to do in relating to their environment on the basis of the foregoing assumptions about reality and the nature of human nature. In one's basic orientation to life, what is the appropriate level of activity or passivity? At the organizational level, what is the relationship of the organization to its environment? What is work and what is play?
6. *The nature of human relationships*: The shared assumptions that define what is the ultimate right way for people to relate to each other, to distribute power and love. Is life cooperative or competitive; individualistic, group collaborative, or communal? What is the appropriate psychological contract between employers and employees? Is authority ultimately based on traditional lineal authority, moral consensus, law, or charisma? What are the basic assumptions about how conflict should be resolved and how decisions should be made?

How institutional participants respond to these questions yields various assumptions that define and shape the core elements of institutional culture that, in turn, form a powerful milieu within which the processes of education ensue.

According to Schein (1985), organizational culture serves to solve group problems of both external adaptation (i.e., what a group must do to maintain survival in a changing environment) and internal integration (i.e., what the group must do to maintain internal relationships and functioning). As the character Tevye in *Fiddler on the Roof* responded emphatically to the question, How do we keep our balance?: "That I can tell you in one word," he says, "Tradition!" Problems of external adaptation include establishing a core mission, specific goals derived from that mission, a means to attain the goals, criteria for measuring success, and strategies for remediation when goals are not being met. Internal integration tasks include establishing and maintaining a common language and set of concepts, determining criteria for membership, deciding how power is used, delimiting relationships, discerning the nature of rewards and punishments, and defining an ideology that helps the group face inexplicable events (Schein, 1985).

From the paradigm of organizational culture, it can be argued that residence halls, classes, informal student groups, and formal campus organizations are all institutional subcultures that assist participants, staff as well as students, in making meaning of the college experience. In effect, they are powerful tools in socializing students to the goals and purposes of higher education, what it means to be a member of a community, and how to go about the business of being a college student. At times, these cultures can be at cross purposes with the educational goals of an institution, as in the case of the proverbial zoo or animal house culture evident where students place a premium on hedonistic and disruptive activities (Moffatt, 1989). At other times, they can be expressly supportive of institutional goals, as in the case of an honors hall or a residential learning community.

Understanding campus environments from a cultural perspective entails application of the tools of qualitative inquiry—personal interviews, participant observation, and document analysis—in the form of a culture audit (Kuh et al., 1991, 2005). The meaning of various events, personalities, regulations, programs, traditions, symbols, stories, and interactions are discovered, described, and understood, from the perspective of the members of those environments, as reflections of a core set of beliefs and assumptions that is organizational culture. For example, at the University of Michigan, it is important to understand the assumptions of selection, membership, and participation in Martha Cook Hall, where formal Sunday sit-down dinners, rather than the more usual cafeteria-style, mark the beginning of each week for its all-female residents. At the University of Virginia, fourth-year students vie for the prestige of living in one of forty-seven, nine-by-eleven-foot single rooms on "the Lawn," forsaking the convenience of a personal bathroom, as recognition for their academic achievements and overall contributions to the university. Also, at Morehouse College in Atlanta, room numbers assigned to Martin Luther King, Jr. and other noted "Morehouse Men," who were once undergraduates in Graves Hall, are committed to memory by many students.

To understand the intent of Xavier University of New Orleans's six ladder programs, designed to increase the number of underrepresented groups in the health professions, one must learn of the Xavier way, which means "high expectations for academic performance within a highly structured and supportive academic and social environment" (Kuh et al, 1991., p. 233). Likewise, to know Earlham College requires an understanding of Quaker values and beliefs, and to know a Mount Holyoke is to know the history and expectations of its founder, Mary Lyons. That places, too, are important pieces of the campus cultural fabric becomes clear when one understands the significance of Red Square at the Evergreen State College, the Forum at Grinnell College, the Red Barn at the University of Louisville, and the bicycle repair shop at the University of California at Davis. Participant perceptions and understandings of campus organizational culture are an important source of information for designing responsive educational environments, and educators must be particularly sensitive to any discrepancies between their views of the institution and those of students.

The concepts of environmental press, social climate, and campus culture reviewed in this chapter share a common focus on participant perceptions, impressions, and systems of meaning making in understanding the nature of campus environments. They all stress the importance of consensual interpretations and constructions of various elements of campus environments as key sources for understanding behaviors of individuals within those environments. In addition, these models offer conceptual templates, useful in deciding which aspects of various campus environments might warrant greater attention than others, and what resources to prioritize for purposes of environmental redesign. In many ways, common practices of campus branding (Moore, 2004) today, whereby features of colleges and universities are cast into an integrated picture of distinct impressions, represent attempts to capitalize on these collective social constructions. Such information is important for understanding from whence an institution has come and where it might be going.

Questions for Discussion

1. What is most impressive about your college or university to a first-time visitor to campus?
2. What messages and images about your campus are conveyed by its institutional website? What do they say about its brand?
3. How would you go about increasing the Relationship Dimensions of your institution's classroom, residence, work, and group environment social climates?
4. What artifacts of campus culture (physical, verbal, behavioral) at your institution are most memorable to alumni?
5. How are institutional rituals and rites used to enculturate new students at your college or university?

Part Two

Designing Campus Environments That Foster Student Learning and Success

The first part of this book articulated and discussed the principal dynamics of human environments as a function of their physical features, the aggregate characteristics of their inhabitants, their organizational structures, and the collective perceptions or social constructions of those who participate in them. With these basic components of environmental design, this second part attends to the conditions thought to be seminal to the effectiveness of environments committed to purposes of student learning and success: a sense of inclusion and safety, opportunities for involvement or engagement, and experiences of community. Recognizing and understanding these conditions are important steps in shaping institutions to achieve educational purposes. Equally important, though, is acquiring a more complete understanding of learning itself.

Nature of Student Learning

For at least 300 years the dominant narrative on learning in American higher education had been about what happens between faculty and students. Learning was the result of having been taught by a teacher. Mention of peers in the process was inconsequential, if at all, except as a potential source of distraction or dishonesty. The learning site was focused almost exclusively on the classroom, with an occasional use of a laboratory or perhaps a field trip. Regardless, learning was characterized principally for most of that time as a one-way passive experience that resulted perhaps more in limited recall than in deep understanding.

There has been a revolution in such matters over the past fifty years in the U.S. postsecondary system. As colleges and universities have embraced commitments to access, have enrolled an increasingly diverse student body, and have begun focusing more intently on student learning outcomes, the conversation has changed dramatically, especially with greater urgency the last twenty years. This paradigm shift has resulted in a new narrative of student engagement and success. In response, the academy has also begun to alter its thinking about how, where, and with whom students learn. Instead of thinking of learning as a one-dimensional activity, we understand it better now as a multidimensional experience involving multiple intelligences and a wide range of styles and preferences. Instead of planning from behind closed classroom doors, we now sample from a full palette of varied sites and venues—real, virtual, and distant. Instead of focusing on the vertical path from student to teacher, we now explore horizontal webs, where experts, peers, practitioners, and other resource persons ground the holistic processes of discovery, insight, and application in a dynamic community of learning. Creating institutions of consequence requires such a broader perspective on learning. Our review of campus environments here recognizes that point, and reviews the extant literature with that in mind.

Numerous authors have contributed to an expanded understanding of student learning, with forays, for example, into the spirit of teaching and learning (Palmer, 2010) and the many forms of learning styles and preferences (Kolb & Kolb, 2012). In his focus on creating significant learning experiences, L. Dee Fink (2013) stretched us to think about how students and instructors refer to what they have learned in the course of their educational experiences. He identified six kinds of significant learning. *Foundational knowledge* involves understanding and remembering the key concepts, principles, relationships, and facts that constitute what is usually referred to as the content of the course. *Application* is being able to engage in thinking about the subject (e.g., critical thinking, creative thinking, problem solving, and decision making), developing other key skills, and learning how to manage complex projects. *Integration* includes identifying the similarities and interactions among realms of knowledge, specific ideas, and people. *Human dimension* is interacting with oneself and others in new and better ways and discovering the personal and social implications of new knowledge. *Caring* involves changing one's interests, feelings, or values related to a subject. Finally, *learning how to learn* is acquiring better studenting skills, learning how to inquire and construct knowledge on a specific subject, and learning how to become a self-directed learner.

One solution to the limited effect of much of what is offered in the name of learning in our institutions is to create significant learning experiences, or "learning that makes a difference in how people live—and the kind of life they are capable of living. We want that which students learn to become part of how they think, what they can and want to do, what they believe is true of life, and what they value—and we want it to increase their capability for living life fully and meaningfully" (Fink, 2013, p. 7). In this context, Fink made a very interesting observation that we suspect is quite true: he characterized what students do about learning in terms of filling files—their course file and their life file. The course file is "where they put everything they learn in school or in the university; they draw on this file only when they take tests, do homework, and so on." On the other hand, in their life file they "put the lessons from their everyday life, and they draw on this file for all their life decisions, questions, actions, and so on" (p. 7).

Although both files might be filled with a breadth and depth of knowledge, it is Fink's observation that the "two files are totally disconnected" (p. 8). Herein lies the point of significant learning: "If we want to promote significant learning, we need to help students connect what they learn in our courses with their life file. In general this means drawing from students' past and current life experiences when building the basis for their learning and then linking new learning to possible future life experiences" (p. 8). The goal is that, as a result of significant learning, students will have enhanced their individual lives and their social interactions with others, as well as become more informed and thoughtful citizens. The distinction between students' course and life files is reminiscent of Palmer (1998) reference to the small story of our lives and the big story of the disciplines, which he also suggested must be integrated if real learning is to flourish.

Our takeaway from this analysis is that learning must be viewed as a whole experience, across a wide range of formal and informal settings and involving an immersion in a community of learning. Thus, learning entails engagement with new experiences and opportunities that challenge an individual's current ways of viewing, understanding, and functioning in the world. The expected outcome is the replacement of these views, understandings, and behaviors with new and more adequate forms. For example, research on the cognitive development of students during the college years (Love & Guthrie, 1999) suggests that students' viewing of the world in absolute, categorical terms soon gives way to more complex forms of uncertainty and flexibility—what King and Kitchener (1994) identified as a shift from prereflective to quasi-reflective thinking.

Inherent to any successful learning experience is the element of risk. Acquiring a new system for making meaning and learning new ways of functioning in the world is fundamentally a risk. Familiar, tried-and-true ways of thinking and doing offer a sense of personal comfort that is not easily forfeited as new situations arise. To do so is to risk a system that has become safe and secure over time. What if the new way of interpreting the world, or the new way of doing things, fails? What is the price of letting go of current ways of approaching and understanding the world? What assurances are there that new ways of thinking and doing will be more effective? Such concerns and doubts are an expected and normal feature of the learning process as challenges unfold in the educational environment.

From this perspective, learning may also be seen most broadly as a progression in meaning making and understanding toward increasingly complex and advanced ways of viewing and interacting with the world. This process requires both the acquisition of new information and access to opportunities for the exercise of new skills, competencies, and ways of thinking and acting. Ultimately, the goal of learning might be seen as the merging of personal identity, values, beliefs, knowledge, skills, and interests toward a purposeful endpoint of fulfillment and human actualization.

Such a conception is at the heart of the classic model of human development and motivation articulated by Maslow (1968). Accordingly, the basic needs of all humans form a hierarchy, beginning with physiological, safety, belongingness, and love needs and progressing upward toward needs of esteem and self-actualization. A basic assumption in Maslow's model is that needs lower in the hierarchy must be met sufficiently before other needs in the hierarchy can be addressed. Therefore, physiological, safety, belongingness, and love needs take precedence over esteem and self-actualization needs. As issues of basic "security, stability, dependency, protection, freedom from fear, anxiety, and chaos, need for structure, order, law, limits, strength in the protector, and so on" (Tribe, 1982, p. 50) are addressed, greater energy can be devoted to higher-level capabilities.

Furthermore, as the needs to belong and to be loved are satisfied, successful adjustment is imminent. The goal in Maslow's model is the development of healthy people who "have sufficiently gratified their basic needs for safety, belongingness, love, respect and self-esteem so that they are intrinsically motivated ... to strive toward self-actualization as an unceasing trend toward unity and integration within the person" (Tribe, 1982, p. 59).

A Hierarchy of Environmental Design

Complementary to Maslow's model of human needs, we propose a hierarchy of environmental design, wherein the need for environments that promote inclusion and safety precede the need for environments that encourage engagement and community (Figure II.1). Furthermore, should concerns of inclusion and safety be in question, the promises of engaging and communal environments are compromised. Ultimately, the success of the conditions of learning community depends largely on the effectiveness of the two previous strata.

We begin our analysis in Chapter Five with an overview of the basic environmental conditions of inclusion and safety. According to our model, an educational institution must first present an inclusive, safe, and secure environment for all students. Without a fundamental sense of inclusion and security, the pursuit of more

Figure II.1. Hierachy of Environmental Design

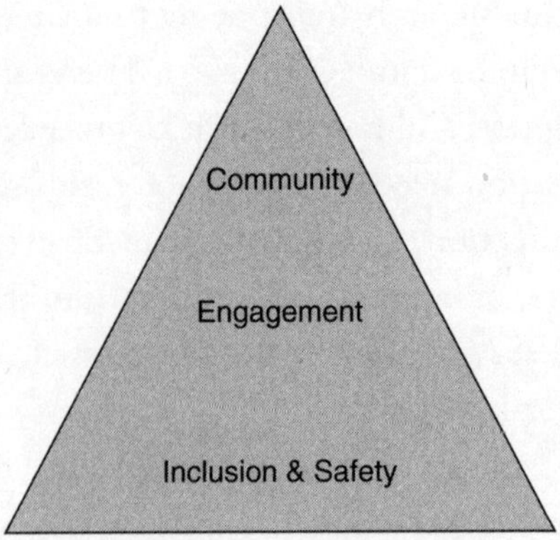

Source: Revised from Strange & Banning, 2001.

fulfilling educational experiences is a daunting task for any student. Without a basic sense of belonging to the campus community, free from threat, fear, and anxiety, attempts at other more lasting goals will likely fail. The first step for campus leaders, then, is to ensure that the physical, human aggregate, organizational, and socially constructed aspects of campus environments create such conditions and serve such purposes.

Inclusion and safety are not the endpoints, though, but rather just the beginning steps. As explained already, education is fundamentally about engaging students in a process that calls for risk-taking and challenge (Sanford, 1966). Thus, if campus environments are to be educationally purposeful, they must also engage students in effective learning experiences that require taking on meaningful roles and responsibilities, both in and out of the classroom. Without access to structures for participation and engagement, the focus of Chapter Six, students remain detached from the kinds of opportunities that call for their investment and responsibility for their own learning, key requisites for powerful educational outcomes.

Finally, it is presumed that while inclusion, safety, and engagement are all necessary conditions for the achievement of educational purposes, they alone are insufficient to ensure an integrated, whole learning experience for students. This requires, as we discuss in Chapter Seven, conditions of community, where goals, structures, values, people, and resources come together in a seamless experience for purposes of self-actualization and fulfillment. It is through the conditions of community—whether in the form of a class, a student organization, a peer training program, or a residence hall floor—that participants experience a complete sense of membership in a setting. They become such a part of the history and culture of the setting and leave their unique imprint on the environment that when they leave they are missed.

Each of the four components of campus environments discussed in Part One (physical, human aggregate, organizational, and socially constructed) has the potential to contribute to or detract from the inclusive, safe, engaging, and communal experience of students. Furthermore, as implications of the emerging digital campus are further understood, the dynamics of educational environments promise to change significantly the way students attend to their educational needs, a point of discussion in Chapter Eight. The following chapters discuss and illustrate the nature of each environmental condition and then suggest various design strategies or options for fulfilling a resolution of each, based on findings and examples noted in the literature.

Finally, Chapter Nine argues for systematically incorporating this environmental knowledge by considering the impact of and response to the total campus ecology. However, rather than an exact prescription for achieving the aforementioned conditions, the intent here is to offer broad strategies, the design specifics of which must be determined within the context of each campus.

5

Promoting Inclusion and Safety

Inclusion and safety are distinct but related constructs: both reflect campus conditions thought to be important requisites for student learning and development to occur, and contributing to one undoubtedly enhances the other. It can also be said that failure to attend sufficiently to one jeopardizes the other. Limited outdoor lighting on campus (a safety issue), for example, may make it less attractive to some students (an inclusion issue), and failure to attract, welcome, and retain sufficient numbers of diverse students (an inclusion issue) may make it psychologically too risky (a safety issue) for the few who do matriculate. Addressing issues of campus inclusion and security necessarily involves aspects that are both physical and psychological in nature. Being present may meet the technical requirements of inclusion, but experiencing a sense of belonging may require another standard. Freedom from physical harm is one thing; feeling secure is another. Both goals must be addressed in an integrated manner should an institution hope to fulfill its educational mission. Absence of either condition can result in a potentially hostile environment for students' engagement in learning, ultimately diminishing the quality of their college experience and the overall effectiveness of the campus community.

The goals of campus inclusion have been pursued for some time in various affirmative programs and federal legislative initiatives over the years. Beginning with the Civil Rights Act of 1964 and proceeding to Title IX of the Higher Education Amendments of 1972, Section 504 of the Rehabilitation Act of 1973, and the Americans with Disabilities Act of 1990, American higher education has placed increasing emphasis on including individuals who have been left out of the opportunity (Schuh, 1993) and on ensuring that they are not limited in their participation, denied benefits, or subjected to discrimination on the basis of race, color, national origin, sex, or disability.

Concerns for safe environments have also drawn considerable attention over the years, perhaps since the very beginnings of campus-based education. Turner (1995) suggested that the placement of early American colleges in the countryside outside towns was an attempt to remove the students "from the corrupting forces of the city" (p. 4). The enclosed quadrangle also "functioned as a defense against potential enemies, who were the townspeople themselves as much as outside armies" (p. 10). In addition, "the ability to close off a college at a few gate-points also gave college authorities the advantage of greater control over students, a concern that was a major factor in the growth of the collegiate system" (p. 10). Smith and Fossey (1995) noted that the custom of having the sheriff of Middlesex County attend Harvard graduation ceremonies stemmed from early Harvard commencements where the sheriff was needed to help control students and to make ceremonies safe.

These early concerns about campus safety have fueled a growing perception that the traditional view of campuses has eroded and that cracks in the ivory tower are increasing (Hopkins, 1994). The safe haven image has been replaced by an awareness of the college campus as a "microcosm for a larger increasingly violent society" (Whitaker & Pollard, 1993, p. xi), leading two authors to observe recently that over the past twenty years campus crime has been constructed as the new social problem and campuses characterized as dark-sided breeding grounds of violence, vice, and victimization (Sloan & Fisher, 2010). Whether or not such claims are warranted, based on the data it is clear that colleges and universities have elevated their vigilance and duty to care in recent years with regard to such matters.

Recognition of the need to do more for campus security is reflected not only in the numerous recent publications about the topic (e.g., Jackson & Terrell, 2007; Jang, Kang, Dierenfeldt & Lindsteadt, 2014; Janosik & Gregory, 2009; Kaminski, Koons-Witt, Thompson, & Weiss, 2010; Katel, 2011; Nicoletti, Spencer-Thomas, & Bollinger, 2010) but also in the federal laws enacted over the years that now govern how colleges and universities address such issues (e.g., the Drug-Free Schools and Communities Act Amendments of 1989, Public Law 101–266; Jeanne Clery Disclosure of Campus Security Policy and Campus Crime Statistics Act (20 U.S.C. §1092 (f)); the 2005 Violence Against Women Act Reauthorization). In addition, the establishment by the U.S. Department of Justice of the first National Center for Campus Public Safety at the University of Vermont, in 2013, suggests that such initiatives have been institutionalized for the long run. Campuses are now held accountable for the transparent reporting of safety and criminal activity, placing at risk their student financial aid should they not comply (Schuh, 1993). Furthermore, they can be held liable for injury since they have a duty to warn if there is any measure of forseeability with respect to such concerns.

Whether motivated by educational purposes or mandated by law, strategies to promote the inclusion and safety of students have been adopted on most campuses in recent decades. All of the environmental components discussed in the previous chapters (physical, aggregate, organizational, and constructed) can serve to either detract from or support the inclusion and security of students. Understanding how such components factor into defining the problems and their solutions is the focus of the following sections. What frames inclusion also serves to support safety, and what maintains security extends from a foundation of inclusion. Nonetheless, each environmental goal deserves its own attention.

Designing Environments for Inclusion

Creating a sense of welcome on campus for all students is where inclusion begins. Absent a basic feeling that one belongs at an institution or that one's identity or characteristics pose significant personal risk in the setting, the prospects of individual success are limited. Students who do not feel included and who encounter inordinate levels of risk tend to check out first psychologically and then physically; in short, they are much more likely to leave an institution where, for a variety of reasons, success seems beyond their reach. Factors that influence this decision are related to the physical designs of campuses, the aggregate characteristics of individuals who inhabit them, aspects of how they are organized, and artifacts of campus culture.

Physical Factors

From the perspective of physical design, the literature is clear that a number of campus features relate directly to the goals of inclusion, in some cases drawing students into the setting and in others excluding them. For significant numbers of students each year, moving into a residence hall is the signature moment of their entry into the postsecondary experience. Choices about where to live and in what type of facility can have an immediate impact on their sense of inclusion. Research on campus housing options suggests that various designs (e.g., suite style, single room, apartments, traditional double-loaded corridors) have differential effects on the kinds of experiences students will encounter and ultimately on their opportunities for learning, growth, and development. Gifford (2007), in a review of thirty years of research on the effects of high-rise living, concluded that "high-rises are less satisfactory than other housing forms for most people, ... social relations are more impersonal and helping behavior is less than in other housing forms, [and] that crime and fear of crime are greater" (p. 12). To the extent that such effects are related to the kinds of welcoming environments most likely to include newcomers makes it clear that such structures, while perhaps economical in the short run, are antithetical to the end goals of education.

An alternative design popular among current students is the suite-style or cluster arrangement, which stands in stark contrast to the traditional double-loaded corridor construction of past campus residences. Students today seem to want their personal space and requisite amenities, perhaps an artifact of most having never had the experience of living with another person in the same room while growing up. Satisfying such wants, though, has led to unintended consequences for the kind of environment institutions try to encourage for supporting the goals of student learning. In a study of residential architecture and students' sense of community at a liberal arts college in the Northeast, a team of researchers (Devlin, Donovan, Nicolov, Nold, & Zandan, 2008) examined (among other factors) residence halls that were recently renovated on campus to support cluster-style or suite arrangements. Although rated higher for comfort, quiet, and storage options, these new designs resulted in a lower sense of community among students than that found in traditional corridor-style halls. Differences were apparent in the extent to which residents kept their doors open and ultimately how much they interacted with other residents, both results favoring the traditional style halls. Similar studies have concurred with the observation that residents of traditional halls interact with others more often than their counterparts in suite-style buildings (Brandon, Hirt, & Cameron, 2008). One conditional effect was attributed to such a comparison, however, by Rodger, Johnson, and Wakabayashi (2005), where more introverted, conscientious students were found to be at higher risk for feeling out of place in traditional-style buildings. However, to the extent that greater interaction among students promotes a sense of community, opportunities for being included and learning from one another are better supported by some designs than others, a point that corroborates earlier findings (Heilweil, 1973) on the topic. Ultimately, any design that isolates students or distances them (physically or psychologically) from one another is less effective in sustaining a learning community (see Chapter Seven). Such designs also tend to diminish the kind of academically related peer interaction that supports students' learning, perhaps as much as if not more than student–faculty interaction (Moran & Gonyea, 2003).

Student density, as measured by number of students per square foot, is another design culprit (Banning, 1997). Research (Baum & Valins, 1977; Bell, Greene, Fisher, & Baum, 2001) has shown that high density leads to behaviors less likely to foster inclusion or to build community, and such effects may occur differentially by gender (Regoeczi, 2008). For example, high density in residence halls is associated with less positive attitudes toward people and places and leads to social withdrawal, interrupts social networks, reduces a sense of neighborliness, and encourages withdrawal and more aggressive behaviors, especially among males. Perhaps the same criticism can be leveled at large classrooms, where anonymity often encourages higher absenteeism among students (Cuseo, 2007).

The need for connectivity as a condition for inclusion is being considered carefully by a number of institutions while they lay out plans for campus renovation and new construction that include intentional campus neighborhoods. Michigan State University, East Carolina University, Elon University, and Western Michigan University are all examples of institutions that share in common their designs of on-campus residential neighborhoods, with convenient services, to support a human scale experience for students while building community. Using a similar strategy, Bowling Green State University has undertaken the construction of a Greek Village, where student members of fraternities and sororities will live in townhouse-style units, connected to a common courtyard and experience community engagement and leadership. As one university administrator commented, "Residential neighborhoods provide students with a sense of belonging and connection to [the university]" (Zipp, 2013), and as one design firm concluded, "Students who develop a close sense of belonging to their college environment are not only likely to remain in student housing, but also to complete their degree and become active alumni" (Lawless, 2012). In building the new campus Cy-Fair College, referenced in Chapter 1 (Troyer, 2005), planners commented on the implications of this aspect of their design: "The campus environment is intended to convey a sense of accessibility, safety, and openness and to encourage students to remain on campus to interact informally with other students and faculty members" (p. 6).

For obvious reasons, the role of the physical environment is also particularly important for the inclusion of certain groups on campus who for reasons of mobility find it difficult to negotiate campus spaces. It stands to reason that without fundamental access to the campus, its facilities, and opportunities, students' sense of inclusion is clearly jeopardized. Jones (1996) pointed to the social construction of disability as an important perspective in campus modification efforts when addressing access and other challenges. He called for the inclusion of both those with and those without disabilities: for example, a moderately sloped entrance serves all without calling unnecessary attention to a few. Rather than focusing on the limitations of individuals, Strange (2000) called for the creation of environments of ability, so recognized for their capacity to include and welcome a wide variety of students. Architectural designs of all too many traditional campus structures disqualify them for such distinction, as they fail to accommodate some students. Both American Disabilities Act standards and universal design principles offer helpful guidelines for rectifying this situation, as institutions work their way through cycles of renovation and reconstruction.

Human Aggregate Factors

The dynamics of human aggregates are particularly relevant to understanding the challenges of creating inclusive campus environments for students. From this perspective, campus environments take on unique features due to the collective characteristics of their inhabitants (Strange, 1993). Dominant campus features often reflect the influence of dominant groups. The essential challenge in the achievement of campus inclusion is the fact that those who share the dominant characteristics are more likely to feel included whereas those whose characteristics differ may not (see Chapter Two). Groups less welcomed on campus are most often in the minority in terms of overall membership. This majority versus minority dynamic sets up conditions that promote a chilly climate for those in the minority, similar to the experience reported by many women on campus (Hall & Sandler, 1982, 1984). Such conditions for women often include a variety of behaviors from men in the majority, including lack of recognition, devaluation of women's abilities, placement of limits on opportunities for participation, and at times subjection to hostile and harassing remarks.

Similarly, ethnic minorities can face a less than welcoming environment, one that is antithetical to inclusion (Gunnings, 1982; Johnson et al., 2007). The chills can occur in admission policies, distribution of financial aid, academic programs, housing programs, and various campus incidents (Hawkins, 1989). Gay, lesbian, bisexual, and transgendered students also face potentially hostile campus environments (D'Augelli, 1989; Evans & Rankin, 1998; Evans & Wall, 1991). Not only does minority status place some students at risk for inclusion, but also it usually limits their access to visible role models for purposes of mentoring and support (Sandeen & Rhatigan, 1990). The majority versus minority distinction, while illuminating the noninclusive nature of the environment, often brings with it significant problems that may hinder rather than enhance necessary environmental changes. For example, Jones (1996) suggested that minority group thinking—while often used to identify issues related to the unjust distribution of power, status, and privilege in the campus environment—lumps members together, forfeits their individuality, and builds on a deficit model, too often justifying the setting apart of minority groups and ultimately jeopardizing the goal of inclusion. Although this seemingly separatist approach (such as offering a minority student orientation or creating a multicultural student center) is important for accomplishing an initial sense of congruence for students in the minority, it may ultimately result in greater exclusion from the campus environment in the long run if subsequent steps are not taken to integrate with the campus at large. For example, one interesting strategy that has shown some promise in that regard has been the assignment of different-race housing roommates, resulting in an increase of interracial friendships on campus beyond the roommate (Mark & Harris, 2012; Stearns, Buchmann, & Bonneau, 2009) and thus encouraging further social integration, especially of dominant group members.

Organizational Factors

Organizational factors in the environment also affect inclusive behaviors and attitudes (Strange, 1993), two examples of which warrant particular attention: organizational mission and organizational size.

Institutional missions vary across a number of dimensions (Lyons, 1993), and what the mission statement of a campus says about inclusion and diversity is important to the interface between organizational concepts and the inclusion of all persons in the campus environment. Kuh et al. (1991) outlined a fourfold commitment necessary for any campus to become an inclusive learning community: "advance knowledge and intellectual understanding of differences among groups of people"; "encourage interaction among members of different subcommunities [sic] (ethnic, cultural, gender-based, academic living groups)"; "promote the appreciation and valuing of commonalties across all students"; and "build on commonalties while acknowledging the importance different groups can make to the academic community" (p. 294).

Especially since the 1970s, most campuses have embedded within their mission statements an institutional commitment to increase enrollments of diverse students in response to a changing multicultural society and to improve the quality of the educational experience for all students. While missions are espoused, they must also be enacted in concrete ways to support the goal of inclusion. Whether it be the University of Miami's pride in "the diversity of our University family" (Miami University of Ohio, 2014), Ithaca College's promise to "embrace diversity as an integral part of the educational experience and of the community we create" (Ithaca College, 2014), or Oakland Community College's stated goal to "promote and advocate a collaborative vision of diversity and inclusion" (Oakland Community College, 2014), numerous like institutions have initiated a range of programs and services designed to welcome students of all backgrounds and to guide their successful matriculation.

The size of a campus also figures prominently in its capacity to include a wide range of students. Ironically, while larger institutions seem to be more successful in attracting diverse students, they also present more challenges to their success. This point can be understood in the concept of manning theory presented in Chapter Three. Accordingly, when the number of inhabitants in an environment exceeds the number needed to complete the various tasks in the setting (a condition described as being *overmanned*), those not engaged feel less commitment to or responsibility toward maintaining the environment (Wicker, 1973)—in other words, less of a sense of inclusion. In addition, high density or crowding, often a consequence of environmental overmanning, "has been found to result in less liking for others (especially in males), and ... is associated with withdrawal from interaction ... [greater] aggression and ... lower incidence of prosocial behavior" (Bell et al., 2001, p. 365). Such effects can indirectly influence the overall campus climate for inclusion. In addition, overmanned environments do little to engage individuals in the activities in the setting. Current emphasis on creating multiple organizational subunits, such as freshman interest groups, academic learning communities, and various theme houses on many campuses, suggests that higher education administrators are becoming more aware of and responding appropriately to the challenges of oversizing by creating more human-scale opportunities for students. The significant positive results associated with such experiences (Price, 2005) indicate that they are well-placed strategies in terms of bolstering students' sense of inclusion.

Carry capacity, or the ability of an environment to sustain itself with current resources, is also affected by oversizing. As campuses or living units become larger in terms of the number of inhabitants, there is seldom the necessary increase in support staff or programs to accompany the larger entity. Goldstein (1996) pointed to institutional size as a correlate to "nonparticipation in governance, impersonalness, and crowding" (p. 38). Such outcomes are descriptive of the condition of deindividuation (Zimbardo, 1969), where individuals begin to feel anonymous, becoming a small or unknown fish in a big sea, and their inhibitions toward antisocial behavior are lowered. While this phenomenon has been most often associated with high-density urban settings, it may be relevant in examining the effects of size as a campus organizational feature. Ultimately, inclusion is strengthened by personalized and affirming encounters. The dynamics of oversizing too often mitigate against such possibilities.

Socially Constructed Factors

While the physical, aggregate, and organizational dimensions directly shape conditions of campus inclusion, it stands to reason that how these dimensions are socially constructed, that is, given meaning by participants, is also a potential predictor of their consequences. A case in point is found in the growing concerns over campus graffiti (Hemphill & LaBlanc, 2010; Rankin, 2005). Students from large urban areas may react more benignly to their presence compared with students whose backgrounds have not exposed them to such conditions or who are not targets of the noninclusive messages embedded in these acts (e.g., when windows in an adjacent Jewish Synagogue are broken, or the doors to the campus women's center are defaced with sexist remarks). However, campus graffiti often targets race, ethnicity, religion, gender, and sexual orientation, and through various social constructions can evoke strong feelings of exclusion and hostility. Banning (1992, 1995) and Banning and Luna (1992) published photographs of campus graffiti that targeted women, Latinos/as, and gay and lesbian students. Their content often included messages telling the targeted students that they don't belong on campus, threatening their safety, and suggesting that they will have limited equality and opportunities within the setting (Banning & Bartels, 1993). Hostility in all its forms is destructive to all groups and diminishes the ability of the campus to foster learning and development. In effect, it "is like a cancer of bricks and mortar. And the side effects are erosion of campus spirit as well as public confidence in the institution" (Taming Campus Vandals, 1980, p. 44).

Verbal harassment, including the use of spoken or written language, is another category that warrants attention in a discussion of campus inclusion (Palmer, 1996). "It may take many different forms, including (but not limited to) racist, sexist, homophobic, or anti-Semitic slurs or other comments that are obscene, demeaning, intimidating, [and] threatening" (p. 270). Although graffiti may send like messages, Palmer's verbal harassment category focuses on the verbal nature of the communication. Every student on campus is a potential victim for harassment, although the most likely targets are groups distinguished by race, ethnicity, religion, gender, and sexual orientation. Nearly two-thirds of college students report having been sexually harassed, with unwanted comments, jokes, gestures, and looks being the most common forms (Hill & Silva, 2005). Although harassment is found in college women's dating relationships (Amar & Gennaro, 2005;

Sugarman & Hotaling, 1989), it is also found in other sectors of the campus environment. Dziech and Weiner (1984) reported that 30 percent of college women were sexually harassed by academic instructors, a problem that continues to have significant negative consequences for many students (Huerta, Cortina, Pang, Torges, & Magley, 2006). Previous reports by Hall and Sandler (1982, 1984) and Boyer (1987) support these general findings to the point that Hall and Sandler's chilly climate critique, applied originally to describe the experience of women on campus, has become part of the standard discourse on campus inclusion.

Feelings of psychological inclusion entail not only the absence of hostility or harassment but also a positive sense of mattering (Schlossberg, 1989) and validation (Rendon, 1994), especially among those who differ from the dominant campus norm or are marginalized in some manner. Mattering includes five aspects: *attention* (i.e., feeling noticed), *importance* (i.e., feeling important enough to be cared about), *ego extension* (i.e., feeling empathy from others for accomplishments or failures), *dependence* (i.e., being needed), and *appreciation* (i.e., feeling appreciated by others for one's efforts) (Rosenberg & McCullough, 1981; Schlossberg, 1989). Feeling that one matters is an important "precursor to students' becoming involved in activities and academic programs that would facilitate development and learning" (Schlossberg, 1989, as cited in Evans, Forney, & Guido-DiBrito, 1998, pp. 27–28). Rendon (1994) underscored the need for validation, especially in the early stages of a student's experience, and for creating supportive spaces for those whose diverse racial, ethnic, and cultural backgrounds have predisposed them to doubts or low self-esteem concerning their abilities and experiences on campus. This process of "enabling, confirming, and [supporting]" (Rendon, 1994, p.46) can occur in any campus setting (classroom, student organization, adviser's office) and be offered by any campus agent (classmates, instructors, staff). Again, active interventions are important for encouraging these students to become involved in campus life.

The role of campus culture in effecting or detracting from a sense of inclusion among some students can be understood further in the issues surrounding various recent challenges to the appropriateness of sports team mascots and symbols at some institutions. For example, the University of Illinois retired Chief Illiniwek as a mascot in 2007 following a controversy that embroiled the campus since 1989, pitting alumni, state legislators, congressional representatives, and the governor against representatives of Native American tribes. At stake was the meaning of Illiniwek's display and ritual at various sporting events on campus. Alumni clung fiercely to the mascot, which they claimed was a symbol of honor that elevated the sacred qualities and history of the Native American tradition. Native American students, on the other hand, then under the leadership of Native American graduate student Charlene Teter, challenged the authenticity and decorum of the costume and dance and suggested that such displays during sporting events were demeaning, humiliating, and an affront to their people's culture, spirituality, and heritage. One Native American student specifically commented on the effect of seeing Chief Illiniwek's crests, in full headdress, hanging in storefront windows of area merchants in Champaign, Illinois, particularly during homecoming events. While these crests were a symbol of pride for the majority Caucasians, they reminded her of the time in Illinois history when bounties were placed on the heads of banished Native American tribes ($7 for males, $5 for females, $3 for children) by advertising with similar storefront effigies. Although both groups claimed high motives for their objections (to either keep or eliminate the current mascot), for the fewer Native American students this controversy created a campus environment that threatened not only their inclusion in it but their safety as well. Acts of hostility had become regular fare among some students and alumni when they returned to campus to face the protests of these offended groups. In such cases, pride confronts pride, and what elevates one group denigrates the other.

Similarly, other campuses have changed their institutional symbols (College of William and Mary removed feathers from its logo) or renamed their teams (University of Massachusetts, Amherst, once Redmen, are now Minutemen), and some have even forgone the use of a nickname altogether (University of North Dakota dropped the use of Fighting Sioux). Acknowledging that traditions indeed run deep and are not easily changed, Florida State University has retained its identification as Seminoles, and a board member of Miami University of Ohio resigned when its team name, Redskins, was replaced with Redhawks.

A similar example, with consequences of social exclusion for Black Americans, raised concerns of campus administrators at the University of Mississippi. Although the university had officially disassociated itself with the rebel flag as an official institutional symbol, throngs of alumni and students continued to wave it at various sporting events while the fight song, "Dixie," and the cane-toting, mustachioed, Southern gentleman mascot, Colonel Rebel, led the charge. Again, what was at stake here was the meaning and interpretation of history as reflected in these symbols. For some of the Caucasian majority, such symbols embodied the university's heritage, but for students of color these same symbols were painful reminders of deep racial division, social exclusion, and oppression. Once again, tradition conflicted with awareness and sensitivity. An interesting consequence of this debate spilled over even into the academic arena where the institution's scholarly reputation was being questioned by a panel of external reviewers considering its application for installment of a chapter of Phi Beta Kappa. Apparently this prestigious academic honor society had reservations about affiliating with an institution where such symbols threatened to exclude some constituents. Symbols create powerful images that carry their messages in forms of pervasive social constructions, regardless of their high intent.

Concerns for inclusive environments are not just about racial and ethnic differences. Images and symbols related to gender distinctions and religious traditions also have captured the attention of campus constituents, with considerable debate. For example, at Southwest Missouri State University, charges of sexism were once leveled at proponents of the so-named Sugar Bears, a female cheerleading squad. Also, the use of the mascot, Princes, was at one time questioned at Heidelberg University (OH) as insufficiently masculine or not aggressive enough to be supportive and symbolic of the male athletic teams. The placement of Christmas holiday decorations and the recognition of Easter break at many campuses continue to draw concerns and criticism from those whose religious traditions do not share such observances. The point of all of these examples is that symbols of campus culture serve to wall in some constituents and wall out others. What any particular symbol actually means is nearly indeterminate, although its effects on various campus groups can be readily observed. It is the nature of constructed environments to emerge from consensual interpretations. The dilemma is such that inclusion for one group often rests on the exclusion (intentional or not) of other groups, ultimately challenging their sense of inclusion, physical or psychological.

Designing for Safety and Security

Questions of campus safety and security, it seems, have dominated news about colleges and universities recently, especially in the wake of the tragic shootings at Virginia Tech (2007) and Northern Illinois University (2008). Numerous publications and reports have revealed, too, that American colleges are increasingly becoming places of risk in terms of institutional and campus-related violence and crime. In collective data released for the 2012 academic year (U.S. Department of Education, 2012), American campuses reported a total of thirty-one murders, two negligent manslaughters, 4,837 forcible sexual offenses, seventy-four nonforcible sexual offenses, 4,396 robberies, 4,664 aggravated assaults, 20,486 burglaries, 5,701 automobile thefts, 2,148 fires, 797 incidents of arson,

402 hate crimes, 1,902 illegal weapon possessions, 30,717 drug arrests, 41,708 violations of alcohol use statutes, 110 body injuries, forty-seven citations for larceny, 327 for intimidation, and 402 for vandalism. In addition, on-campus disciplinary actions were taken for 1,670 illegal weapon possessions, 58,339 drug arrests, and 204,244 liquor law violations. While such numbers are probably not out of line for (and perhaps are even less than) a comparable population size and variety of locations as are represented in the composite of colleges and universities reporting, they are clearly cause for concern and challenge the capacity of any institution to carry out its educational mission. Crime, violence, vandalism, harassment, assault, and hazing all make it very difficult for any college or university to foster students' learning and development. Building on the aforementioned mechanisms for inclusion, factors associated with the physical, aggregate, organizational, and socially constructed components of the environment can contribute to the achievement of a sense of safety and security among students, as presented in the following sections.

Physical Factors

In a list of key physical environment categories, Moos (1974) included geographical, meteorological, and architectural design variables for consideration in examining issues of campus safety and security. Campus geographic variables pertain to both macro- and micro-design features. At the macro level, concerns related to regional location emerge. For example, patterns of campus violence in terms of type and time of year may vary with climate, terrain, and urban versus rural location. Strange (1993) suggested that a campus in a natural wooded setting may influence student behavior different from a campus located in the "middle of a massive urban metropolis" (p. 137). Although rural areas are not without crime (Phillips, 1982), census data suggest that felonious assaults against persons are strongly related to city size, underscoring a simple fact: "There is more crime per person in urban areas than rural areas" (Martin & O'Connor, 1989, p. 28). Although these data do not directly speak to campus environments, they do describe the nature of institutional environments for many campuses. The relationship among climate, weather, and specifically heat and aggression has been a long-standing research interest of environmental psychologists. Bell et al. (1996) concluded their review of the topic, suggesting that moderately uncomfortable heat increases aggression. They also pointed out that the Federal Bureau of Investigation itself "has listed climate as a variable of importance in explaining the incidence of crime" (p. 203).

Campus micro-geographic design variables, such as placement of buildings, also influence campus crime. Outlying buildings on school grounds, those located in poorly lit areas, and buildings that are not easily seen are most likely to be a target of vandalism (Pablant & Baxter, 1975). The relative location of rooms can also influence social contacts and therefore indirectly predispose some individuals to safety risks more so than others. For example, rooms next to elevators or stairwells or in remote sections of a building are more likely to expose occupants to contact with others, friend or foe.

The role of architectural design in the affording of campus safety, particularly its role in the reduction of vandalism, is well documented. A rather interesting position is found in Weinmayer (1969), where the author claimed that the real vandals in our environment are the designers. Concurring with this perspective, Zeisel (1976) suggested that about half of the vandalism that occurs in schools results from poor design.

In addition to the initial design and layout of buildings, there is evidence to suggest that vandalism is also a function of buildings' physical appearance and maintenance (Pablant & Baxter, 1975). Given that many American postsecondary institutions are rapidly pursuing master planning, facility upgrades, and new construction, the relationship of poor building appearance and maintenance to vandalism and other crimes becomes an urgent campus management concern. This is especially the case as we come to understand more about the connections between various micro-level design features of aging buildings and the perceptions of insecurity and fear they may evoke from users. Three factors associated with such perceptions are victim prospect (how far, how well, and how much they can see), offender refuge (the availability of places for offenders to hide), and victim escape (access of an escape route from the area) (Nasar & Fisher, 1992). Fear is heightened by "poor prospect for the passerby due to inadequate lighting, blocked escape for the passerby, and concealment for the offender" (Nasar & Fisher, p. 48).

Macro-design issues involving campus layout and location are equally troublesome. This is especially the case at institutions in large urban areas where there may be an "opportunity for victimization presented by potential targets (students, faculty and staff), a supply of motivated offenders nearby (neighborhoods with poor socioeconomic conditions), and poor guardianship (open access with varying levels of security among students)" (Nasar & Fisher, 1992, p. 48). Ironically, some of the same characteristics that contribute to the richness of possibilities campuses offer to students also render them especially vulnerable to victimization. As and Nasar and Fisher (1992) observed: "Campuses tend to have easy access, free movement at all hours, and the diversity that allows offenders to remain unnoticed, all of which contribute to a lack of guardianship" (p. 36). In summary, the authors cautioned about the broader enrollment implications of these concerns, noting, "If parents or students believe that a campus is unsafe, they may voice demands for greater security or simply decide to go elsewhere" (p. 63). "At a time when universities face safety issues, due, in part, to increasing fear of crime on campus, the design of the physical environment should not be overlooked as a safety strategy" (Fisher & Nasar, 1992, p. 63). Based on their assessment, Fisher and Nasar (1992, p. 63) recommend the development of design criteria and audit processes focusing on the three aspects of victim prospect, offender refuge, and victim escape:

> Specifically, campuses might try to improve areas that have low prospect, high refuge, or poor escape. This might involve reducing the height or increasing the permeability of visual barriers, such as shrubs and walls, and eliminating or opening up alcoves and other confining areas. These changes have particular importance near heavily used paths [adjacent to] an offender population... because of the coincidence of offenders and innocent passersby make such areas likely targets for crime.

While the effects of architectural design variables in campus living environments have been reviewed broadly in the literature (see Blimling, 1988; Heilweill, 1973; Moos, 1979; Schuh, 1980; Strange, 1993), one feature important to the reduction of vandalism due to rowdiness is related to the concept of behavioral zoning (Jackson & Schroeder, 1977). This idea underscores the need for stimulation behavior zones, particularly in the design of residence halls. If not accommodated in the original design, students will create their own, and usually in ways that are unproductive or that inflict damage on the facilities, for example, using a corridor for an impromptu bowling alley or floor hockey match.

Aggregate Factors

The composition of campus human aggregates may also contribute indirectly to campus violence and therefore to its solution. Goldstein (1996), in a comprehensive review of the related research, concluded, "At the university level also, males are more vandalistic than females. [First-year students] commit more vandalism than [upper-class students], and regardless of class level, alcohol consumption is a frequent concomitant of such behavior" (p. 24). A similar pattern is found in other crime forms. Men, usually Caucasian, are cited the most in hate crimes, rape, and sexual harassment. Finley and Corty (1993) reported in their study that approximately one-third of men on campus indicated being perpetrators of nonconsensual and pressured sexual penetration. More often than assault by physical force, this group also implicated the involvement of alcohol. Kilmartin (1996) also noted the serious problem of campus sexual assaults and domestic violence perpetrated by males. Several authors (Dietz-Uhler & Murrell, 1992; Koss, Gidycz, & Wisniewski, 1987; Warsaw, 1988) concurred on the importance of sex-role attitudes in these matters. Not all men make the campus unsafe for women, but as the previous studies suggest, college men who have less respect for women, see them as inferior, or have callous attitudes toward rape victims do create a hostile environment for women in particular. The point of these observations is not to suggest the exclusion of certain types of students on campus but rather to understand that knowledge of the aggregate population is necessary for planning the kinds of interventions that will challenge prevailing norms and contribute to an increased sense of security for all. Antirape and sexual violence websites directed toward males on campus (Masters, 2010) are examples of the kinds of institutional strategies that are challenging constructed images of masculinity and male sexuality within certain segments of the campus aggregate.

Organizational Factors

Although organizational features might not appear to directly address issues of campus safety and security, it can certainly be argued that some factors may lend themselves broadly to potential influence within this dimension of campus environments. For example, studies of secondary school settings have shown that the larger the school environment the more incidents of vandalism per capita (Garbarino, 1978; Goldman, 1961). In some ways, large bureaucratic environments, to the extent that they function anonymously through centralization of authority and higher degrees of formalization, might diminish the kinds of relationships that would support greater vigilance and awareness of others. On the other hand, organizational environments or subenvironments of a more human scale may hold claim on individuals in a much more personalized way, promoting a greater sense of belonging and attachment. In other words, as dynamic designs engage individuals they may be more personally accountable and, as a result, more inclusive and safe. However, more than a few tragic examples of workplace violence have recently heightened awareness of organizationally induced stress and anxiety, as individuals are compelled to produce more at an even quicker pace. Such pressure in the absence of personal control, flexibility, or decision-making authority is apparently a formula for disaster in some situations.

Constructed Factors

Much of the previous discussion with regard to the goals of inclusion also apply to understanding how constructed factors of campus environments contribute to the safety and security of students. Just as with the potential consequences of aforementioned stress, the cumulative effects of person–environment incongruence associated with physical, aggregate, and organizational features of an environment often render some individuals as outsiders, whose sense of psychological security and safety must be negotiated daily in the setting. Often symbols and artifacts of campus culture, as already illustrated, can be sources of security or stress, depending on the individual engaging them. Arguably, campuses that place greater emphasis on developing relational social climates might prove more secure for all students involved.

In conclusion, all of these examples highlight the importance of environmental design in effecting a sense of inclusion and safety among students. Learning is inherently a social activity, and decisions about campus design must include strategies that promote a wide embrace of students and their connection to one another. This is the basis of the applications discussed next.

Strategies for Inclusion and Safety

A number of strategies have emerged on the college campus in recent years that address issues of inclusion and safety for various subpopulations. Among these are the application of universal design principles for widening the accommodating capacity of campus facilities and learning opportunities, the creation of safe and brave spaces designed to facilitate social justice intergroup exchanges and dialogues, the implementation of institutional ethnic cultural centers established to affirm various subgroup identities, and the institution of campus living learning communities to capitalize on the benefits of territoriality and defensible space. These methods combine a holistic use of physical, aggregate, organizational, and socially constructed environment components to elevate both the sense of inclusion and safety, especially for students whose experience would place them at risk for either.

Principles of Universal Design

One of the major contributions to understanding campus inclusion and safety has been the development and articulation of principles of universal design. This term, if not the idea, originated with the work of the architect Ronald L. Mace, who used it to name the "concept of designing all products and the built environment to be aesthetic and usable to the greatest extent possible by everyone, regardless of their age, ability, or status in life" (retrieved from http://www.ncsu.edu/ncsu/design/cud/about_us/usronmace.htm). Originally framed around seven core principles, the application of universal design has been extended to a variety of campus physical settings and educational approaches including "instruction, websites, distance learning courses, software, multimedia, libraries, computer labs, career centers, advising offices, tutoring and learning centers, and conference exhibits" (retrieved from http://www.washington.edu/doit/Resources/ udesign.html). In brief, these principles and associated guidelines emphasize the importance of any design manifesting the following features (Exhibit 5.1) (retrieved from http://www.ncsu.edu/ncsu/design/cud/about_ud/udprinciplestext.htm).

Exhibit 5.1. Principles of Universal Design

PRINCIPLE ONE: Equitable Use

The design is useful and marketable to people with diverse abilities.

Guidelines:

1a. Provide the same means of use for all users: identical whenever possible; equivalent when not.

1b. Avoid segregating or stigmatizing any users.

1c. Provisions for privacy, security, and safety should be equally available to all users.

1d. Make the design appealing to all users.

PRINCIPLE TWO: Flexibility in Use

The design accommodates a wide range of individual preferences and abilities.

Guidelines:

2a. Provide choice in methods of use.

2b. Accommodate right- or left-handed access and use.

2c. Facilitate the user's accuracy and precision.

2d. Provide adaptability to the user's pace.

PRINCIPLE THREE: Simple and Intuitive Use

Use of the design is easy to understand, regardless of the user's experience, knowledge, language skills, or current concentration level.

Guidelines:

3a. Eliminate unnecessary complexity.

3b. Be consistent with user expectations and intuition.

3c. Accommodate a wide range of literacy and language skills.

3d. Arrange information consistent with its importance.

3e. Provide effective prompting and feedback during and after task completion.

PRINCIPLE FOUR: Perceptible Information

The design communicates necessary information effectively to the user, regardless of ambient conditions or the user's sensory abilities.

Guidelines:

4a. Use different modes (pictorial, verbal, tactile) for redundant presentation of essential information.

4b. Provide adequate contrast between essential information and its surroundings.

4c. Maximize "legibility" of essential information.

4d. Differentiate elements in ways that can be described (i.e., make it easy to give instructions or directions).

4e. Provide compatibility with a variety of techniques or devices used by people with sensory limitations.

PRINCIPLE FIVE: Tolerance for Error

The design minimizes hazards and the adverse consequences of accidental or unintended actions.

Guidelines:

5a. Arrange elements to minimize hazards and errors: most used elements, most accessible; hazardous elements eliminated, isolated, or shielded.

5b. Provide warnings of hazards and errors.

5c. Provide fail safe features.

5d. Discourage unconscious action in tasks that require vigilance.

PRINCIPLE SIX: Low Physical Effort

The design can be used efficiently and comfortably and with a minimum of fatigue.

Guidelines:

6a. Allow user to maintain a neutral body position.

6b. Use reasonable operating forces.

6c. Minimize repetitive actions.

6d. Minimize sustained physical effort.

PRINCIPLE SEVEN: Size and Space for Approach and Use

Appropriate size and space is provided for approach, reach, manipulation, and use regardless of user's body size, posture, or mobility.

Guidelines:

7a. Provide a clear line of sight to important elements for any seated or standing user.

7b. Make reach to all components comfortable for any seated or standing user.

7c. Accommodate variations in hand and grip size.

7d. Provide adequate space for the use of assistive devices or personal assistance.

Source: Copyright © 1997 NC State University, The Center for Universal Design. Reprinted with permission.

While the previous foundational tenets focused initially on concerns of physical design, access, and use, an extension of this work is found in a related set of ideas addressing how students learn. The resulting principles of *universal design for learning* (UDL) add to the previous work in the context of classroom learning and include three additional provisions: multiple means of representation, multiple means of action and expression, and multiple means of engagement. The first principle, *provide multiple means of representation* (i.e., the what of learning), recognizes that students vary in the "ways they perceive and comprehend information that is presented to them" (CAST, 2011, p. 5). Whether for reasons of sensory or learning disabilities, cultural differences, or a differential preference for visual or auditory resources over printed text, this principle suggests that for a learning environment to be optimal for all learners, a variety of modes of representation is essential. The second principle, *provide multiple means of action and expression* (i.e., the how of learning), emphasizes the point that learners "differ in the ways that they can navigate a learning environment and express what they know" (CAST, 2011, p. 5). For some with significant movement impairments, executive process challenges, language barriers, or simply a preference for either written or oral means of expressing what they know, a range of techniques and approaches is warranted. As this principle suggests, while the overall outcome of learning remains constant, the means to achieve it must vary to anticipate a variety of individual differences. Finally, the third principle, *provide multiple means of engagement* (i.e., the why of learning), underscores the significance of learner affect in the success of the learning process. Accordingly, "learners differ markedly in the ways in which they can be engaged or motivated to learn" (CAST, 2011, p.5). Consistent with other research on personal interests (Holland, 1973), strengths (Clifton & Harter, 2002), learning styles (Kolb, 1983), and personality types (Myers & McCaulley, 1985), some students are "highly engaged by spontaneity and novelty, while others are disengaged, even frightened, by those aspects, preferring strict routine. Some learners might like to work alone, while others prefer to work with their peers" (CAST, 2011, p.5). In all of these options the goal is to optimize level of learner engagement (Kuh, 2003). Thus, offering multiple approaches is key to success for involving and engaging students in their learning. Meyer, Rose, and Gordon (2014) extended these principles into action with examples of educators' current classroom strategies and practices. These principles are proactive in that they attempt to anticipate the range of accommodation required ahead of time rather than adjust to what doesn't work after the fact. Such a strategy will go a long way in reducing the need for some students to justify their desire for inclusion and security on campus.

Safe and Brave Spaces

Encounters of campus diversity in recent decades have generated new ways of thinking about campus space with regard to the inclusion and security of those who inhabit it. Numerous institutions have initiated safe space programs, which focus on raising institutional awareness and understanding of disenfranchised groups on campus, especially members of the lesbian, gay, bisexual, transgendered, queer, and questioning (LGBTQQ) community. Such goals are typically pursued through staff training opportunities and the identification of supportive spaces on campus (typically offices), so designated by placement of a safe space sticker or placard. At Millsaps College (MS), for example, such a program states among its purposes to "provide a supportive environment for LGBTQQ individuals"; "support parents, family members, and friends of LGBTQQ individuals"; "foster a social climate in which others do not feel the need to express anti-gay attitudes in order to 'fit in'"; "dispel negative stereotypes and present factually accurate information about LGBTQQ individuals"; and "publicize other support resources or structures that are available on or off campus." Participants are encouraged to expect that, when they see a safe space sticker or placard on an office door, they can engage with a person who is "informed with accurate and current information on LGBTQQ issues"; will "help to create an atmosphere of safety and support, including how it affects LGBTQQ students and staff"; "will respect confidentiality concerning questions about LGBTQQ issues"; "will be aware of services available to LGBTQQ youth and adults, including support groups, hotlines, and other community resources"; "will challenge hate speech, name-calling, harassment, and discrimination, and real or threatened violence as it pertains to LGBTQ students, faculty, staff, families or those perceived to be LGBTQ" (retrieved from http//www.millsaps.edu/student_life/safe_space_ program.php).

Following a survey indicating incidences of harassment, bullying, and discrimination on campus at the University of Arizona, an evaluation of a similar program found that a majority of LGBTQQ community members agreed that safe zone markers (either placard or button) made them feel more comfortable in talking with a person they didn't already know (57 percent), feel safer on campus (74 percent), and feel better about campus climate toward LGBTQQ people (92 percent). A majority of safe zone allies also reported that the program successfully trained them to respond more effectively to LGBTQQ people (92 percent), provided helpful resources (88 percent), increased their awareness of LGBTQQ issues and concerns (90 percent), and changed their behavior (55 percent) or language (66 percent) because of information provided. More than seven of ten allies also reported having made greater efforts, as a result of their participation in the program, to increase their comfort in discussing LGBTQQ issues, educate themselves about LGBTQQ issues, avoid generalizations or stereotypes, and use inclusive language in everyday conversations with friends and in campus contacts (e.g., in a classroom, an office, or department). According to the author (Crockett, 2011), "Whether reinforcing positive ally behaviors or helping participants to make a conscious behavior change, it appears that Safe Zone is producing allies that are actively combatting the negativity of homophobia and heterosexism on campus" (p. 11).

The traditional safe space approach to encounters of diversity has not been without criticism, although challenges to it have mostly evolved in the form of further articulations and refinements to the strategy. One such example is found in Arao and

Clemens (2013) who argued for the provision of brave spaces as an alternative. According to the authors, the conflation of safe spaces with presumptions of being free of discomfort or difficulty restricts engagement and learning in the authentic exchange between *agent* (dominant) and *target* (minority) groups, mostly due to insidious differences of power, privilege, and oppression. They further contend that "authentic learning about social justice often requires the very qualities of risk, difficulty, and controversy that are defined as incompatible with safety" (p. 139). In conclusion, they recommend cultivating "brave spaces rather than safe spaces for group learning about a broad range of diversity and social justice issues," including examinations of "sexism, homophobia, heterosexism, ableism, religio-spiritual oppression, ageism, U.S.-centrism, and other manifestations of oppression" (p. 141). By reframing the traditional safe space ground rules to encourage deeper participation of all, conflict and civility pair up to allow "room for strong emotion and rigorous challenge" (p. 144), leading to further clarification and understanding. In essence, such encounters of different sociocultural groups call participants to be *brave* rather than *safe* as they approach questions of social justice.

Ethnic Culture Centers

Since the 1960s American colleges and universities have witnessed the emergence of numerous ethnic culture centers on campus (Patton, 2010). These have become important spaces of identity and resistance, as members of various ethnic and other minority groups come together to acknowledge common concerns and issues, while challenging the broader institution to embrace a wider range of differences. One of the antidotes to the hegemony of a dominant-culture institution is the establishment of subculture enclaves, where those who differ from the normative institutional press can find refuge, experience affirmation of identity, connect to peer support, and gather the necessary motivation and energy to continue resistance. Patton (2010) characterizes such centers as "counterspaces, a home away from home, and a haven in a hostile territory" (p. xiv). They serve to mitigate prevailing assumptions and expectations that, on a day-to-day basis, students in the minority often find debilitating. In essence, such centers provide a place to charge one's psychological batteries and interact with kindred spirits in a common affirming experience.

The power of campus culture centers, whether organized around differences of race and ethnicity, gender, sexual orientation, age, religion, or citizenship status, is that they capitalize on the dynamics of proxemics, homophily, engagement, and culture to effect a sense of belonging and security for participants, even if only for brief interludes. They also bring a visible focus to the concerns of campus subgroups, whose ordinary experience is not necessarily one of fitting in (Johnson et al., 2007). Perhaps they are at their best when they serve as a counterforce to the prevailing culture; in doing so, they offer the promise of congruence and consistency to strengthen these students' attraction, satisfaction, and stability in an otherwise unfamiliar and challenging setting. The range of such efforts can be found at large research universities (e.g., *Paul Robeson Cultural Center* at Penn State University), regional state institutions (e.g., *LGBT Resource Center* at St. Cloud State University), liberal arts colleges (e.g., *Women's Center* at Georgia College), and community colleges (e.g., *First Nations Student Union* at Central Oregon Community College), to cite a few examples. The previous strategies employ physical (proxemics), aggregate (heterogeneous groupings), organizational (structural dynamism), and socially constructed (language, culture) components to challenge barriers to inclusion and security in an environment. Such mechanisms are critical in shaping any setting for diversification of the norm as they build communities of identity that welcome and invite students to become involved in their learning.

Territoriality and Defensible Space

Over the past two decades American higher education has greatly expanded with significant success the use of learning communities (residential and otherwise) as mechanisms for engaging students in their learning. The quality of such experiences is partially a function of their capacity for sustaining among students a sense of territoriality and defensible space. Territoriality speaks to the behaviors and thoughts persons or groups exhibit, underlying their perceived ownership of physical space. This concept includes both claiming and defending the identified space (Bell et al., 1996). Newman (1972) expanded on the concept of territoriality in his development of the idea of defensible space. Similar to residential learning communities and campus-based fraternity and sorority houses, the culture centers discussed above serve as territories and defensible spaces dedicated to specific purposes. The benefits of defensible spaces are both physical and psychological; a design "which makes use of semi-private and private space, as opposed to public space is more defensible" (Newman cited in Jeffery, 1977, p. 193). Bechtel (1997, p. 190) summarized Newman's four characteristics of defensible space:

> Territoriality, as manifested by architectural barriers and markers; surveillance, as defined by what people can see from windows, or lines of sight; image, which is conveyed by architectural design, presence or absence of trash and vandalism, and evidence of maintenance; and milieu, which is the numbers and kinds of people and the frequency of their habitancy.

There are three ways defensible spaces contribute to campus safety (Bell et al., 2001). First, if campus spaces look defended, then potential offenders have to assume that their inhabitants will likely respond to intrusions. For example, a campus building that is well lit and showing signs of activity is less likely to be vandalized than a remote, unlit, and unoccupied unit. Second, defensible campus spaces may also encourage inhabitants to develop closer relationships and therefore a greater awareness of potential offenders from outside. For example, traffic patterns associated with housing complexes can be designed to bring people into social contact with one other, through a common, centrally located entrance, rather than individual ones. Third, defensible space may inhibit crime by increasing inhabitants' feelings of territoriality and the desire to protect their space. For example, Schroeder (1978–1979) and Phelps (1990) both suggested that encouraging students within a residence wing or floor to paint a wall mural leads to greater group identity and personalization, increasing their sense of territoriality and their willingness to protect the facility against potential intruders. The same can be said for other facilities such as student organization offices in a university union. Encouraging students to make their mark on the space enhances their sense of ownership and therefore their willingness to defend it.

Given the importance of architectural design in the creation of defensible space, the positions of Weinmayer (1969) and Zeisel (1976), emphasizing the role of designers in campus vandalism, become more evident. Campus housing personnel are recognizing the importance of this design issue across the United States. In a 1995 survey (Banning, McGuire, & Stegman, 1996), housing officers reported that, next to the cost, designing for security was their highest priority in various building projects. In Smith and Fossey's (1995) major work on campus crime they concluded with strong support for Newman's theory of defensible space, encouraging campus administrators to give serious consideration to parking, lighting, locking systems, key control, and building maintenance. It is clear that campus physical design plays a crucial role in campus inclusion and safety but is also important is the collective role of persons within those campus environments.

Campus Assessment and Response

Issues of campus inclusion and safety are complex and require a variety of institutional responses to succeed in creating conditions that promote a sense of belonging and security. Perhaps the place to begin, in terms of campus policies and practices, is an audit of current institutional conditions, both in terms of how they contribute to or detract from students' of all backgrounds sense of belonging and being valued on campus and their basic experience of safety and security.

Harper (2008) and colleagues authored a comprehensive overview of inclusive campus environments through a cross-cultural lens, suggesting a variety of strategies and practices designed to promote learning and student engagement concerning such issues. Among practices considered are: working through student resistance to cross-cultural learning and engagement (Jones, 2008), identifying and training cultural practitioners on campus (Jenkins & Walton, 2008), applying ecological principles to the creation of multicultural learning environments (Kinzie & Mulholland, 2008), engaging underrepresented students in campus activities and student organizations (Griffin, Nichols, Perez, & Tuttle, 2008), partnering with various campus units on cross-cultural programming (Patton & Hannon, 2008), and assessing campus cultures to enhance cross-cultural engagement (Museus, 2008). The volume concludes with Hill and Magolda's (2008) suggestions for breaking through the totalizing effects of dominant communities by enacting multicultural democratic ideals. Acting on such a vision is an ongoing institutional quest that includes "assembling individuals committed to these ideals; supporting and advocating for seldom-heard voices from subcultures; monitoring and challenging normalizing expectations; facilitating border crossings; creating environments and attitudes that embrace cultural differences; and mediating conflict" (p. 258). Focusing on the potential of ethnic cultural centers themselves,

Patton (2010) recommended the organization of a campus audit team (adapting a model presented in Kuh, Schuh, Whitt, & Associates, 1991) to evaluate the center's mission and philosophy, the students served, the overall campus culture and climate for engaging in multicultural learning, programs and services offered, and the requirements of current policies and staffing needs. The goal is to discover how the center, in the context of the broader institution, exercises its countercultural role in effecting a more inclusive campus environment. What is applied here to challenges of ethnic cultural differences on campus might also transfer to other distinctions relative to gender, sexual orientation, age, religious belief, and disability. Using a systems approach, like those previously recommended, while anchored in a visible internal community (e.g., LGBTQQ Center, Adult Learner Office) may be the most effective strategy for engaging the campus in assessments and dialogues of inclusion.

The creation and maintenance of safe college campuses has also been the focus of several recent publications (Gregory & Janosik, 2013; Jang, Kang, Dierenfeldt, & Lindsteadt, 2014; Janosik & Gregory, 2009; Kaminski, Koons-Witt, Thompson, & Weiss, 2010; Katel, 2011; Miller & Sorochty, 2015; Nicoletti, Spencer-Thomas, & Bollinger, 2010). Jackson and Terrell (2007) recently edited a sourcebook for evaluating and enhancing campus safety programs. Beginning with an overview of the complexity of campus safety legislation (see Miller & Sorochty, 2015, on the topic of risk management in student affairs), the participating authors focus on the culture of high-risk drinking among students (Ceglarek & Brower, 2007), the nature of campus hate crimes (Cole, Orsuwan, & Sam, 2007), the dangerous forms of hazing (Kimbrough, 2007), and the campus climate for LGBTQQ students (Rankin, Millar, & Matheis, 2007) and women (O'Callaghan, 2007). Also considered are the special security contexts of community colleges (Dukes & Harris, 2007) and minority-serving institutions (Gasman & Drezner, 2007) and the role of campus police and security departments (Perrotti, 2007), the incompatibility of weapons on campus (Cychosz, 2007), and the legal context for student affairs responses to such concerns (Lowery, 2007). The volume concludes with a review of best practices in public safety (Stewart & Schuh, 2007), relevant resources for college administrators (Reason & Lutovsky, 2007), and basic elements of a campus safety plan (Champagne, 2007). In this last chapter, the author conducted a content review and analysis of campus security websites at twenty-five institutions located near recent disaster areas, in addition to a sampling of 100 online institutional safety plans, to yield the following seven essential elements found in a comprehensive approach to the problem:

- Coherent organizational structures developed through collaborative efforts of many departments and constituent groups.
- Recognition of multiple sources of threats.
- The ability to address the needs of potential victims or targets of the threats on a particular campus.
- Planning for prevention and response measures, interpersonal threats, and natural crises.
- Effective communication systems.
- Comprehensive education and training measures.
- Ongoing appraisal and reworking in light of new developments.

Much like concerns for environmental inclusion, needs of campus safety and security are better served through planning and anticipation rather than response.

Challenges of campus safety have long been part of the experience for many postsecondary institutions. Nearly three decades ago the American Council on Education (1985) first issued a report on campus self-regulation initiatives, making many recommendations, including the appointment of an explicitly designated administrator who will ensure that security needs are considered in the design, maintenance, and operation of buildings, grounds, and equipment; that students and others are informed about security risks and procedures; that security staff are properly screened, trained, equipped, and supervised; that the number of security staff is adequate to perform necessary functions; and that security data are collected and periodically reviewed. Among the concerns reviewed for campus design, maintenance, and operation are the provision of adequate lighting, appropriate contact information, escort services, clearance of obstructions to pathways and entrances, and monitoring of campus access through selective issuance of entry devices and heightened sensitivity to unauthorized visitors. In addition to the importance of adequate numbers of well-trained and supervised security staff, professional and paraprofessional alike, the report calls for informed communication with campus constituents concerning various security procedures and incidents, and cooperative arrangements with local law enforcement personnel.

Strategies for campus assessment

Postoccupancy evaluation (POE). POE (see Chapter One) is retrospective evaluation of physical environments and buildings where the results are used to suggest modifications for improvement (Bell et al., 1996), in this case for reasons specific to personal safety and security. Elements of POE for monitoring safety might incorporate some of the environmental design issues noted in Goldstein (1996): target hardening, that is, the use of devices or materials, such as security screens, to obstruct vandals; access control, such as placement of reception desks in residence halls, making it more difficult to enter a space; deflecting offenders, that is, redirecting behavior to more acceptable outlets, such as providing graffiti boards in campus restrooms; target removal, that is, removal of potential crime targets, such as returning outdoor tables and chairs after special events; and removing inducements, that is, physical alteration of potential targets, such as quickly removing graffiti to help prevent its spread.

Archival records review. Institutional archival records, from police, disciplinary proceedings, and other campus incidents, should be reviewed on a periodic basis for trends, events, and issues related to safety and inclusion. After a complete debriefing of the records, more insightful intervention strategies can be planned.

Photographic assessment techniques. Banning (1992) presented a series of pictures of campus artifacts that could send messages of sexism. Photographs can be taken and then presented to various campus groups for their interpretation of messages and suggestions for interventions, if necessary. Since then, Banning (1997) has conducted an assessment by photographing a housing system and using the photographs for training purposes. One item of the housing system's mission statement was to ensure resident safety. These photographs served to expose both compliance and contradictions of mission. For example, one photograph demonstrated a security door properly locked, conveying a message of security. Another exposed a dislodged window screen, calling into question the safety of the setting. The photographs were assembled into a slide show and presented to the housing staff personnel for discussion and recommendations, serving to further sensitize staff to issues of safety and to more effective solutions.

With respect to potential intruders, Smith (1988) argued for the "erection of perimeters of protection that can deter, hinder, or prevent penetration of the facility ... Appearances are important; discouragement of would-be intruders is of greater value than apprehending those who do intrude" (pp. 110–111). Citing Territo (1983), Smith recommended consideration of several potential campus safety concerns: surveillance of problem locations (where incidents have occurred); maintenance of recommended lighting standards; checking groundskeeping with a focus on placing and trimming shrubs or hedges to eliminate hiding spots; scheduling classes to avoid secluded locations at night; checking for availability of emergency phones that do not require coins near walking routes, parking lots, and recreational areas; provision of adequate protection in residence halls; arranging after-hours and weekend work schedules so that staff are not left in isolated areas; organizing rape prevention programs; and offering of crime prevention programs for security personnel.

How campuses are responding to these assessments and suggestions for intervention is captured in a framework of five types of campus safety and security initiatives reported initially in a survey of 701 institutions (Beeler, Bellandese, & Wiggins, 1991) but highly relevant today:

- Traditional services: campus police, patrols, security services, outreach programs, prevention and response services, security technology, and communications
- Educational and support programs: from general security precautions to in-depth crime victim advocacy, including orientation programs, class meetings, residence hall programs, and symposia
- Planning, policy, and information strategies: crime reports, safety studies and reviews, research and use of broad-based safety information to guide decision-making
- Environmental/technical modifications: construction or landscaping to minimize crime opportunities, reducing places where crime is likely to occur; electronic technology (phones, personal entry device [PED] access, cameras)
- Community action: use of campus and community groups to enhance safety strategies

These initiatives suggest that the goal of securing campus life is multifaceted and requires the application of a wide range of strategies.

Finally, recommendations from the Council of Ontario Universities (1991) continue to be instructive of the importance of student characteristics in achieving a sense of security. Their report concluded, "The environment is experienced differently according to a person's ethnicity, race, class, age, ability and sexuality" (p. 10). Thus, campus safety audits should be conducted with the needs of various campus groups and constituents in mind. For example, concerns about sexual harassment and assault are more apparent among women. In such cases, "the goal of safety audits is to improve the physical environment in ways that reduce the opportunities for sexual assaults and to effectively make the campus a more equitable environment" (p. 9). "An environment designed to discourage sexual assault will minimize the opportunity for other kinds of assaults and for crimes involving property" (p. 4). A focused audit of this kind might include the following:

- Surveying places where people feel most unsafe or uncomfortable.
- Visiting these identified places in different seasons and times of day.
- Use an audit checklist at each site to focus on general impressions, lighting, signage, sight lines, degree of visual and sound isolation, number of people in the area at different times, distance from emergency services, frequency of security patrols, predictability of movement along routes and paths, availability of alternate routes, location of hiding places, location and security of possible assault sites (indoors and out), availability of escape routes, nature and usage of adjacent land, maintenance of facilities, sense of care

displayed for the location, overall layout and design.

- Consider aspects of the nonphysical environment as well (policies and programs). Do the people around seem trustworthy? Would they respond sensitively to an assaulted person? Is information about assaults in the vicinity publicized? What are the lengths of wait for transportation or escort service? Are there policies on sexual assault/harassment on campus? Policies to deal with racism? Sexism? Homophobia? Are free self-defense courses available? Is there an escort or walk-home service available?

The authors concluded that "women's safety is affected not only by the physical design of spaces but also by a variety of other design factors such as policies, practices and services. Universities and colleges must examine environments that encourage a climate of sexual exploitation and must challenge social values, attitudes and practices which are prejudicial to women" (Council of Ontario Universities, 1991, p. 10). Implicit in these suggestions is that measures taken on behalf of one campus group (women) might also improve conditions of inclusion and safety for other groups (e.g., lesbian, gay, bisexual, transgendered students, students of color, students with disabilities).

Inclusive and safe environments are created physically (in the classroom, residence halls, campus offices, campus grounds), in human aggregate groupings (targeted services and programs focusing on the needs of particular groups of students), organizationally (the curriculum, student organizations, departments), and through socially constructed perceptions of the setting (through images, symbols, cultural variations). Experiencing a fundamental psychological sense of belonging on campus and being free from physical threat and harm are important conditions for the pursuit of opportunities to learn and succeed. At the very least, student time and energy spent on coping with feelings of exclusion and insecurity can only detract from efforts applied to more positive growth experiences.

Although identification of problems associated with inclusion and campus safety is rather straightforward, implementing solutions is a much greater challenge. The dilemma created by many of these suggested strategies is that an approach designed to attend to one concern may actually create another concern of equal difficulty. Sometimes the trade-off is between strategies that assure anonymity and strategies that support identity. Such is the case of special housing arrangements (by hall or floor) on some campuses, designed to meet the needs of particular groups of students (racial and ethnic minorities, lesbian, gay, bisexual, and transgendered students). The emphasis on identity recognition and support for purposes of inclusion and safety might also expose students, rendering them ready targets of vandalism and other forms of harassment.

Target hardening, another often recommended strategy to secure campus facilities, illustrates a similar dilemma. As educational settings, colleges, and universities traditionally have been committed to openness and accessibility, encouraging the free flow of diverse peoples and ideas in a rich mix of intellectual pursuit. That mix contributes to the unique and powerful qualities of educational institutions, but it also renders them highly vulnerable. Securing the campus environment tightly (target hardening) diminishes its overall openness and accessibility. The price of these approaches is perhaps not yet well understood, but the direction charted by such strategies certainly raises significant questions about institutional purposes and goals.

A balance or compromise of strategies may be inevitable in addressing these concerns. Whatever the case, the importance of inclusive and safe environments is that they free individuals to pursue more active engagement and higher purposes in the setting, that is, to become involved as engaged participants in the educational environment, the focus of the next chapter.

Questions for Discussion

1. What physical, human aggregate, organizational, and socially constructed features of your institution serve to welcome students to campus?
2. What environmental features (physical, human aggregate, organizational, and socially constructed) of your college or university tend to exclude what kinds of students?
3. How does the physical layout of your institution support or detract from the sense of security students experience on campus?
4. What spaces on your campus best reflect the principles of universal design?
5. If you were to increase the sense of inclusion and security for one particular group of students on your campus, how and for whom would you go about doing so?

6

Encouraging Participation and Engagement

Whether in the form of a classroom, student organization, residence hall, department offices, or an entire campus, educational environments exert their influence long before students enter them. Such influence is recognized in the degree of attraction a student may feel for any particular setting, and those environments found most attractive are presumed to exert the greatest influence in terms of encouraging individuals to participate in them. The obvious corollary is that environments seen as least attractive are most likely to repel individuals.

This theory of attraction is a fundamental dynamic of every institution's efforts to successfully recruit students who can benefit from its educational programs and opportunities. Providing the right kind of student–institution match that is further supported by features of inclusion and safety, as the previous chapter discussed, maximizes the chances that personal satisfaction and stability will result. Thus, retention is encouraged and attrition is minimized.

However, creating conditions that support the desire of students to remain in a particular setting is only the first step. With active learning as the goal, institutions must also look beyond issues of belonging, comfort, and stability to consider the nature of environments that encourage significant investments of time and effort on behalf of members—in other words, those that call for participation and engagement in the setting. The National Institute of Education (NIE) report (1984) concluded, "The most effective education is one which most fully involves the student in the learning process and the opportunities for enriching experiences in the college setting… The quality of education can be improved by three critical conditions: student involvement, high expectations, and assessment and feedback" (Pace, 1990, pp. 7–8).

This chapter characterizes and discusses features of campus environments, from the perspectives of physical design, human aggregates, organizational structures, and participants' social constructions of them, that encourage student engagement in learning, both within and beyond the classroom. At the heart of current debates about institutional effectiveness are issues of student learning. What learning constitutes a credible college education? What conditions promote student learning? It is clear from numerous studies that the benefits of learning are related directly to degrees of student participation and involvement. Students who engage themselves as active learners, regardless of setting, show greater gains from the learning experiences encountered. What are the environmental conditions and mechanisms that promote engagement of students in their learning?

Theories of Student Engagement

While the catchphrase on today's postsecondary scene is *student engagement*, the roots of this concept are buried deep in the earlier work on student involvement by Alexander Astin and C. Robert Pace. According to Astin (1985, p. 133), the key to successful learning and, indeed, to developing students' talents can "be simply stated: Students learn from becoming involved." Student involvement then is recognized more by actions than by attitudes:

> Involvement is neither mysterious nor esoteric. Quite simply, student involvement refers to the amount of physical and psychological energy that the student devotes to academic experience. A highly involved student is one who, for example, devotes considerable

> energy to studying, spending a lot of time on campus, participates actively in student organizations, and interacts frequently with faculty members and other students. Conversely, an uninvolved student may neglect studies, spend little time on campus, abstain from extracurricular activities, and have little contact with faculty members or other students. (p. 134)

Although a person's motivation is a potentially important indicator, Astin (1985) concluded that "it is not so much what an individual thinks or feels but what he or she does that defines and identifies involvement" (p. 135). Likewise, Pace (1984) concluded that "what counts most is not who they [students] are or where they are, but what they do" (p. 1). Thus, involvement is most clearly manifested in behaviors and actions such as joining, participating, attaching, committing, engaging, immersing, and volunteering.

Astin (1985) outlined five basic postulates of his involvement theory:

> 1. Involvement refers to the investment of physical and psychological energy in various "objects." The objects may be highly generalized (the student experience) or highly specific (preparing for a chemistry examination).
> 2. Regardless of its object, involvement occurs along a continuum. Different students manifest different degrees of involvement in a given object, and the same students manifest different degrees of involvement in different objects at different times.
> 3. Involvement has both quantitative and qualitative features. The extent of a student's involvement in, say, academic work can be measured quantitatively (how many hours the student spends studying) and

qualitatively (does the student review and comprehend reading assignments, or does the student simply stare at the textbook and daydream?).

4. The amount of student learning and personal development associated with any educational program is directly proportional to the quality and quantity of student involvement in that program.
5. The effectiveness of any educational policy or practice is directly related to the capacity of that policy or practice to increase student involvement. (pp. 135–136)

Following suit in this line of inquiry, Pace and Kuh (1998) revised the College Student Experiences Questionnaire, which resulted in a systematic inventory of 142 activities that are reflective of a range of undergraduate experiences constituting forms of student involvement. These activities are arranged within fourteen different categories (or subscales), which provides a useful map through various arenas of student participation on a typical college campus, including the following: course learning; library experiences; activities related to science and technology; use of cultural facilities, student union, and athletic and recreation facilities; experiences in residence halls and fraternity or sorority houses; experiences with faculty; writing activities; participation in clubs and organizations; personal experiences; student acquaintances; and topics and information in conversations. The six to twelve items within each category assess a descriptive litany of observable activities that students may engage in and that indicate quantity and quality of their campus involvement within that category. For example, within the category of *experiences with faculty*, students report on the frequency with which they have talked with a faculty member, discussed career plans and ambitions, or worked with a faculty member on a research project. Exemplars from other categories include, for purposes of further illustration, heard a speaker at the student union or center (*student union*), asked other people to read something you wrote to see if it was clear to them (*experience in writing*), and had serious discussions with students whose philosophy of life or personal values were very different from yours (*student acquaintances*). The items in each subscale vary in intensity of activity, ranging from those more passive to those more active. Implicit in this scheme is that each of these activities is presumed to contribute to students' learning and development. Therefore, campus environments that make available and encourage such activities are thought to be involving. What is it that characterizes such environments? According to Pascarella and Terenzini (1991), "The environmental factors that maximize persistence and educational attainment include a peer culture in which students develop close on-campus friendships, participate frequently in college-sponsored activities, and perceive their college to be highly concerned about the individual student, as well as a college emphasis on supportive services (including advising, orientation, and individualized general education courses that develop academic survival skills)" (p. 64).

Engagement in Learning

Building on this agenda further, the National Survey of Student Engagement (NSSE) (Kuh, 2003) was created as a joint undertaking of the Indiana University Center for Postsecondary Research and Planning and the National Center for Higher Education Management Systems. This assessment measures institutional quality in reference to how students report using their time (in terms of activities and experiences inside and outside the classroom) and what instructors and student affairs staff do to engage students in empirically proven effective educational practices. Much like its predecessor (Pace, 1990; Pace & Kuh, 1998), survey results are issued to campuses in an institutional report that evaluates them on a range of engagement indicators or thematic benchmarks inclusive of best practices known to be related to powerful educational outcomes. Thus, within the *Academic Challenge* theme, best practices in higher-order learning, reflective and integrative learning, learning strategies, and quantitative reasoning are assessed. Reflecting *Learning with Peers* are two engagement measures: collaboration and discussions with diverse others. The *Experience with Faculty* theme includes student–faculty interaction and effective teaching practices, and the *Campus Environment* theme focuses on items related to quality of interactions and supportive environment. The last theme, *Participation in High-Impact Practices*, captures students' reports of their engagement in learning communities, service learning, research with faculty, study abroad, internships and field experiences, and culminating senior experiences. These activities are labeled high impact because of their "positive effect on student learning and development, [and they] call on students to invest considerable time and effort, facilitate out-of-class learning, engage students meaningfully with faculty, encourage interaction with people unlike themselves, and provide frequent feedback on performance. Students often describe their participation in these activities as life changing" (McCormick, Gonyea, & Kinzie, 2013, p. 13).

College students get involved in all kinds of activities that consume their time and energy. The significance of the aforementioned research on student engagement is that it cuts through all the noise of the college experience to focus sharply on educationally purposeful activities: those that make a significant contribution to students' learning and success. Students who engage in these high-impact practices simply get more out of going to college. However, this also seems to be a conditional effect, as suggested by Hu and McCormick (2012). They found that engagement depends partially on the type of student experiencing it (see Chapter Two). As reported in their descriptions of an engagement-based student typology (Table 6.1), *Academics*, although well above the mean on

Table 6.1. Cluster Centers (*z* scores) on Engagement Benchmarks for Seven Student Types

	Academic Challenge	Active & Collaborative interaction	Student-faculty experiences	Enriching educational environments	Supportive campus	N (%)
Academics	.757	1.000	.636	.568	−.294	284 (12.4)
Unconventionals	−.235	−.025	−.264	.936	.292	398 (17.4)
Disengaged	−1.392	−.970	−.865	−.873	−1.065	303 (13.2)
Collegiates	−.538	−.667	−.540	−.763	.296	393 (17.2)
Maximizers	1.041	1.469	1.755	1.064	1.140	233 (10.2)
Grinds	.214	−.211	−.473	−.394	−1.094	335 (14.6)
Conventionals	.572	.028	.427	−.254	.797	344 (15.0)
All	0	0	0	0	0	2,290 (100.0)

Source: With kind permission of Springer Science+Business Media

four of the engagement outcome measures, scored below the mean on supportive campus environment, suggesting limitations on their social relations and perceptions of campus support. *Unconventionals* were well above the mean on enriching educational experiences, and *Disengaged* students were well below the mean on all five measures. Collegiates were above the mean on supportive campus environments but fell short on the other four indices. *Maximizers* excelled on all five measures, and *Grinds* distinguished themselves only on the measure of academic challenge. Last, *Conventionals* were right in the middle of the pack in terms of active and collaborative learning and above on academic challenge, student-faculty interaction, and supportive campus environment. What accounts for these differences from one institution to another is a matter of specific design, the focus of the following sections. We now turn to a consideration of the range of physical, aggregate, organizational, and socially constructed environment concepts that illuminate the dynamics of environments that may promote student engagement.

Physical Dimensions of Engagement

Several key concepts emerge from the study of physical environments relevant to a discussion of student engagement. Among the more salient are notions of campus location, human-scale design, layout, and flexibility.

Campus Location

The location of an institution itself is perhaps the most obvious factor in considering the degree of involvement and engagement encouraged among students. Although the dynamics of a small, rural campus differ significantly from those of a large urban campus (to cite two variations among others), opportunities abound in either type of setting. As Kuh et al. (1991) observed in their study of fourteen exemplary institutions recognized as "involving colleges" (and confirmed in a subsequent study of twenty documenting effective educational practices twenty DEEP colleges documenting effective educational practices (Kuh, Kinzie, Schuh, Whitt, & Associates, 2005): "No matter where a campus is located—geographically isolated, a short distance from a city, or surrounded by a metropolitan area—that location can be used to educational advantage" (p. 307).

For the small rural, residential campus, in spite of predictable student complaints about nothing to do, motivation for engagement may emerge from physical isolation and the need to create a whole, meaningful life as full-time students. Much like the workings of a small village or town, decisions need to be made with respect to purposes and goals of programs, allocation and expenditure of resources, the social and intellectual needs of citizens, and the nurturing of a sense of pride of place. Each of these aspects offers numerous opportunities for students to become engaged in practices of good citizenship and assuming responsibility for the quality of life encountered. Grinnell College, for example (see Kuh et al., 1991), located in a small Iowa town, sixty miles from the nearest city of any size, perhaps works best in engaging its talented students precisely because of the fewer distractions demanding student time and energy in its immediate environs. Students there take great pride in the creation of their own engaged learning environment. Berea College in rural Kentucky and Earlham College in southern Indiana are other examples of this same dynamic. Isolation becomes the motive for on-campus involvement.

On the other end of the spectrum, the location of a large urban campus, ensconced in a thriving, or in some cases deteriorating, metropolis presents a different challenge. On the one hand, issues of campus safety and security may mitigate against access of students to various resources and locations in limited ways. Evening hours, traditional times for student meetings, events, and gatherings, may be especially risky in such settings for students who are cautioned not to venture out across campus alone at night. On the other hand, such settings may offer a wealth of opportunities for students to participate in a wide range of community activities, from cooperative learning positions to group service learning programs. In fact, an understanding of involvement in such settings may need to be expanded to include activities and roles that students—particularly those of nontraditional ages—bring with them to campus (Schuh, Andreas, & Strange, 1991). This is especially the case with many community colleges where the multiple commitments and challenges of their students make it difficult to capitalize on the limited capture time these institutions have in which to engage students (McClenney & Greene, 2005). Whether internal to the institution or a combination of campus-based and community-centered programs and leadership opportunities, it is essential to identify initiatives with potential for drawing students into them as a means both of complementing classroom learning and of contributing to the quality of life in the institution and its environs.

Human-Scale Design

Another principle derived from the physical dimensions of an environment has to do with its overall scale. As Nock (1943) observed, "All Souls College, Oxford, planned better than it knew when it limited the number of its undergraduates to four; four is exactly the right number for any college which is really intent on getting results" (p. 51). Clearly, settings characterized as human-scale in design tend to encourage greater participation and engagement of members. Just as their location served to generate opportunities for involvement, the human-scale physical properties of involving colleges further encouraged participation and investment of time among students (Kuh et al., 1991).

> The concept of human scale is multifaceted. Taken together, human-scale properties permit students to become familiar with and feel competent in their environment. In this sense, human-scale environments

> engender a sense of efficacy and confidence ... Human-scale environments are not over-crowded, blend in with the natural surroundings, and accommodate small numbers of people in structures usually no more than three stories above the ground ... For example, smaller, low-rise dormitories seem to be more cheerful, friendly, relaxing, and spacious than larger, high-rise dormitories. A greater sense of community and increased incident of helping behavior are exhibited by residents of low-rise units when compared with counterparts in high-rise units. In addition, cohesion and social interaction characteristic of small living units seem to mediate tensions and stress common to academic communities. (p. 110)

The importance of human-scale design to the central purposes of higher education becomes quickly evident when considering the experiences of students in a typical large-scale, introductory course often encountered during the first year of college, especially at large, public institutions. From the literature on intellectual development during the college years (e.g., King & Kitchener, 1994), it is clear that students bring varying assumptions about knowing and appropriate sources of knowledge to any learning experience. The economies of large-scale classes, not to mention the potentially intimidating qualities of such settings, all but preclude many of the conditions related to active learning. Given the standard fifty-minute time period, it is practically and physically impossible to include all students in the type of active learning strategies known to promote intellectual development (e.g., constructing, presenting, and defending a point of view in the presence of peers; leading a group discussion about a significant issue; or authoring a paper synthesizing a range of resources on a particular topic). Too often such conditions dictate the use of standardized, objective assessments, and generally a much more passive format than smaller, human-scale settings.

Design Layout and Flexibility

Finally, it is clear that the design, layout, availability, and flexibility of campus settings (see Chapter One) also have much to do with their ability to encourage involvement. The extent to which the design and layout facilitates interaction of participants is thought to be an important antecedent to student engagement. Spaces that encourage individuals to spend time interacting with others are described as *sociopetal* or *socially catalytic* spaces. Intentionally planned or not, these designs support the social qualities of campus life and mitigate against the personal isolation that may evolve over time in a competitive academic milieu. Kuh et al. (1991) underscored the importance of these institutional spaces.

> Interaction among community members is fostered by the availability of indoor and outdoor spaces where people can come together without much effort. Institutions should consider whether their campuses have adequate places that encourage spontaneous, informal interaction among students. Examples include: accessible departmental lounges; alcoves, benches, and chairs in the hallways of classroom buildings which allow faculty members and students a convenient place to continue class discussions; residence hall and union areas that encourage impromptu interaction, such as lounges with comfortable furniture, wide hallways, and side stairwells; and meeting facilities with space dividers that permit the creation of small, quiet gathering spaces. (p. 309)

In addition to public spaces, providing personal space may be equally important for purposes of engagement. Students need places to call their own, where a sense of ownership, personalization, security, and identity offer a base from which to venture out and seek involvement with others. In the words of Virginia Woolf, a person needs a room of one's own to be creative and successful. As Kuh et al. (1991, p. 120) point out:

> [Most involving colleges] provide places to which students can escape and find solitude if desired ... Escape places are more than a library carrel or a single room in a residence hall. The availability of personal space—such as the foothills at Stanford, the Miller farm and back campus at Earlham, the pond at Western College at Miami University, the river at Mount Holyoke, and the organic farm and Puget Sound at The Evergreen State College—allows students to relax and to think.

Related to this notion of personal space is the importance of a third place (Oldenburg, 1989) in students' lives (see Chapter One). A third place is distinguished by its characteristic setting, that is, a place where one neither lives nor works but goes to relax and enjoy the moment. Much like a familiar hangout, a third place tends to bind people together in a defined space where typical roles and responsibilities are lifted temporarily while new relationships and connections are explored in a unique and comfortable culture. The corner pizza pub, coffee shop, or bookstore has served such purposes for many. On college and university campuses the need for a third place is often met in the facilities of a student union or commuter center.

Ultimately, space most likely to contribute to student involvement must be flexible in its design. The ability to move walls and to rearrange seating capacities and designs allows for the maximum use of space and the accommodation of the greatest number of needs. Thus, a small-tiered lecture room by day becomes a comedy club stage by evening, encouraging students to share time and talents. The availability of multiple spaces amenable to multiple uses seems to be the key to an engaging physical design.

Aggregate Dimensions of Involvement

Concepts from human aggregate theory (see Chapter Two) suggest that individuals are most attracted to and involved in groups of people who share interests and activities (principle of homophily), and such groups are most likely to reinforce those interests and activities as congruence between personal needs, skills, and environmental rewards is maximized. In Holland's (1973) terms, highly differentiated (dominated by a single type) and consistent aggregates (comprised of similar compatible types) create characteristic environments that have greater potential for attracting, supporting, and retaining those most similar to the aggregate's dominant features (see Chapter Two). Thus, person-environment fit, rather than incongruence, is presumed to encourage engagement. This basic dynamic of human aggregates is evident in the synergy of any student organization or activity group where individuals of like minds and spirit come together in the interest of a common goal, program, or event. One of the long-standing principles in psychology is that opportunities for individual reinforcement are increased by joining a group (Skinner, 1953). The influence of peers in the college experience is undeniable.

Another principle worth exploring here is the potential connection between homogeneous groupings and degree of student involvement. The use of common interest groupings is on the rise among academic and student affairs planners. On some campuses this takes the form of establishing residential-learning communities where students are assigned rooms, floors, wings, or entire residence halls based on a commonality of academic interests (such as women in sciences or business majors). In other places (such as the University of Missouri), freshman interest groups (FIGs) are organized around a core set of learning experiences. In many ways the standard academic department reflects a similar dynamic, as faculty and students come together in a curriculum designed to focus on a particular set of interests.

Specialized offices and organizations serving the needs of particular students (adult learners, students of color, women, lesbian, gay, bisexual, and transgendered students) also function as supportive aggregates that, in turn, encourage engagement. In Spitzberg and Thorndike's (1992) analysis, such centers sustain the community of the parts in an institution, in effect offering homogeneous groupings of individuals who share common cultures, experiences, and values that distinguish them from others in the setting. This is particularly important when considering involvement of those who differ from the dominant culture and characteristics of the campus at large (Harper & Quaye, 2009). Thus, the Latino student union, multicultural affairs office, and the lesbian, gay, bisexual, and transgendered student organizations become important not only as a source of support and security for select students but also as a secure base from which to become engaged in the larger campus.

Organizational Dimensions of Involvement

Engagement entails the involvement of individuals in significant roles and activities. As participants assume responsibilities, settings make greater claims on them, exacting commitments and uses of their time and energy in support of specific goals. This is the nature of organized behavior, a dynamic basic to engagement and learning, whether in the classroom, conference room, or student activities planning room. What aspects of the organizational environment contribute to or detract from participant engagement? Answers to this question may lie in an understanding, once again, in the consequences of organizational scale and the dynamics of organizational structure (see Chapter 3).

The overall organizational scale of a setting has significant impact on the level of involvement in that setting. According to Moos (1986), "The results on organizational size are highly consistent. As ... group size increase[s], morale and attitudes become less positive, and absenteeism is more frequent" (p. 410). From this perspective it becomes clear why large-scale organizational settings might discourage involvement indirectly through attenuating participants' enthusiasm, morale, and ultimately retention. Simply stated, if individuals have few reasons to show up, they have even fewer reasons to become engaged in the setting. For example, large settings encounter the problems of overmanning (Wicker, 1973) or redundancy (Chickering & Reisser, 1993). Redundant or overmanned environments simply have too many people for too few opportunities for meaningful achievement among participants. The opposite condition, undermanning (too many opportunities for too few people), also has consequences for involvement. As Moos (1986, p. 408) observed:

> People perform more activities in undermanned settings, and they are required to accept more positions of responsibility. These settings have a greater "claim" on people, because they require more effort and because relatively more difficult and important tasks are assigned to the occupants. It is less likely that a person will achieve great proficiency at any one task, since each person must fulfill several tasks. Each person has greater functional importance in the setting, more responsibility, and a greater feeling of functional self-identity. However, there may be greater feelings of insecurity, since each person is in greater jeopardy of failing to carry out the tasks assigned, and the tasks are more important for the maintenance of the setting.

To encourage involvement in an overmanned setting, either the overall size of the membership needs to be reduced or the number of opportunities must be increased (perhaps by starting another group or section). In undermanned settings, increasing the number of participants or reducing the number of tasks and responsibilities becomes the challenge. In essence, it is the overall ratio of number of individuals to number of opportunities in a setting that is most important for consideration in creating an engaging environment.

Related to this discussion of the effects of organizational scale is the design of organizational structures (see Chapter Three). The degree of organizational complexity and the way power is distributed in an organization often determine the level and significance of engagement for participants. Insufficient structural complexity, combined with centralization of power and decision-making and maintained by higher degrees of formalization and stratification, usually means that fewer individuals become involved. In such cases, a minimal number of individuals do most everything, leaving little room or reason for others to participate. On the other hand, as structural complexity increases (to a point) and power and decision-making are distributed more equitably throughout, greater opportunities emerge for the participation of greater numbers of individuals. For example, the history of most new student organizations can illustrate this dynamic. Although functioning as a committee of the whole might be quite satisfactory initially while the group is small, success in attracting additional members is dependent on the extent to which the organization can create multiple tasks and assignments establishing a need for additional members. This goal is typically achieved by the creation of subcommittees or task groups with their respective charges and functional responsibilities within the organization. In effect, this step increases structural complexity (horizontally), and, as long as this change is accompanied by a decentralization of power and decision-making, opportunities for significant engagement increase.

An interesting parallel is seen in the growth and development of megachurches (e.g., Mars Hill Church in Seattle), particularly among the rapidly growing evangelical sects. As church membership increases, greater and varying needs emerge, calling for the establishment of new ministries (increasing horizontal complexity), which in turn engages additional members in the decision-making and work of the church. When optimum size is surpassed, additional churches break off from the larger body to form a new smaller scale unit, and the process continues (Graham, 2015).

Perhaps the key to any involving organizational environment has most to do with the distinction between a dynamic and static design. Recall from Chapter Three that the structural arrangements of dynamically organized environments combine a higher degree of complexity with lower degrees of centralization, formalization, stratification, efficiency, and routinization and a relative emphasis on the quality (rather than quantity) of the organization's products or services. An organization oriented toward the status quo might be characterized by lower degrees of complexity but higher degrees of centralization, formalization, stratification, efficiency, and routinization and a relative emphasis on the quantity (in contrast to quality) of the organization's products or services. In general, a dynamic organizational design encourages and supports innovation, while the static design tends to discourage change (Hage & Aiken, 1970).

Both designs might contribute to engagement, to some extent, at differing points in the life cycle of the organization. For example, any organization (e.g., residence hall government, student activities club) that is up and running, complete with clearly delineated structures, functions, and programs, offers an identifiable framework for potential members to become involved with, especially as vacancies occur. The familiar request of, "We need someone to take over this responsibility this year," becomes a direct invitation to become more involved. Simply stated, there's something to join. A dynamic structure, on the other hand, might also encourage participation through its potential for innovation. Change brings opportunities for program development and leadership, especially for those who are more capable of functioning within ambiguous and fluid leadership situations. Perhaps an extreme of either design might discourage involvement—the static organization through its limited flexibility and the dynamic design through its limited definition of direction and structure.

Support for these notions of a dynamic and involving organizational design is reflected in the recent growing interest in models of classroom teaching, variously labeled *cooperative*, *collaborative*, and *peer learning based*. These forms of academic teamwork call for a restructuring of the more traditional centralized, formalized, and stratified classroom to include group-oriented strategies, with students assuming major responsibilities for their own learning in collaboration with peers and instructors (high-impact practices) (Kuh, 2008). Benefits of these pedagogical designs have included greater student achievement, more positive relationships among students, and greater psychological well-being.

Constructed Dimensions of Involvement

The notion that socially constructed aspects of an environment contribute to a degree of participant engagement is immediately recognized when consideration is given to the consequences of various social climate and organizational culture features of the setting. From a social climate perspective (see Chapter Four), Moos (1986) concluded that settings emphasizing relationship dimensions "exert a consistent positive influence on morale and satisfaction in all environments" (p. 415). Whether in work settings (where involvement, peer cohesion, and staff support form the components of this dimension), task-oriented groups (emphasizing cohesiveness, leader support, and expressiveness), or living environments (emphasizing involvement and emotional support), relationship dimensions serve to invite participation and to sustain those who do become involved. From an institutional view, the importance of relationship dimensions may lie in their capacity for evoking a sense of attachment from students. As Moos (1986) observed, "Colleges with a high sense of Community and Awareness (Relationship dimensions) have a high proportion of students who feel a strong emotional attachment to the college. In addition, it is rare for students to report not having participated in any extracurricular activities in college environments that are high on Cohesion" (p. 337).

The effects of this dynamic are apparent in specific institutional subenvironments as well: "Students express greater satisfaction, show more interest in their course material, and engage in more course-relevant activities in classes that are high on Relationship dimensions" (Moos, 1986, p. 338). The pervasive influence of relationship dimensions on engagement makes sense given the social nature of human beings and the potential for reinforcement gained by joining a group (Skinner, 1953). Clearly, a group that alienates others has little potential for attracting, satisfying, or sustaining involvement of members. Thus, taking the time to build and nurture connections and relationships in a setting may be the single most important strategy a group leader can pursue if continuing engagement and satisfaction of members are the goals.

The role of customs, symbols, beliefs, values, and other artifacts of organizational culture must also be considered in this discussion of engagement. Cultural artifacts not only invite others to join and participate but also instruct members on how to participate fully and identify with a group. The study of Amish society has yielded some interesting observations in that respect (Hostettler, 1993), underscoring the power of nonverbal communication in shaping members' behavior.

Among the strongest communities are those that emphasize nonverbal modes of communication—a practice, a style, an expression, a tradition, a ritual. Communities most at risk for losing their identity tend to emphasize verbal communication. The same might be said about colleges and universities that promote engagement in learning. Institutions that are most successful at enculturating a tradition of involvement among students are culturally distinctive in the sense that they create an attractive and powerful feel, apparent immediately to prospective participants in the setting. Perhaps this is why such campuses concentrate many of their resources (e.g., recruitment materials, orientation programs) prior to or at the beginning of the college experience, in the interest of communicating to prospective students the nature of those cultural artifacts. Learning the Aye-Ziggy-Zoomba cheer, for example, at Bowling Green State University, or the O-H-I-O gesture at The Ohio State University, are equally important for connecting new students to the symbolic culture of each institution.

Campus culture creates a signature impression on students prior to their enrollment, inviting them to join the legacy that has served others well. Recall the opening scenario in Chapter Four when Clare learned about the unusual involvement history and tradition of Adams College at the first-year convocation ceremony. There is something special about such a place that encourages students to become part of the experience. This is the tacit power of institutional culture.

Involving Campuses and Engaging Institutions

Colleges and universities most successful at inviting students to become engaged in them seem to do so through offering a continuous and seamless experience of learning, both within and beyond the classroom. After visiting fourteen exemplar institutions perceived to engage students in out-of-class involvement as a complement to the academic mission, Kuh et al. (1991) concluded the following about what characterizes such places that encourage student involvement: they "have a clear mission, kept plainly in view" (p. 341); "value and expect student initiative and responsibility"(p. 345); "recognize and respond to the total student experience" (p. 347); "provide small, human-scale environments and multiple sub communities" (p. 351); "value students and take them and their learning seriously" (p. 359); and "generate feelings of loyalty and a sense of specialness" (p. 363).

In subsequent research Kuh et al. (2005) studied a sample of twenty institutions, selected for their capacity for achieving student engagement and persistence in learning, even beyond what the entering characteristics of students in them would have predicted. What they found in common with these DEEP schools was their commitment to a living mission and lived educational philosophy, an unshakeable focus on student learning, environments adapted for educational enrichment, clearly marked pathways to student success, an improvement-oriented ethos, and shared responsibility for educational quality and student success.

In terms of institutional mission, these colleges and universities all go to great lengths to articulate and communicate their respective value placed on talent development as a guide to decision-making, action, and ultimately student success. As educational institutions they take students and their learning seriously, pursuing a range of engaging pedagogies, inside and outside the classroom, while "harnessing the power of peers to make learning more interesting, relevant, and socially rewarding" (Kuh et al., 2005, p. 88). These DEEP schools are also "place conscious" and "use their settings to educational advantage by creating engaging [human-scale] spaces for learning" (p. 105). "Through buildings, signs, and the landscape of the campus, the physical environment [of these institutions] communicates messages that influence students' feelings of well-being, belonging, and identity" (p. 106). In addition, they acculturate students to "what the institution values, what successful students do in their context, and how to take advantage of institutional resources for their learning" (p. 110). In doing so, the many routes to student success are clearly marked. By and large, these colleges and universities sustain an institutional culture of improvement, supported by dynamic structures that encourage experimentation and innovation; they seek to do better what they already do well. Last, DEEP schools are inherently inclusive institutions that invite across departmental lines the collaboration of diverse campus constituents while expecting students to be responsible and holding them accountable. In summary, these six properties form the institutional infrastructure of institutions intent on student engagement and success as a prelude to holding high academic expectations, accommodating diverse learning styles with active and collaborative strategies, fostering student–faculty interaction, making available an array of complementary learning opportunities, and offering supportive programs, services, and resources.

Together the lessons of these involving colleges and DEEP schools are ones of intentionality and design. Student engagement is an outcome of purpose-directed policies and practices, instead of leaving it to chance. Descriptions of what these learning-oriented institutions achieve are replete with examples of the many environmental strategies discussed in this and previous chapters. Physical design and layout, human aggregate groupings, dynamic organizational structures, and collective social constructions all come together to leave little doubt as to the purposes of the setting—to join, participate, and become actively engaged in learning.

Institutional Assessment and Response

To promote more student engagement, institutional leaders must first become aware of the extent to which the environments they create and participate in exhibit the kinds of characteristics most likely to capitalize on students' sense of belonging and security, to promote a more active presence among them in the form of opportunities for involvement. The following might serve as institutional probes for identifying factors that encourage or inhibit student engagement:

1. Engaging environments contain physical features of human-scale dimension, flexible design, and the capacity for encouraging interaction as well as providing for individual needs. Is there sufficient meeting space? Where do students and faculty gather? How accessible are these places? What spaces isolate individuals? What spaces encourage individuals to gather informally? What are the traffic patterns of those who participate in the setting?

2. Engaging environments encourage the development of campus subgroupings, characterized by a commonality of purposes and interests. To what extent does the institution support and sustain its community of the parts (Spitzberg & Thorndike, 1992)? Are various campus groups given adequate resources for sustaining an ongoing agenda of educational purposes? How do students learn of the various group participation options? How is participation in campus groups facilitated, recognized, and rewarded?
3. Engaging environments offer an optimum ratio of individuals to opportunities, with sufficient structure to allow for the identification of significant roles and sufficient flexibility to accommodate the imprint of participating members. Are there sufficient opportunities for students to join and participate in various leadership roles on campus? In residence halls? In student organizations? In classrooms? What is the average class size? What is the ratio of faculty to students? Are resources available to cover start-up costs of new student initiatives?
4. Engaging environments tacitly encourage participation through cultural artifacts that signal the availability, importance, and value of engagement. What nonverbal messages are communicated to prospective students about the role of campus involvement? What would a campus culture audit (Whitt, 1993) say about the prevailing value placed on participation and involvement in classes? In student organizations? In campus governance? Who is included in campus culture? Who is excluded?

Depending on what information is generated from such assessments, campus policies and practices can be directed more intentionally toward the development of engaging milieus. For example, where overmanned settings prevail (such as large introductory classes), small, human-scale subgroups can be organized to promote greater participation and investment of time and energy. Democratic and collaborative decision-making practices can be modeled to create opportunities and expectations for involvement. Gathering spaces can be identified and enhanced through new construction or renovation of current facilities (as is happening with student union buildings and recreation centers on many campuses) to encourage interaction of various campus constituents. Social events (such as a campus-wide picnic) can be featured to enhance the relational and hospitable qualities of campus life. Last, campus traditions, practices, and symbols can be highlighted in ceremonies and publications for purposes of enhancing student identification, attachment, and engagement with the institution.

Involvement or engagement in an environment extends beyond mere physical presence and sense of security. While such conditions promote participant fit and stability, they may do little to encourage the level of engagement required for learning, growth, and development. The latter outcomes are more effectively addressed by more active modes of participation. Thus, engagement includes the investment of time and energy in significant roles and responsibilities, where individuals' strengths, skills, and talents are called upon under conditions of challenge and support to contribute to the processes and outcomes of the setting (Sanford, 1966). Physical scale, design, flexibility, the affiliation and organization of people, and the integration and support of campus culture can all serve in the interest of promoting this degree of environmental response. However, as the next chapter suggests, engagement is just the beginning of yet another level in this model—the experience of community.

Questions for Discussion

1. Are the challenges to student engagement at your institution related mostly to conditions of over- or undermanning? Explain.
2. To what extent does your college or university feature high-impact practices known to support student engagement?
3. How do out-of-class engagement opportunities at your institution complement the in-class experiences of students, and vice versa?
4. What engagement-based student types tend to be most active on your campus?
5. What institutional changes (physical, human aggregate, organizational, socially constructed) would you recommend at your college or university for purposes of increasing student engagement on campus?

7

Building Communities of Learning

We have claimed in previous chapters that environments offering inclusion and safety and that engage participants in significant and meaningful roles fulfill two primary conditions for promoting learning, growth, and development: a sense of belonging and security and mechanisms for active involvement. We also suggested that if the learning potential of any environment is to be realized, a third and more complete condition must be achieved: the experience of full membership in the learning setting. This last condition is present most powerfully in an environment that is characterized by the dimensions of community.

A recurrent interest in the importance of community has emerged in recent decades within society in general and within higher education in particular. Etzioni (1993) charted a communitarian agenda as the means to restore a civil society in America. The Carnegie Foundation for the Advancement of Teaching (1990), noting earlier the historical tension between individuality and community in the undergraduate experience, underscored the need for a "larger, more integrative vision of community in higher education" (p. 7) that is purposeful, open, just, disciplined, caring, and celebrative. Spitzberg and Thorndike (1992) presented a theory of campus community to guide institutional renewal in the form of a compact for a pluralistic community. Tierney (1993) used ethnographic case studies to illuminate the challenges of building communities of difference on college campuses. And Cross (1998) and Tinto (2003) have been among a chorus of voices calling for the creation of campus learning communities to support greater student success.

While such calls have long served to rally proponents, in an age of increasing social division and fragmentation, especially along lines of class and culture, the image of *community* has remained deeply embedded in our views of powerful educational environments, and for very good reasons. The concept of community contains all the essential features associated with powerful educational experiences, as unifying purposes and values, traditions and symbols of belonging and engagement, and mutuality of care, support, and responsibility encourage a synergy of participation and worth, checking and cross-checking, to create a positive human learning environment. It is no surprise, then, that conditions of community are often prescribed in the literature on higher education reform (e.g., Carnegie Foundation for the Advancement of Teaching, 1990; Chickering & Reisser, 1993; Palmer, 1987; Smith & MacGregor, 2009; Smith, MacGregor, Matthews, & Gabelnick, 2004). As Parker Palmer concluded in his observations of the status of American higher education and continues to promote (Palmer, Zajonc, & Scribner, 2010): "Community must become a central concept in ways we teach and learn" (Palmer, 1987, p. 25). In fact, Palmer (1998), drawing on the transformed "images of reality—from fragmentation and competition to community and collaboration" found in "virtually every academic discipline over the past fifty years" (p. 96)—takes his recommendation one step further to suggest that "community is the *essential* form of reality" and that "we know reality *only* by being in community with it ourselves" (p. 97, emphasis added). Thus, community building and its associated tasks has become a major focus in how we think about the goals of education and the means to achieve them.

Perhaps no one in the higher education and student affairs literature first addressed these issues more directly than Crookston

(1974, p. 57) in his seminal proposal for an intentional democratic community (IDC) as a model for campus residential living (which is still employed at the University of Connecticut where it was first created). In that proposal, Crookston outlined the essential characteristics of such a community to include (much like a dynamic organizational environment design) shared power and decision-making, open communications, flexibility, and organizational and individual symbiosis. Crookston argued, "As the individual contributes to the enrichment of the community, so the community is able to enrich the individual" (p. 58). Implicit in Crookston's analysis is an understanding that community is as much a process as it is a condition.

What is community? What does it mean to build community, to engage in community living, to learn as a community? These questions are addressed in this chapter with consideration of the role and design of physical, human aggregate, organizational, and socially constructed aspects of campus environments.

Characteristics of Communities

Communities offer a sense of belonging, security, and engagement of participants, but they also do much more. Communities establish a status of full membership for participants in an environment, offering them opportunities to engage in and shape over time a distinct history, tradition, and culture. Historically, the qualities associated with community have included a common location, common ties of purpose and direction, and forms of social interdependence (Gardner, 1990). McMillan and Chavis (1986) further distinguished a psychological sense of community to include "a feeling of belongingness, a perception of one's ability to have influence in the community, a shared belief that members' needs will be met by their commitment to be together, and a shared emotional connection" (as cited in Wells, 1996, p. 4).

The literature on human community is vast and rich and draws from many disciplines and insights. Wells (1996, pp. 15–16) distilled ten overlapping and intersecting themes from this material to include:

> A sense of history and longevity (Bellah et al., 1985; Selznick, 1992) ... a distinctive identity (Selznick, 1992) with explicit group norms and values (Gardner, 1990) ... a healthy pluralistic differentiation of personal, family, ethnic, and occupational groups (Gardner, 1990; Selznick, 1992; Warren & Lyon, 1983) ... interdependent, reciprocal, genuine, caring relationships (Selznick, 1992) that provide a sense of fellowship and confirm "otherness" (Friedman, 1983) ... equilibrium between the preservation of individual rights and the maintenance of systems that serve the common good (Boyer, 1987; Etzioni, 1993; Friedman, 1983; Newbrough & Chavis, 1986) ... full participative inclusion of all people without regard to difference in formal status, race, gender, political ideology, sexual orientation, age, etc. (Palmer, 1977; Peck, 1987) ... structural mechanisms for conflict containment and accommodation (Cottrell, 1983) ... institutional provisions and processes for self-regulation (Gardner, 1990) and for facilitating participant interaction and decision-making (Cottrell, 1983) ... on-going linkages and relationships with the larger society (Cottrell, 1983; Gardner, 1990; McMillan & Chavis, 1986), using it as a reference point for self-examination (Peck, 1987) ... [and] a celebrative ceremonial life which honors, affirms and renews a sense of shared identity (Boyer, 1987; Dunne, 1986; Gardner, 1990).

Synthesizing this list further, it appears that communities, at their most fundamental level, are recognized by their distinct and celebrated historical identities, their balance of interdependent roles and relationships, their norms and procedures for functioning, and their linkages to the larger society.

Successful Communities

Wells's (1996) review is also instructive on the characteristics of successful communities, suggesting that they can be assessed using three criteria: "(a) commitment to the community, (b) a sense of empowerment, and (c) a sense that one 'matters' to others within the community" (p. 18). Genuine commitment that is instrumental, affective, and moral (Kanter, 1972) is possibly the most important criterion of successful communities. Commitment is most apparent when members' "(a) observations of how [the community] acts and is acted upon has a vital impact in their lives and their chosen values, (b) they find that they have a significant role in [the community], and (c) they see positive results in their efforts to participate in [the community's] life" (Cottrell, 1983, as cited in Wells, 1996, p. 17). The commitment's manifestations are high retention, cohesiveness, and an acceptance of social control (Kanter, 1972). With respect to empowerment, the second criterion, successful communities influence members to act, in effect, to move beyond a sense of security and belonging to become actively engaged. Successful communities are places where it is "safe for taking risks and trying out new behaviors" (Peck, 1987), where "members participate fully and freely (Cottrell, 1983; Selznick, 1992) and share the tasks of leadership (Gardner, 1990)" (as cited in Wells, 1996, pp. 17–18). The third criterion, mattering (Schlossberg, 1989), is apparent when members move from a marginal (invalid or invisible) state to a feeling that others depend on them, are interested in them, are concerned about their fate, and share pride or empathy for their successes or failures. Crucial to this quality of successful communities is the measure of responsible concern members demonstrate, including "not looking away when a member is in need, a known set of community values, and the obligation to confront a member when he deviates from these values" (Mandell, 1981, as cited in Wells, 1996, p. 19).

Although this analysis thus far draws primarily from the insights of modern behavioral sciences to define the characteristics of successful community, it is interesting to note their similarity to features that have distinguished an ancient and persistent form of community life in Western culture—the monastery. Strange and Hagan (1998) identified six hallmarks of monastic communities committed to the Rule of St. Benedict, a defining document for men and women called to this form of life since the sixth century (Fry, 1981). Benedictine community members share a routine of daily life informed by both a written rule and a tradition of practices and customs; a commitment of stability to a specific place, a people, and a teacher (such as an abbot or prioress); a willingness to pursue personal change and growth in relationship with others; a heightened sensitivity to other members, expressed in the form of careful listening and mutual obedience; a balance of active work and reflection; and an openness to and intentional hospitality toward those outside the community. Whether in the form of ancient rituals of prayer or designer artifacts of modern corporate culture, the characteristics of community, however manifested or expressed, elevate individuals to a purpose greater than self. For an institution of higher education that purpose becomes the learning, growth, and success of students.

Dimensions of Community

Not surprisingly, communities evolve from the same components that define inclusive, safe, and engaging environments. That is, communities depend on various natural and synthetic physical features of their location, the collective characteristics of their members, the manner in which community relationships and tasks are organized, and the distinctive and tacit qualities of their dominant cultures. Thus, each component can potentially contribute to or detract from a sense of community in the environment. Among strong communities there is a synergy of components as physical features define spaces where members pursue common purposes over time in ways that are sustained by their shared characteristics and compatible with their unique collective qualities. What is impressive about any community is not the nature of any singular component but rather how all their components resonate to form a more complex and seamless whole—the community. Nonetheless, certain forms of these environmental dimensions seem to support the development of community more so than others.

Among the physical features that most clearly shape the direction of any community is territory, both physical and psychological. Communities, by nature, tend to be territorial; they need space in which to exist and to carry out their functions. Territory (in both natural and synthetic forms) serves to orient the community and to create a sense of a home place, a space where artifacts of material culture are maintained and the company of members enjoyed. Proximity establishes the common ground from which the community's agenda can grow. Drawing from principles of the architecture of community (Krier & Thadani, 2009), Levy (2009) identified the following features to consider in designing the student union of today: grand, inviting interior spaces (e.g., atria, stairways, balconies, ballrooms); well-developed transparency mix (i.e., using glass to separate large spaces); action/activity (e.g., running water, areas for formal and informal activity); light and sound (i.e., mix of low light and bright spaces); a sense of student (i.e., art, furniture, and facility components fitted to current constituents); flexible, technical spaces (e.g., lounges, common spaces, meeting rooms, technically savvy facilities); and a sense of spontaneous connectedness and comfort (i.e., spaces that engender true interpersonal connectivity). Such features are important for drawing students together in a location of community to interact and engage with one another.

Commonly shared interests are also important features of most communities. Human aggregate concepts (see Chapter Two) suggest that the collective characteristics of people in communities are more highly differentiated and consistent, reflecting a higher proportion of similar types. Homogeneous aggregates exhibit clearer characteristics that, in turn, attract, satisfy, and sustain individuals who share those same interests. Joining in the group then reinforces the characteristics already present, ultimately strengthening its dominant features. This accentuation effect (Feldman & Newcomb, 1969) or press toward conformity (Astin & Panos, 1966) weaves a very tight fabric for most communities, adding to a stability of roles, rewards, and expectations over time. The initial development of a community may depend on the attraction of a critical mass of involved participants whose common interests create a momentum that becomes self-sustaining. As time passes, and a community history and culture emerge, the capacity for incorporating and sustaining a consistent membership improves. The power of this community development dynamic is apparent in the establishment of theme houses or first-year interest groups on many campuses, for example, where students of like majors are assigned to live in one location for purposes of creating a living learning community (Blimling, 2015).

Organizationally, communities are often a paradox of design. They must be structured sufficiently to offer a framework of stability for involvement yet be flexible enough to respond and adapt to changing conditions and circumstances. Maintenance of traditions, customs, and practices—the collective memory and lifeblood of most communities—requires certain degrees of formalization, stratification, and routine (see Chapter Three). These organizational structures tend to preserve the status quo and resist change. Innovation—the capacity of any organized system for responding to changing conditions—depends on a more dynamic design, one that deemphasizes the way things have always been done. Communities also require structural flexibility as new demands call for changing roles, expectations, and rewards. Successful living communities can point to the way things were and to the way things are. For them, adaptability assures continued viability. This capacity for responsiveness is probably facilitated by a balance of defining authority and a decentralized democratic distribution of power and decision-making within the community.

Finally, in terms of the socially constructed dimensions of communities, the importance and power of organizational culture cannot be overstated. Strong communities exhibit and are recognized most often by their distinctive, well-defined presses, climates, and cultures. Values, beliefs, symbols, and artifacts form a seamless and, for the most part, tacit synergy of influence over all aspects of community life. How this works is illuminated by the difference, noted by Hall (1976) and cited in Hostettler (1993, p. 18), between high-context and low-context cultures.

> A high-context culture is one in which people are deeply involved with one another. Awareness of situations, experience, activity, and one's social standing is keenly developed. Information is widely shared. Simple messages with deep meaning flow freely. There are many levels of communication—overt and covert, implicit and explicit signs, symbols, and body gestures, and things one may and may not talk about. Members are sensitive to a screening process that distinguishes outsiders from insiders ... The nonverbal, or unstated, realms of culture are extremely important as conveyors of information. High-context cultures are integrated, for members are skilled in thinking comprehensively according to a system of the common good. Loyalties are concrete and individuals work together to settle their problems. If one person has a problem, others are expected to know what is bothering that person.

Such a description (typically reserved for more traditional communities) seems highly appropriate in the context of some departments, classes, or campus organizations where many experience the sense and intensity of community. In contrast, Hall's description of low-context cultures, as paraphrased in Hostettler (1993, pp. 18–19), might lend an understanding to the challenges other departments, classes, or organizations face as they fall short of the goals of communal life.

> Low-context cultures emphasize literacy and rationality. Highly bureaucratized segments of culture within American life are "low" in context because information is restricted primarily to verbal communication. Other levels of awareness are underdeveloped or dormant. Ways of perceiving are restricted primarily to a linear system of thought, a way of thinking that is considered synonymous with truth. Logic is considered the only road to reality. Low-context cultures use primarily mathematical models to explain nature and environment. People are highly individualistic and somewhat alienated in contexts that require little involvement with other people. Low-context culture is fragmented rather than integrated, and people live more and more like machines. The contradictions that compartmentalize life are carefully sealed off from one another. Persons in low-context cultures are prone to use manipulation to achieve their goals and are also prone to be manipulated. Failures are blamed on the system. In times of crisis, individuals expect help from institutions, not from persons.

Hall suggests that these differences do not emerge through conscious design but rather unconsciously through "the hidden currents of culture that shape the lives of people living under its influence. These differences are rooted in how people express themselves, the way in which they think, how they move, how problems are perceived and solved, ... and how people arrange their time and space" (Hostettler, 1993, pp. 18–19). Perhaps all of this is to say that socially constructed dimensions form the glue that holds a community together.

In summary, communities seem to thrive when space is available for (or dedicated to) a group of individuals who share characteristics and interests; when organizational designs invite participation, role-taking, and decision-making; and when artifacts of culture express and support a common vision and purpose. This synergy of environmental conditions creates a life of its own, recognized by those within its boundaries, as well as by those beyond, to be whole and distinctive.

Challenges of Building Community

Understanding the dimensions of community in higher education is one thing; implementing policies and practices to create and sustain them is another. Yet, as Wells (1996) noted, the "creation of a sense of community on college and university campuses is viewed as one of the central tasks of leadership" (p. iv). Spitzberg and Thorndike (1992, p. 145) articulated the timely challenge facing higher education leaders committed to building community in a pluralistic world:

> Those who work to strengthen community on American campuses walk hand in hand with paradox. In the face of increasing complexity and diversity, they seek ways to connect individuals to sub communities and sub communities to community of the whole. Those aspiring to community have always possessed the ability to see the promise of wholeness in the apparent contradiction of competing individual and small-group needs and rights. Today the challenge is greater than it has ever been.

The creation and maintenance of community on campus is particularly challenging to educators today, especially at institutions that are overmanned and fragmented by various subgroups. The dilemma is that what contributes to strong subcommunities most often detracts from the community of the whole and what sustains the whole community usually does so at the expense of various subcommunities. The solution from Spitzberg and Thorndike is rather elusive, but ever more urgent: "In our travels, we found many people who share our concern that healthy sub-communities are not enough, that in today's complex and diverse world, more than ever, students, and everyone else working on our campuses, must connect with the institution" (p. 151). However, for large campuses, the structural accommodation of subcommunities is a necessary step in making that connection:

> Such a campus must affirm the centrality of its sub-communities, for it is through these that people are most likely to connect to the whole. In addition, a large campus could choose to create a variety of crosscutting learning communities, no larger than five hundred members (students, faculty, staff), in order to reduce the scale of the institution. These intermediate networks could connect the smaller sub-communities to the campus as a whole. (p. 161)

The challenge of building authentic campus communities was addressed by Schroeder (1993) in the context of residentially based programs. For purposes of encouraging and assessing the development of communities, the author applied four criteria: involvement, influence, investment, and identity. He defined these criterion elements as follows:

> 1. *Involvement.* A true community encourages, expects and rewards broad-based member involvement. The environment is characterized by a high degree of interaction, with students, not staff, assuming a multitude of roles. As a consequence, everyone is

important and everyone is needed. Returning residents assume responsibility for orienting and integrating "new" members through formal and informal rites of passage. High-involving floors are characterized by supportive interactions, with students naturally helping one another with personal and academic problems.

2. *Influence.* In floor units that exhibit a high degree of influence, control is vested in members, and students exert maximum control over their physical and social environments. For example, residents are encouraged and expected to personalize their rooms and hallways, through painting and decorating them, and to recruit and assign members. They are also expected to develop a social contract whereby group standards are affirmed, both individually and collectively. In such units, students feel important, their perspective is valued, and their contributions are essential to the welfare of the group.
3. *Investment.* Investment is a reflection of psychological ownership and flows naturally from involvement and influence. Students care about one another and their group. Boundaries with respect to other groups are clear, and group or institutional property is guarded rather than damaged. Interactions are often characterized by gentle confrontation rather than polite or passive-aggressive behaviors. Students are simply unwilling to have staff assume responsibility for them—they understand and appreciate the need for open, honest, and assertive communication with one another. Finally, there are clear variations in status and roles, as well as longevity of association. Rewards are provided for being a "good" member.

4. *Identity*. Floor units characterized by a high degree of identity are ones that focus on commonalties and transcendent values. Students in such units have shared symbols, similar to those fraternities and sororities use to signify their identities. In such living units, members describe themselves in collective terms such as we and us, not I or they, thereby reflecting their emphasis on common purposes and unity. (pp. 524–525)

Although these prescriptions were first proposed two decades ago, they are as current today as any time, and the value of the four elements is apparent beyond their specific residential application, when consideration is given to what might characterize a strong academic department, a student activities organization, or a classroom. Certainly, achieving the goals of involvement, influence, investment, and identity as outlined already will go far in building a sense of community in these settings as well.

Schroeder (1994) extended this framework with a six-point prescription for creating learning communities in general. Learning communities are "generally small, unique, and cohesive units characterized by a common sense of purpose and powerful peer influences" (p. 183). They include: "Student interaction [that is] characterized by the four I's—involvement, investment, influence, and identity; involve bounded territory that provides easy access to and control of group space that supports ongoing interaction and social stability; [are] primarily student centered, not staff centered, ... [that is] staff ... assume that students are capable and responsible young adults who are primarily responsible for the quality and extent of their learning; [are] the result of collaborative partnerships between faculty, students, and residence hall staff ... designed to intentionally achieve specific educational outcomes; [and] exhibit a clear set of values and normative expectations for active participation ... [with] normative peer cultures ... [that] enhance student learning and development in specific ways. (p. 183) The role of physical, human aggregate, organizational, and constructed dimensions discussed in preceding chapters is apparent in these prescriptions. Homogeneous groupings, facilitated by defined territory, participative organizational structures, and an integrative culture sustains communities capable of supporting learning in powerful ways.

Chickering and Reisser (1993) also suggested a formula for the development and maintenance of community, conditions they proposed for optimum development of students. They concluded:

> the community, whether it takes the form of residence hall unit, sorority or fraternity house, student organization, or informal circle of friends, should have the following characteristics ... regular interactions between students [as] a foundation for ongoing relationships ... opportunities for collaboration—for engaging in meaningful activities and facing common problems together ... small enough so that no one feels superfluous ... [inclusion of] people from diverse backgrounds ... [and] it serves as a reference group, where there are boundaries in terms of who is "in" and who is "out," [with] norms that inform those with different roles, behaviors, and status that they are "good" members or that what they are doing is unacceptable. (pp. 276–277)

Brower and Dettinger (1998) also offered a comprehensive model for learning communities, incorporating academic, social, and physical components in the interest of developing students' professional, ethical, and civic responsibility. These components are defined respectively in terms of the "curriculum content" (academic), "interpersonal relations among students, faculty, and staff" (social), and the "place or facility where the community meets or resides" (physical) (p. 17). They argued that "for a program to create a community effectively and enhance learning... it must integrate these three components to some degree" (p. 17). They further described seven characteristics common to all learning communities:

> All learning communities are purposefully designed to do the following:
>
> 1. Develop a sense of group identity in which all participants recognize one another as learners, while still valuing the contributions of each individual. Students recognize that participants are neither solely independent nor dependent.
> 2. Provide facilities or spaces in which people can come together to meet and engage in transformative learning activities.
> 3. Create a supportive environment that engages new students in the life of the institution. Activities and programs are designed to engage a continual stream of new members.
> 4. Develop a seamless student experience that integrates social and academic experiences. Although the level of integration will vary, activities and programs are designed to enable students to bring their personal interests into their academic work, as well as to bring their academic work into their personal and social activities.
> 5. Develop connections among disciplines, recognizing that although ways of knowing may be discipline specific, knowledge and concepts are not.
> 6. Provide the context for developing complex thinking skills—including divergent, flexible, and critical thinking—and social cognition, creativity, and metacognition, whether the focus is on civic,

professional, or ethical responsibility. Programs and activities are designed so that students interact with material at a much deeper level than simply receiving information.

7. Continually evaluate both the process and the outcomes. Modifications should be made as necessary. A learning community continually evolves as new members enter. Although this is essential to the vitality of the community, it also requires that the community be continually evaluated to ensure that its stated objectives continue to be met. (pp. 20–21)

The ultimate goal of any community-building initiative is that students themselves recognize its most important outcome: a high-quality sense of community. From student responses at one institution in a large urban area (Cheng, 2004), a sound campus community was deemed to "(a) have an open environment where free expressions are encouraged and individuality is accepted and respected; (b) engage faculty and students in teaching and learning; (c) provide an active social and learning environment in residence halls; (d) foster positive relationships among ethnic and cultural groups through programs and student activities, (e) celebrate traditions and heritage of the institution, and (f) provide assistance to students when they feel lonely or depressed" (p. 226).

The aforementioned authors' prescriptions closely parallel those of other observers and theorists summarized in the present and preceding chapters, insofar as they understand the development of community as an integrated process, involving physical, aggregate, organizational, and socially constructed dimensions along a dynamic, evolutionary path. Successful communities never come to be, in any fixed formula; rather, as organic entities, they must continue to grow and develop in response to their own environs, both internal and external to their boundaries. One particularly successful model of community building on many college campuses is found in the growing trend toward establishing campus learning communities (Zhao & Kuh, 2004).

Campus Learning Communities

Since their inception, campus learning communities have abounded as educational options for students and faculty alike at numerous colleges and universities. Living-learning communities (LLCs) or programs (LLPs) are but one form that has grown in popularity among students seeking opportunities for support and engagement during the college experience. For example, at Virginia Polytechnic Institute and State University (Virginia Tech), a research extensive land-grant institution of 31,000 students (82% undergraduates), options are extended to incoming and continuing students for four different models of learning communities (Virginia Tech Division of Student Affairs Housing and Residence Life, 2014):

Academic major learning communities

"bring together students pursuing a common professional field such as engineering or biological and life sciences. The majority of the participants are first-year students. Students are encouraged to continue living in the community serving in various leadership roles and creating a multigenerational living environment." Names such as *inVenTs* (an engineering and sciences community), *Da Vinci* (a biological and life sciences learning community), and *Hypatia* (an engineering community for women) promise a full agenda of inclusion, security, and engagement as members pursue common interests of a discipline.

Enhanced learning communities

"explore a specific area of interest (e.g., service learning or leadership) through academic courses and co-curricular experiences. These communities are open to students of any academic major." So named *Serve* (Students Engaging and Responding through Volunteer Experiences), *Morrill Community* (focusing on sustainability through experiential learning and civic participation), and *Thrive* (employing a strengths-driven philosophy (using StrengthsQuest and helping students discover their inherent talent and then teaching them how to use that talent to benefit academics, careers, involvements), these communities reflect a range of student interests that capitalize on students' out-of-class experiences.

Residential colleges

"are multigenerational and multidisciplinary, and host first-year, sophomore, junior, senior and graduate students from a full range of academic backgrounds. The residential colleges are led by a live-in faculty principal and a student life coordinator from the Division of Student Affairs, as well as a host of faculty and staff Fellows who mentor students.

Members of the residential colleges are expected to participate in governance, budget management, event planning and student conduct. Curious and engaged students will love living in one of our residential colleges. Students may elect to live in a residential college for as many as four years." Options such as *Residential College at West Ambler Johnston* (where members participate in a variety of academic and social activities, with the goal of creating a sense of community and tradition that fosters an environment where students know and are known) and *Honors Residential College* (a community of faculty, staff, and students who share a deep intellectual curiosity) employ many of the best practices discussed in the present volume to include, secure, engage, and invite students into communities of learning.

Themed housing

"offers students with common interests the opportunity to live together. Residents are encouraged to create a community by engaging in shared activities. These programs are open to first-year through senior-level students." Thus, *Oak Lane Community* houses students engaged in fraternities and sororities, and *The Well* offers students opportunities to construct community guidelines for living together and, among other outcomes, gain practical experience in leadership, teamwork, and time management. Again, these student-centered communities offer a human-scale and holistic pathway through the college experience. The added value of such experiences has been documented in the research on college outcomes, including being linked to higher levels of engagement, student self-reported outcomes, and overall satisfaction with the college experience (Zhao & Kuh, 2004), especially among first-year students (Rocconi, 2011). A national study of LLPs confirmed the general academic and social benefits in LLCs (Brower & Inkelas, 2010), especially for first-generation students (Inkelas, Daver, Vogt, & Leonard, 2007).

Learning communities have also enhanced faculty effectiveness on many campuses (Cox & Richlin, 2004; Lenning, Hill, Saunders, Solan, & Stokes, 2013; Sipple & Lightner, 2013). Distinguished from other kinds as *faculty learning communities* (FLCs) or *professional learning communities* (PLCs), they have been described as a "group of trans-disciplinary faculty, graduate students and professional staff group of size 6–15 or more (8 to 12 is the recommended size) engaging in an active, collaborative, yearlong program with a curriculum about enhancing teaching and learning and with frequent seminars and activities that provide learning, development, transdisciplinarity, the scholarship of teaching and learning, and community building." Two such examples include a *cohort-based* FLC, which is designed to "address the teaching, learning, and developmental needs of an important cohort of faculty or staff that has been particularly affected by the isolation, fragmentation, stress, neglect, or chilly climate in the academy," and a *topic-based* FLC "designs a curriculum to address a special campus or divisional teaching and learning need, issue, or opportunity" (Miami University Center for Enhancement of Learning, Teaching and University Assessment, 2014). Examples of FLCs for the 2014–2015 academic year, sponsored by the Center for Faculty Excellence at Bowling Green State University, include *Evidence Based Teaching for High Achieving Students, Active Learning and the Transition to Digital, Strategies for Teaching in a Large Classroom, Service Learning Faculty Learning Community*, and *Creating a Community of Care*. These communities are limited to eight to ten members, excluding the facilitator assigned to each group, and meet to focus on their selected concern six to eight times each semester.

In a review of extant research on the impact of these faculty and professional learning communities on teaching practice and student learning, Vescio, Ross, and Adams (2008) concluded, "Participation in learning communities impacts teaching practice as teachers become more student-centered. In addition, teaching culture is improved because the learning communities increase collaboration, a focus on student learning, teacher authority or empowerment, and continuous learning; ... students benefit as well, as indicated by improved achievement scores over time" (p. 88). Parallel positive outcomes from such experiences for students also include greater "student success, broadly defined [as] enhanced academic performance, integration of academic and social experiences, positive perceptions of the college environment, and self-reported gains since starting college" (Zhao & Kuh, 2004, p. 133).

Assessment and Institutional Response

In addition to the features that contribute to a sense of belonging, security, and engagement, assessment of campus characteristics that support the development of community, whether in the classroom, academic department, student organization, commuter student center, or residence hall, should include the following questions:

- Do students, faculty, and staff have opportunities and spaces to connect with others on campus around their common interests, values, and experiences?

- Are differences of interests, values, and experiences accommodated in caring and supportive ways?
- Do decision-making structures and practices facilitate participation?
- Do symbols, traditions, and other cultural artifacts reflect and celebrate the community of the whole as well as the community of the various parts?

The importance of common interests, values, and experiences in learning underscores the role of identity and affiliation in students' lives. Individuals seek educational experiences to explore dimensions of self (Chickering & Reisser, 1993). Who am I, what can I do, and where am I going are all questions that converge in a state of transition (Levinson, 1978; Levinson & Levinson 1996) as life structures are unpacked, examined, and reassembled for the next phase of life. Experiencing a community of interests during such a time affirms and supports the emergence of a sense of identity, one of the most powerful and consistent overall outcomes of the learning process. Institutional administrators should inquire as to what extent gathering spaces and resources are allocated and opportunities created to facilitate multiple communities of interest on campus. How and when are these opportunities communicated to students? What are the expectations concerning these opportunities and their role in student learning? The resurgence of first-year experience programs on many campuses may offer the best model for introducing new students to these communal dimensions of learning.

The dynamics of selection and identification necessary for developing a community of interests will sooner or later lead to a divergence of interests and inevitable moments of conflict and tension. However, as Palmer (1987) noted, conflict is not the absence of community but rather its heart: "Knowing and learning are communal acts. They require many eyes and ears, many observations and experiences. They require a continual cycle of discussion, disagreement, and consensus over what has been seen and what it all means" (p. 25). Thus, conflict, rather than detracting from community, energizes it. Parker continued, "At the core of this communal way of knowing is a primary virtue ... capacity for creative conflict ... there is no knowing without conflict." In fact, "A healthy community ... includes conflict at its very heart, checking and correcting and enlarging the knowledge of individuals by drawing on the knowledge of the group" (p. 25). The key, then, may lie in how conflict is embraced and responded to, and therein is the importance of communities of learning. As Palmer concluded, "Community ... is precisely that place where an arena for creative conflict is protected by the compassionate fabric of human caring itself" (p. 25).

In addition to an ethic of justice and fairness, campus leaders must inquire as to what extent an ethic of care is manifested during moments of conflict. Can individuals disagree with each other without forfeiting relational bonds? In a pluralistic society this ethic of care must extend beyond the community of the parts to also include the community of the whole. Are individuals and groups willing to give up self-interests for the sake of preserving the larger sense of community?

The importance of facilitating learning through participative, democratic organizational structures has long been a part of the philosophical discussions of educational systems (e.g., Dewey, 1916; Thayer-Bacon & Bacon, 1998). Democratic processes entail the distribution of power and decision-making in a setting (a decentralized organizational design) while inviting participants to assume significant roles and responsibilities. This is the essence of involvement—the exertion of energy and time on task toward the achievement of educational goals. Such an approach recognizes, as Palmer (1987) suggested, that without the investment of community members, education quickly reverts to a one-sided, hierarchical, and at best rote ritual of information giving and receiving. Freire (1972) described this as a banking system, with little capacity for liberating individuals from their oppressive experiences.

Learning is a more active challenge, enhanced by the input and processing of a variety of perspectives and points of view. It also involves a level of risk as participants struggle to construct new ways of thinking and being in the company of others. The participative structures of democratic community offer the conditions most likely to support the outcomes of active learning. Institutional leaders, faculty, and staff interested in encouraging participation must develop an ear and an eye for democratic community wherever it may be found on campus. Classroom instructors, directors of student activities and residence hall groups, and department heads can all begin by asking: Who is in charge here? How are decisions made? In general, the extent to which responses are inclusive of the greatest number of participants in the setting reflects the degree to which this criterion is being met.

The significance of organizational culture in effecting a sense of community on campus has been underscored in numerous studies (e.g., Kuh et al., 1991, 2005). Engaging communities are mission driven and are recognized immediately by a distinctive array of symbols, values, beliefs, practices, and other artifacts that create a compelling vision of where they are going and how they intend to get there. While accommodating the varying needs of subcommunities (the community of the parts), those settings committed to the goals of community building are successful in identifying that which unites all members, regardless of differences; that is to say, they can visualize the community of the whole.

Questions contained in the Involving College Audit Protocol (Kuh et al., 1991), for example, include several probes appropriate to assessing this criterion, such as: "What traditions and events introduce and socialize students to core values of the institution?"; "What opportunities exist to celebrate the campus community?"; "Are there segments of the campus community who feel they are excluded from participating in such celebrations?"; and "What 'terms of endearment' [that is, words and expressions that have context-bound meanings and encourage feelings of belonging in members and express institutional values and beliefs] are used to communicate the special qualities of the institution to insiders and outsiders?" (pp. 403–404).

A number of different models have served as frameworks for understanding the nature and role of educators in colleges and universities. We've grown accustomed more recently, under increasing pressures for accountability, to assessing inputs and outputs as the managers of educational industries, where student achievement scores and degrees are written into annual reports as products, with expectations of increasing various efficiencies from one year to the next. Also familiar to us are the political dimensions of our work. We become monitors and referees in cultural wars on a battleground of ideas, where alliances are struck, persuasions mounted, and power consolidated to accomplish the outcome of debated concerns. While elements of either of these models are perhaps unavoidable in any pluralistic setting, the engaging and generative qualities of community are preferred here for purposes of defining the character of a learning environment. In community, shared interests in time, space, and culture compel individuals to engage one another creatively toward the achievement of specific goals and outcomes. This is the most powerful framework for the pursuit of learning.

Finally, we acknowledge that the elements of community defined here heavily depend on physical proximity for shaping their dynamics. With increasing emphasis on distance learning and the technological capacities of the Internet and World Wide Web emerging on many college campuses, it is becoming a distinct possibility that our thinking about this particular dimension in the lives of students might change significantly in the years to come. The potential for designing digital mobile environments to deliver similar conditions of inclusion, safety, engagement, and community suggests that this is an area deserving of our attention. This is the focus of the next chapter.

Questions for Discussion

1. To what extent does your college or university manifest the characteristics of successful communities?
2. What environmental features (physical, human aggregate, organizational, socially constructed) on your campus most support the experience of community among students?
3. If you were to ask students where on campus they experience a sense of community most, what would they most likely say?
4. What stands out as unique about students' experiences at your institution that distinguishes it from other colleges or universities?
5. What would you recommend to change about the environmental features (physical, human aggregate, organizational, socially constructed) on your campus to increase the experience of community among students?

8

Learning Through Mobile Technology

Since the first edition of our work (Strange & Banning, 2001), three factors have converged in American higher education that promise to radically reshape how it goes about the work of educating students: the emergence of a mobile culture, proliferation of social networking, and a greatly expanded and deeper understanding of the dimensions of human learning. From the perspective of *where* we learn, attachment to a physical campus is no longer necessary for access to information. Proximate learning is rapidly being challenged by mobile learning. Synchronous, one-dimensional pedagogy is giving way to teaching within "blended learning" opportunities (Vaughan, Cleveland-Innes & Garrison, 2013) or the "organic integration of thoughtfully selected and complementary face-to-face and online approaches and technologies" (Garrison & Vaughan, 2008, p. 148). We have truly become a mobile society in which distance no longer limits access to resources or connection to one another. As members of the human community, we have always depended upon our connections to family, friends, colleagues, and acquaintances as both a social and practical matter. Now, however, such networking has evolved into a principal source for learning about the world around us. How we learn has evolved as well. From a once exclusively didactic model we now acknowledge an exceptional range of possibilities responsive to a much broader constellation of learning styles and preferences. Generational shifts have also resulted in students bringing to this new digital shoreline (McHaney, 2011) different expectations for the quality of the learning experience. Thus, social networking and learning have merged on a platform of mobility in higher education, forever altering its path.

The press of such factors on colleges and universities has caused them to reconsider how they contribute to student learning and success. These are shifts occurring at the very foundations of higher education that some have suggested will push it over the tipping point (Gladwell, 2006), far beyond the traditional place it has occupied in the past. Where that may be is difficult to predict with any accuracy. In fact, even writing about this now is a risky proposition, especially given the rapidity with which this revolution has unfolded in postsecondary institutions over the past ten years. Rather than a carefully planned investment, the digital invasion of the American college campus has proven to be a movement that is both organic and self-organizing at its core. Instead of asking, What shall we do?, educators are more inclined to comment, Look what's happening! See what students are doing? Let's go there! Wherever it goes, though, higher education must take the lead if it is to survive as an institution for the learning, growth, and development of students.

On a prefatory note, it is arguable that the conventional distinction between real and virtual environments (Rheingold, 1991), common to our discourse on the topic, has any value for college students today. For most college students, their everyday experience is much more seamless as they navigate between personal encounters and digital likes. Searching the Web or sharing a story with friends on Facebook, responding on Twitter, and displaying on Instagram are just a few of the many different activities they typically engage in while negotiating between their digital and sentient worlds. Maybe for them the whole of it functions as one world, with multiple ways of accessing and engaging it. Perhaps the connotation implicit in conventional circles—that somehow the virtual world is less than authentic than the real world—may not be an issue for them. Entering the new paradigm of mobile learning requires new assumptions and new ways of thinking about learning spaces, real and virtual (Sköld, 2011). If the past ten years are any indication of the scope and speed of change in this new paradigm, what may seem preposterous now might be commonplace tomorrow.

The Scope of Things Present

World Wide Internet use has grown from 14 million, or 0.3 percent of the world's population, in 1993 to nearing 3 billion users, or 40 percent, in 2014, with the largest numbers coming from China, the United States, India, and Japan. China, with 46 percent of its citizens connected to the Internet, has a total of 642 million users, while the United States, with 86.8 percent of its population connected, has 280 million users. The five countries with the greatest proportion of its citizens connected to the Internet are Qatar (96.7 percent), Iceland and Bahrain (each 96.5 percent), Norway (96.2 percent), and Denmark (96.1 percent) (Internet World Stats, 2014).

A Pew Research *Mobile Technology Fact Sheet* (Pew Research Center, 2014) indicated that 90 percent of all adults reported having a cell phone, with equivalent portions across categories of sex, race/ethnicity, age, education level, household income, and type of community (rural vs. urban). A total of 42 percent own a tablet computer, and 32 percent own an e-reader. Within the general population, 58 percent reported having a smartphone, which they use for sending or receiving text messages (81 percent), accessing the Internet (60 percent), sending or receiving email (52 percent), downloading apps (50 percent), getting directions, recommendations, or other location-based information (49 percent), listening to music (48 percent), participating in a video call or video chat (21 percent), and checking in or sharing one's location (8 percent).

In terms of college students' connection to the Internet, data continue to show that they are digitally steeped in new technologies, although differentially so. A 2010 Pew Research Internet Project survey (Smith, Rainie, & Zickuhr, 2011) found that nearly 100 percent of students at four-year colleges access the Internet, and 93 percent of them are home broadband users. Nine of ten also report using wireless connections (laptop or cell phone). Looking at community college students, perhaps reflecting demographic differences, 94 percent are Internet users, 78 percent broadband users, and 85 percent wireless users. An earlier national study (Jones, Johnson-Yale, Millermaier, & Perez, 2009) also demonstrated that acquisition and use of technology among college students is partially a function of student background characteristics. Accordingly, this study found differences by gender, for example, with "female college students [tending] to use the Internet for communicative and academic purposes more frequently than their male counterparts" (p. 259). Racial differences were also apparent in the data, with Black and Hispanic students having begun their use of the Internet at school and White students more often reported having done so at home. Such findings support claims of a certain digital divide in this technological revolution that may or may not persist as time goes on. At the very least, observers of college students should monitor potential differences to account for changes across time as the divide seems to be narrowing. Regardless, it is clear that the Internet is here to stay and continues to grow exponentially. Perhaps as signs of where things are, Van Der Werf (2014) reported that within "the last decade, the compound annual growth rate for online enrollments is 17.6%, while the annual growth rate for overall higher education enrollment is 2.6%. Almost one-third of students take at least one course online," for reasons of scheduling, convenience of travel, enjoyment of computer technology, interest in innovation, and even differences of personality (e.g., introverts prefer online classes) (Harrington & Loffredo, 2010).

The Status of Things as They Are

The uses of Internet technologies by students in colleges and universities fall into several general categories: communicating with others, connecting to peers through social networking, searching for information, accessing online courses and assignments, and collaborating on projects. Such activities have followed suit on the development of a catalog of new systems, applications, technologies, and strategies adapted for purposes of learning. From basic email to complex course management interfaces, with e-reader tablets and the more sophisticated smartphones and much anticipated wearable technology, college students are arriving at our institutions thoroughly wireless and have come to expect a wide range of digital options in the learning environment. Although we are still on the front edge of such developments, much has transpired in the postsecondary setting to suggest that the Internet has firmly embedded itself within the Academy as a major venue for students' learning. This is frontier space that demands much greater exploration.

We preface this review with the claim that, regardless of *where* higher education finds itself in future years, the basic environmental conditions outlined in our model will continue to be highly relevant. Students will always need to know whether they are welcomed and included in the process of learning. They must continue to experience a certain level of safety and security in any opportunity that expects to retain their involvement, and it will always be the case that whatever they gain from such opportunities, their success will be contingent on their degree of engagement in them. Learning is inherently a social activity, so the power of community will always be the ultimate capstone of the learning experience. Thus, the fundamental aims of educational design—that is, to include, secure, engage and invite students into the learning community of higher education—will not change, but the specific methods and techniques employed to do so have and most certainly will continue to evolve.

In a review of twenty-first-century digital age pedagogy, Beetham and Sharpe (2013) suggested that, if not the basic principles, "the methods available to learners and teachers have evolved, and new approaches have proliferated. Learners' independent access to networked technologies has allowed an intermixing of personal, social and academic practices which has made learning both more accessible and more unpredictable, and has led to creative new hybridizations" (p. 13). Citing the work of McGill (2011), the authors also concluded that generational differences lend themselves to greater compatibility between learner ease and learning opportunities.

> Learners themselves are changing. Most young people in Western societies make routine use of the Internet and email, text messaging and social software, file sharing sites, cloud services and mobile devices. Their familiarity with these new forms of exchange is carried over into their learning. Beyond whatever engagement with technology is required by their institution or course of study, learners use the communication and information tools they have at hand to help manage their learning. Indeed some curriculum transformation projects have found that more progress can be made by allowing students to choose their own technologies. (p. 6)

In his review of how social media can be used to enhance student engagement and educational outcomes, Junco (2014) argues persuasively that the digital world has much to offer the academy, the premise of our analysis here. So we ask: How are these new technologies, and the multitude of digital opportunities they have spawned in recent years, reshaping for students the dimensions and dynamics of their college experience, especially with regard to aspects of learning? What is the promise of these new forms of communication on campus? What are its challenges and cautions?

In response to the conceptual framework of this book, what are the implications of this technology for the inclusion, safety, engagement, and experience of community for students? These are the questions that guide our examination in the following pages.

Effecting Inclusion and Safety

Among the earliest uses of digital technology has been to communicate with and welcome students to campus. DeAndrea, Ellison, LaRose, Steinfield, and Fiore (2012) reported on the positive effects of a social media site (*SpartanConnect*) created to enhance feelings of connection between students and their on-campus residential neighborhoods at Michigan State University. Users of the site "could join groups, organized around both interests and residence hall geography, each with its own forum, event calendar, and member directory" (p. 17). The site was developed "to cultivate healthy beliefs about college among incoming students and to model positive social norms" (p. 17). Ostensibly, the intent of the website was to "facilitate the development of a support network during students' first year of college, prior to their arrival on campus" (p. 15). Accordingly, it was assumed that "having students connect with one another on a social media site prior to their arrival on campus may help [them] enter college with a more expansive social network than they otherwise might have had, contributing to [their] bridging social capital" (p. 16). Results of their assessment indicated that website activity positively predicted critical student expectations regarding the discovery and use of a diverse support network, thereby contributing to their successful transition to college. In addition, they observed on the website that many students engaged in peer-to-peer support and information exchange that further facilitated their matriculation process. Another example, blending social-relational and academic goals, is found in Bers and Chau (2010), who described a preorientation program titled Active Citizenship Through Technology (ACT) for incoming students that engaged them in civic dialogue early in their academic experience while fostering a long-term peer support network. Participants used a digital platform to "design and inhabit a Virtual Campus of the Future to express concerns and ideas about community issues that interested them. In addition, they participated in face-to-face activities to promote civic skills and learned about their college community" (p. 1).

Regardless of such efforts, heading to college is an anxious moment for many aspiring students, especially those from first-generation families who have little precedent or models to draw from in easing the transition of a son or daughter. The same can be said for students whose ethnic identity, sexual orientation, disability, religious belief, age, or socioeconomic status differ from the dominant culture on campus. Dedicated websites and invitations to social networks are becoming routine practice on many campuses as they recognize the need to reach out especially to underrepresented entering students whose risk for early withdrawal is quite high in comparison. The capacity of online communities to both identify and to offer anonymity to students makes them an important asset for building inclusive and secure digital environments, although not without risk. Social networking in particular has fallen victim to any number of privacy breaches and threats from beyond as members become comfortable and perhaps share too much information in the course of connecting to others. Open systems, such as are many social networks, are accessible to friends and foes alike and in spite of expressed standards for participation are prey to some with negative motives. Spamming, phishing, data mining, and malware attacks are not uncommon abuses of the unsuspecting in the digital world. However, system blocks and trusted certification mechanisms have made progress on increasing the safety of such networks. Nevertheless, caution is always in order when accessing these systems.

In general, colleges and universities have come to rely heavily on online digital tools for making first contacts with potential enrollees. Institutional websites have become primary sources of information as well for interested students and a principal site for processing college applicants. An institution's online presence is also an important source for communicating institutional mission and identifying important campus cultural artifacts. The ability to attach multimedia presentations and stories to a website portico further strengthens an institution's capacity for establishing personalized relationships with students as they anticipate the college experience.

Inviting Engagement in Learning

While the infusion of digital technology into postsecondary education has created many new opportunities for including and securing students during the matriculation process, it has also brought great promise for engaging students in their own learning (Hu & Hui, 2012), through quick access to information, ease of communication and content collaboration, accommodation of a variety of ways to learn, and situating learning within context (Gikas & Grant, 2013). Although the digital innovations discussed here do not ignore concerns of inclusion and safety, they do seem to focus primarily on getting students involved in becoming more active learners, both within the classroom and beyond. One example of the latter is *CampusQuad* (http://www.campusquad.co), a mobile social networking and analytics app designed to engage students in campus involvement opportunities through real-time communication and information. This approach capitalizes on students' comfort with mobile technologies, for educational purposes, by informing them of campus groups and events that match their interests and experiences while connecting them to peers who share the same. *CampusQuad* is but one of a plethora of social media technologies (SMTs) emerging now on college campuses to engage students in their own learning, to support student services, to build community, and to expand alumni connections and community outreach (Davis, Deil-Amen, Rios-Aguilar, & Gonzalez Canche, 2012).

However, before considering additional options, a few comments about the nature of learning are in order. Over the past few decades a sizeable literature has emerged around questions of how students learn. From a once simplistic claim on the topic ("We taught them; they just didn't learn!"), we have arrived at a much greater sophisticated understanding of the complexity of multiple intelligences (Gardner, 1985, 1999), learning styles (Kolb & Kolb, 2012), strengths and talents (Clifton & Anderson, 2002), and circuits of cognitive functioning in coming to appreciate human learning as a phenomenon of infinite variation and nuance (see Chapter Two).

As theory itself has evolved on the topic, we've also come to understand the active nature of the learning process and the role of learning communities in supporting it. "Learning is fundamentally a social activity, and hence a communicative activity" (Jin, 2002, p. 175); it is also an interpretive activity. Postmodern constructivist approaches emphasize that "learners create their personal interpretation of the world based upon their experiences and their interaction with the world"; we actively construct knowledge rather than receive it. "Knowledge can be jointly constructed, and social interaction can trigger the reconstruction process of what was learned" (p. 175). Chan (1995) argued that "if most knowledge can be regarded as a common consensus of real world society, then learning should naturally take place in a social environment. Therefore, social interaction may play a dominant role in learning; all learning may be considered to be interactive in one way or another" (Jin, 2002, p. 175).

Parker Palmer has long been a strong advocate for the crucial role of community building in the work of teaching and learning in the academy. In a seminal piece on the topic (Palmer, 1987), he averred the point: "knowing and learning are *communal* acts. They require many eyes and ears, many observations and experiences. They require a continual cycle of discussion, disagreement, and consensus over what has been seen and what it all means. This is the essence of the 'community of scholars,' and it should be the essence of the classroom as well"; and again, "Community must become a central concept in ways we teach and learn" (p. 25). More recently reflecting on his own undergraduate experience, Palmer (2002) concluded, "By now we have more than enough research (to say nothing of personal experience) to know that the fastest and deepest learning happens when there is a dynamic community of connections between teacher and student and subject" (p. 185). If anything, campus dialogues about teaching and learning the past twenty years in higher education have shifted focus from learning as a solo activity to learning as a communal achievement. In many ways this is the insight that drives the innovations made possible by new digital technologies.

New approaches to digital pedagogy have also been enhanced in revisiting the concepts of experience and engagement as requisites for learning. These are ideas that date back nearly a century ago to the Progressive Education Movement (Dewey, 1916, 1933) and continue to be monitored on the college campus by assessments like the National Survey of Student Engagement (NSSE). A review of the tenets of Progressive Education might sound strangely familiar to those who have framed much of the work to date on designing virtual and online learning communities. Proponents of progressive education iterate the following defining principles (Progressive Education Network, 2014):

- Education must prepare students for active participation in a democratic society.
- Education must focus on students' social, emotional, academic, cognitive, and physical development.
- Education must nurture and support students' natural curiosity and innate desire to learn.
- Education must foster internal motivation in students.

- Education must be responsive to the developmental needs of students.
- Education must foster respectful relationships between teachers and students.
- Education must encourage the active participation of students in their learning, which arises from previous experience.
- Progressive educators must play an active role in guiding the educational vision of our society.

A list of qualities common to applications of this approach include the following (Wikipedia, 2014):

- Emphasis on learning by doing: hands-on projects, expeditionary learning, experiential learning.
- Integrated curriculum focused on thematic units.
- Integration of entrepreneurship into education.
- Strong emphasis on problem solving and critical thinking.
- Group work and development of social skills.
- Understanding and action as the goals of learning as opposed to rote knowledge.
- Collaborative and cooperative learning projects.
- Education for social responsibility and democracy.
- Highly personalized education accounting for each individual's personal goals.
- Integration of community service and service learning projects into the daily curriculum.
- Selection of subject content by looking forward to ask what skills will be needed in future society.
- De-emphasis on textbooks in favor of varied learning resources.

- Emphasis on lifelong learning and social skills.
- Assessment by evaluation of student's projects and productions.

A number of concepts and applications arising out of the higher education digital revolution, and reflective of the aforementioned emphases on community and experience, seem especially relevant to the goals of student engagement in learning: mobile learning, here-and-now learning, personal learning environments (PLEs), multiuser systems, and personal apps. Very different from traditional models of teaching and learning, these approaches and tools draw from the roots of user-centered design (UCD) (Abras, Maloney-Krichmar, & Preece, 2004) in shaping learning environments that are both context relevant and responsive to individual differences in the learning process. It has been the rapid development of digital technology and systems such as Web 2.0 that has fueled the advancements represented by these techniques and approaches.

Mobile Learning

Mobile is the word that best describes much of the current technology use among college students for accessing online courses and assignments. Such technology, supported by the rapid expansion of pervasive computing and what some have labeled "The Internet of Everything" (Evans, 2012), enables "anywhere, anytime learning" (Vinu, Sherimon, & Krishnan, 2011, p. 3069), an opportunity for which college students are seemingly well prepared. The *Student Mobile Device Survey 2013: National Report on College Students* (Pearson Learning Solutions, 2013) found that 91 percent of college students regularly used a laptop computer, 72 percent a smartphone, 51 percent a desktop computer, 40 percent a tablet, 20 percent an e-book reader, and 11 percent a netbook. One third of those sampled indicated their plans to purchase either a tablet or smartphone within the next six months. Those students most likely to report using tablets are male (44 percent), Black (51 percent), Hispanic (51 percent), and 25–30 years old (57 percent). Those more likely to use smartphones are Black (79 percent) and Hispanic (80 percent) and early adopters (84 percent). Among those who use laptop computers for schoolwork, 94 percent report doing so two to three times a week or more; 73 percent report using their smartphones for schoolwork with the same frequency; and about two-thirds of small and full-size tablet owners also indicate their use for schoolwork two or more times per week. If the survey of students conducted in 2012 at the University of Central Florida is any indication of the current status of things, then mobile learning is well on its way on the American campus. Among the 1,082 students sampled, 91 percent reported owning a small mobile device (e.g., iPhone, Android, iPod Touch), but only 37 percent owned a mobile tablet (e.g., iPad, Android tablet, Kindle Fire) and 27 percent an e-book reader (e.g., Kindle or NOOK) (Chen & Denoyelles, 2013). A total of 82 percent of tablet owners reported using them for academic purposes, while only 58 percent of small mobile device owners and 64 percent e-book readers did so.

Various demographics also figure into the usage of these technologies, with first-year and sophomore students reporting greater use than juniors and seniors of small mobile devices in courses, Asian students more than others in their use of these devices to complete course assignments, and in general a similar pattern describes males more so than females and younger students to a greater degree than older students. Clearly there is a generational tide to this movement. More interesting, though, to the researchers was the inverse relationship discovered between students' GPA and their use of small mobile devices and e-book readers. Perhaps while they are growing in popularity among students, their dedication to academic purposes has yet to be effected completely. In fact, with regard to the five most popular app categories rated by these students, all fell within the social and entertainment genres: 75 percent social networking, 71 percent music, 53 percent games, 48 percent navigation, and 47 percent entertainment. This finding concurs with a previous national survey reporting the use of social networking sites by 86 percent of college students. Another recent study of students enrolled in instructional design and technology courses in one university found that talking on the phone (100 percent) and texting (100 percent) constituted the greatest use of their mobile devices, followed by browsing the Internet (93 percent), and doing schoolwork (83 percent) (Martin & Ertzberger, 2013). Whether students have yet to explore the full potential of these devices for learning or faculty have yet to invite them to do so is unclear; more likely, both are continuing to evolve in the direction of greater usage of digital technology.

Digital gadgets college students use also reflect a range of devices. According to the previously mentioned Pew study, 96 percent of undergrads report owning a cell phone, 59 percent a desktop computer, 88 percent a laptop, 84 percent an iPod or mp3 player, 58 percent a game player, 9 percent an e-book reader, and 5 percent a tablet computer. Among community college students, comparable use of cell phones was apparent, but lesser proportions reported owning a desktop computer (67 percent), a laptop (70 percent), iPod or mp3 player (72 percent), e-book reader (4 percent), and tablet computer (4 percent). Yet a greater proportion of community college students reported owning a game console (61 percent). Again, these data probably reflect demographic differences in the enrollment distributions of these campuses. Nevertheless, community college students were slightly more likely to use their cell phones for Internet connectivity (65 percent) than were four-year undergraduate peers (63 percent). Last, these studies affirmed that the type of device students own makes a difference, with 82 percent of tablet owners using them for academic purposes compared with 58 percent of small mobile devices and 64 percent e-book readers. The data also implicate the need to provide additional faculty professional development opportunities to integrate such technology into the curriculum. Although informative, such studies can offer only a brief snapshot of a rapidly changing scene. Regardless, the ubiquitous nature of mobile technology has enabled and elevated the demand for more relevant and immediate learning opportunities such as those discussed next.

Here-and-Now Learning

First described as situated learning (Lave & Wenger, 1991), the widespread use of mobile devices has led to the evolution of here-and-now mobile learning, or *Mlearning* (Stevens & Kitchenham, 2011). This approach was defined as "the intersection of mobile computing and e-learning and includes anytime, anywhere resources; strong search capabilities, rich interaction, powerful support for effective learning, and performance-based assessment" (Quinn, 2000). Martin and Ertzberger (2013) further articulated the nature of this approach by defining it as "learning that occurs when learners have access to information anytime and anywhere via mobile technologies to perform authentic activities in the context of their learning" and what "gives students the opportunity to be in the context of their learning and have access to information that is related to what they are seeing and experiencing at the moment" (p. 77). Vinu, Sherimon, and Krishnan (2011) describe an advanced form of this approach, pervasive mobile learning, as "learning enhanced with intelligent environment and context awareness" within designated smart space. Accordingly, "information about the learner's context is obtained from the learning environment which is embedded with sensors, tags and so on. While the learner is moving with his/her mobile device, the system dynamically supports his/her learning by communicating with embedded devices in the environment" (p. 3069).

The effectiveness of here-and-now mobile learning is described in terms of a three-characteristic framework: engagement, authenticity, and informality. Such an approach has proven to be both motivating and engaging for students because of its "authentic learning and context based applications" (Martin & Ertzberger, 2013, p. 77). This, in turn, allows "consistent involvement with other professionals, regardless of their geographical, cultural, or socio-political isolation (Beckmann, 2010) ... [leading into] authentic activities by participants" (pp. 77–78). Fundamental to here-and-now learning is "that knowledge should be situated within the context of authentic tasks, because learning can be influenced in fundamental ways by the context in which it takes place" (Bransford, 2000, cited in Martin & Ertzberger, p. 78). Thus, a "mobile-based learning environment, by virtue of its portability, will provide scaffolding [that is, moving students progressively toward stronger understanding and, ultimately, greater independence in the learning process] WHEN and WHERE students need it—whether in the classroom or investigating in the field. Mobile learning can sustain the learning environment regardless of where the student or the investigations are situated" (Bransford, 2000, cited in Martin & Ertzberger, p. 78). Last, mobile learning, because it is situated in context, "has the ability to increase the ease of informal learning" or "learning that takes place naturally and without directed effort" (p. 78). The combining of here-and-now learning with mobile technology, especially in applied fields, raises the bar for student engagement and makes possible a closer correspondence between learning needs and opportunities. Rather than theory and practice being sequential in the learning process, here-and-now mobile technology juxtaposes both within a specific context, allowing students to integrate expectations and applications in a cyclical manner. That sort of immediacy blends well with another feature of the digital revolution—the capacity to shape the learning experience to the individual needs and preferences of students.

Personal Learning Environments

Dabbagh and Kitsantas (2012) explored the emerging integration of social media in the academic experience as a prelude to their examination of the concept of PLEs. Citing the 2010 EDUCAUSE survey, they noted that 49 percent of students reported social networking sites, 40 percent micro-blogs, 38 percent blogs, 33 percent video sharing, 31 percent Wiki use, and 31 percent social bookmarking as social media tools used in coursework-related collaboration. Faculty also have reported increased use of social media (e.g., blogging, e-portfolios, and Twitter) to support teaching and learning activities and to stimulate student engagement. From the *Pew Research Internet Project Social Media Update* (Duggan & Smith, 2013), it was reported that Facebook, now with over a decade of use, remains the dominant social networking platform of choice among adults (73 percent) compared with LinkedIn (22 percent), Pinterest (21 percent), Twitter (18 percent), and Instagram (17 percent), although a significant portion of them (42 percent) are migrating toward the use of multiple social networking sites. All such figures are, of course, moving targets as future generations bring their experiences and preferences into the system. However, this sort of immersion has begun to reshape the parameters of the academy, with education systems or personal learning environments.

PLEs capitalize on the tools made available by Web 2.0 technology. As the name given to a second generation of the World Wide Web, Web 2.0 "includes open communication with an emphasis on Web-based communities of users, and more open sharing of information" (Webopedia, 2014). The claim is that

PLEs "empower students to take charge of their own learning prompting them to select tools and resources to create, organize and package learning content to learn effectively and efficiently" (McGloughlin & Lee, 2010; Rubin, 2010, as cited in Dabbagh & Kitsantas, 2012, p. 4). Being student designed, PLEs focus on each student's learning goals or learning approach "to match his or her personal learning style and pace" (Johnson, Adams, & Haywood, 2011, p. 8, as cited in Dabbagh & Kitsantas, 2012 p. 4). In most postsecondary institutions, learning management systems are controlled by faculty and administrators, and learner control and personalization are all but absent. The power of PLEs is that they place students on the other side of the equation, encouraging them to learn about learning, to recognize their learning preferences, to use tools with which they are familiar, to collaborate with peers, and to design and regulate their own paths toward the learning outcomes they desire.

Adding to previous work on self-regulated learning (Zimmerman, 2000), Dabbagh and Kitsantas (2012) proposed a three-level framework for using social media to support students' self-regulated learning in personal learning environments (Table 8.1). Their model complements Zimmerman's three-phase cycle of student academic achievement, where in the first phase (*forethought*) students "have a predefined set of cognitions (e.g., goal setting and planning) and self-beliefs (e.g., task interest, self-efficacy) that will impact how they will approach the task" (Dabbagh & Kitsantas, 2012, p. 6). In the second phase (*performance*), the student "begins to actually engage in the behaviors required to successfully achieve his or her goals" by monitoring "their learning progress and [using] selected strategies to perform learning tasks" (p. 6). During the third phase, students "use self-monitored outcomes to make judgments regarding their learning performance" (p. 6). In this way self-regulated learners "engage in a cyclic feedback loop until they successfully achieve their goals" (p. 6).

Exhibit 8.1. A Framework for Using Social Media to Support Self-Regulated Learning in Personal Learning Environments (PLEs).

	(Level 1) Personal information management	(Level 2) Social interaction and Collaboration	(Level 3) Information aggregation and management
Blogs	Instructor encourages students to use a blog as a private journal to set learning goals and plan for course assignments and tasks.	Instructor encourages students to enable the blog comment feature to allow for instructor and peer feedback enabling basic interaction and sharing.	Instructor demonstrates how to configure a blog to pull in additional content and how to add the blog to RSS aggregation services.
Wikis	Instructor encourages students to use a wiki as a personal space for content organization and management.	Instructor encourages students to enable the wiki's collaborative editing and commenting features for feedback.	Instructor demonstrates how to view a wiki's history to promote student self-evaluation of their learning across time.
Google Calendar	Instructor encourages students to use Google Calendar for personal planning.	Instructor encourages students to enable the calendar sharing features to allow feedback and collaboration to complete course tasks.	Instructor demonstrates how to archive personal and group calendars to promote student self-valuation regarding time planning and management.
YouTube or Flickr	Instructor encourages students to use Flickr or YouTube to set up a personal media archive related to course content.	Instructor encourages students to enable the sharing feature of the media archive and join similar media archives created by peers.	Instructor demonstrates how to aggregate media from several media archives to refine their personal archive.

	(Level 1) Personal information management	(Level 2) Social interaction and Collaboration	(Level 3) Information aggregation and management
Social networking sites	Instructor encourages students to create an academic and career profile on LinkedIn.	Instructor encourages students to connect to online communities related to their professional goals.	Instructor asks students to engage in self-reflection with the goal to restructure their profile and social presence.
Social Book-marking	Instructor encourages students to use a social bookmarking tool (e.g., Delicious) to organize course content.	Instructor encourages students to collaborate with other classmates and create a shared list of bookmarks related to a specific learning topic or project.	Instructor asks students to self-reflect on their personal and group bookmarks to enhance the desired learning outcome.

Source: Reprinted from *The Internet and Higher Education*, Vol 15, Nada Dabbagh and Anastasia Kitsantas, Personal learning environments, social media, and self-regulated learning: A natural formula for connecting formal and informal learning, pages 3–8, Copyright 2012, with permission from Elsevier.

The intent of Dabbagh and Kitsantas's (2012) framework is to "inform faculty and instructors how to engage students in a transformative cycle of creating PLEs that support self-regulated learning" (p. 6). At Level 1 of the framework, the goal is to "guide students to create a personal or private learning space by self-generating content and managing this content for personal productivity or organizational e-learning tasks such as creating online bookmarks, media resources, and personal journals and calendars" (p. 6). At Level 2, students are "using social media to foster informal learning communities surrounding the course topics thereby extending the PLE from a personal learning space to a social learning space" (p. 6). At the third level of the framework, students are encouraged to "use social media to synthesize and aggregate information from level 1 and level 2 to reflect on their overall learning experience" (p. 6). Each social medium at each level in the framework, along with the various mobile technologies used to access them, can contribute to students' becoming self-directed learners, the enviable goal of any college or university education. Results of such Web-based learning applications have been quite positive in effecting student engagement and achieving desirable learning outcomes. According to Chen, Lambert, and Guidry (2010), not only do students who use "Web and Internet technologies in their learning tend to score higher in the traditional student engagement measures [i.e., NSSE], ... they also are more likely to make use of deep approaches of learning like higher order thinking, reflective learning, and integrative learning in their study and they reported higher gains in general education, practical competence, and personal and social development" (p. 1230). Numerous mobile applications (or apps for short) are adding further to the possibilities students can explore for use in their personal learning journeys, whether in the context of academic offerings or in out-of-class opportunities for engagement, such as the *CampusQuad* app (http://www.campusquad.co).

MUDs and Other Multiuser Systems

First inspired by the game *Dungeons and Dragons*, multiuser dimensions (MUDs) are "software systems that allow multiple people to interact and communicate in pseudo-spatial surroundings" (Curtis & Nicholas, 1993, as cited in Jin, 2001). They are a kind of "user-extensible virtual reality, where participants have the appearance of being situated in an artificially constructed place, and communicate with each other in real time. Participants cannot only explore the virtual world, but also extend it, creating new places and various types of objects. MUDs put special emphasis on collaboration, encouraging interaction in a social setting, [potentially offering] rich opportunities for interactive learning" (Jin, 2001, p. 173).

An extension of this kind of technology that has gained traction on the college campus for purposes of student learning is the multiuser virtual environment (MUVE). All MUVEs "enable multiple simultaneous participants to (a) access virtual contexts, (b) interact with digital artifacts, (c) represent themselves through 'avatars' (in some cases graphical and in others, text-based), (d) communicate with other participants (in some cases also with computer-based agents), and (e) take part in experiences incorporating modeling and mentoring about problems similar to those in real world contexts" (Dede, Nelson, Ketelhut, Clarke, & Bowman, 2004, as cited in Dieterle & Clarke, 2007). One of the more advanced and popular versions of MUVEs is *Second Life* (SL). Launched by Linden Lab in 2003, SL is a three-dimensional virtual environment where multiple users can participate through graphical representations known as avatars that walk, fly, teleport, and talk to each other. Being open-ended, "users are provided with tools and guidance to design, create, and manipulate the in-world environment" (Wang & Burton, 2013, p. 358). Library science was among the first education fields to adopt SL as a platform for distribution of services. Some institutions have created departments or an entire campus in SL to "support synchronous and collaborative learning" (De Lucia, Francese, Passero, & Tortora, 2009 p. 223). As a creative tool, SL "has the potential to support study through the use of in-world artifacts of realistic and detailed design that might be otherwise expensive or impossible in real world" (p. 359). Instructors have focused on SL as a technology itself in courses dealing with gaming, online communities, and emerging technologies; it has also been used as a communication medium for delivering lectures, making presentations, and conducting discussions; and it has been used as a learning space for in-world learning activities, such as role-playing, interactive simulations, and educational games (Gerald & Antonacci, 2009, as cited in Wang & Burton, 2013, p. 359). Educators have looked to SL for "its potential to foster constructivist and experiential learning, such as collaborative learning, community of inquiry, authentic learning, action learning, project-based learning, situated cognition and problem-based learning" (Wang & Burton, 2013, p. 362). In addition, it has sought to motivate learners. As one other example, John Carroll University integrated SL into its first-year seminar courses as a method for engaging students in issues of social justice (Budin, 2009).

For purposes of engaging students further, some institutions have implemented educational MUVEs, such as Harvard University's River City, Indiana University's Quest Atlantis, and North Carolina State University's WolfDen virtual campus (Wang & Burton, 2013). These are learning systems that engage multiple users simultaneously through interactive avatar identities and virtual objects within specific contexts. Thus, according to project developers, one example—River City—was designed to allow students to

> travel back in time, bringing their 21st century skills and technology to address 19th century problems. Based on authentic historical, sociological, and geographical conditions, River City is a town besieged with health problems. Students work together in small research teams to help the town understand why residents are becoming ill. Students use technology to keep track of clues that hint at causes of illnesses, form and test hypotheses, develop controlled experiments to test their hypotheses, and make recommendations based on the data they collect, all in an online environment. (River City Project, 2014)

MUVEs have been applied across a diversity of academic fields, such as engineering, sociology, arts, history, and teacher education, in support of online communities, to immerse students in relevant contexts, to explore new concepts, to engage in scientific inquiry, to take museum field trips, and to experience creative collaboration with other learners. Some of the advantages of MUVEs is their "ability to leverage aspects of authentic learning conditions that are hard to cultivate in traditional classroom settings (Griffin, 1995) … [and] allow for the design of situations … not possible or practical in the real world … that are safe, cost effective, and directly target learning goals" (Dieterle & Clarke, 2007). Perhaps the genius of such new technologies is that they have managed to synchronize learning and play, ironically a return to the ancient Greek's understanding of school being equated to leisure. These applications offer educators "new ways of deploying knowledge and skill," which they must understand further "if their learning interventions are to make sense to communities of practice forming in spaces like Second Life" (Bell, 2009, p. 517).

Mobile Apps

The rapid rise of mobile technology (mostly smartphones, watches, and tablets) has also brought with it an entire industry of new apps. According to an August 2014 Apps Store Metrics Summary report, there are more than 1.25 million active apps available for download from 311,856 publishers (Pocket Gamer.biz, 2014). This represents a doubling of these products since 2012. During the same recent month observed, 31,169 new apps were submitted to the Apps Store, for an average of 1,113 apps per day. Among the most popular active apps categories are games (20 percent), education (10 percent), business (9 percent), lifestyle (8 percent), and entertainment (7 percent) apps. The top five mobile apps, as measured by the number of unique visitors recorded, included Facebook (115 million), You Tube (83 million), Google Play (72 million), Google Search (70 million), and Pandora Radio (69 million) (comScore, June, 2014). By 2013, a majority of Americans (56 percent) owned a smartphone and app store downloads topped 40 billion, with

20 billion in 2012 alone (Pew Research Center, 2014). In 2014, Facebook purchased the messaging app *Whatsapp* for $19 billion. The business of attending to the application needs and interests of mobile technology users has reached immense proportions and continues to increase at an immeasurable pace.

For the college-age user (18–24 years old), a profile of their share of app time spent includes Facebook (14.8 percent), Pandora Radio (9.1 percent), Instagram (6.6 percent), YouTube (5.2 percent), and Snapchat (3.4 percent). In 2014, 45 percent of users ages 18–29 in serious relationships indicated that the Internet has had an impact on their relationship. The average person has downloaded at least forty-one apps, and further development of new platforms like Kleverbeast promises to accommodate even more as users are given the tools to create their own apps. A recent feature in the *New York Times* (Kaminer, 2014) highlighted the growing use of student-built apps that are being pressed into service to solve scheduling problems students encounter in course selection and registration at large universities. Perhaps this is the sense of things to come as these technologies become more readily available and user-friendly.

Colleges and universities have hopped on the bandwagon as well, with the creation of institutional apps that assist student users in navigating campus opportunities and services and monitoring their academic progress. In an August 21, 2014, *U.S. News & World Report* article (Sheehy, 2014), campus apps were among the five "must downloads" recommended for college students, along with those that promote time management (e.g., Rescue Time), tracking and organizing bibliographies (e.g., RefMe), collaborating on group projects (e.g., Google Drive), and managing ideas and notes (e.g., Evernote). The facility of these various apps makes them incredibly creative mobile tools for students as they pursue learning and negotiate the college experience. Increasing numbers of institutions are also featuring their use in various classes with significant positive outcomes. For example, Junco, Heiberger, and Loken (2011) found that the use of Twitter for educational purposes in a first-year seminar resulted in greater engagement of students (as measured by NSSE scores) and a positive effect on grades as well as more active faculty participation.

Engaging the Community of Peers

Following on the heels of the introduction of email to higher education came one of the earliest adaptations of digital technology to the college experience: social networking. Students had always networked socially, but the immediacy of the Internet and convenience of mobile devices soon set a new pace for human connection that has since transformed the college campus into a virtual playground of digital encounters. The proverbial bell used to signal the end of class but now seems to alert students to wake up their smartphones and scroll through text messages; review recent posts and updates on Facebook, Twitter, and Instagram; and check phone messages they have received while they were in class. Even to the most casual observer, it is apparent that much of a college student's life today goes on within the recommended 16-inch distance between his or her face and a mobile device. In many ways the ease of social networking has created a whole new level of communal experience for students on campus, who now gauge their participation by numbers of friends, likes, and tweets. While the appeal of specific platforms has tended to shift over time, the presence of college students on various social networks is well established.

According to comScore data released by DIGIDAY (January 2014), 88.6 percent of U.S. college-aged adults (age 18 to 24) participate in Facebook, maintaining it as the most widely used social network on campus (retrieved from http://digiday.com/platforms/social-platforms-college-kids-now-prefer/). Inevitably, others are rapidly increasing their subscriptions among Millennials, who continue to exert their preferences for more convenient, succinct (140 characters or six seconds), visual, and ephemeral communication. Thus, Instagram (52 percent), Twitter (44 percent), Tumblr (36 percent), Snapchat (26 percent), and Vine

(25 percent) all have recently gained users over this time period. As older generation subscribers continue to invade these venues, though, younger, college-age participants are migrating quickly to newer and more selective platforms, such as Blend, a retail marketing platform that masquerades as a social network (our conclusion, not theirs). Novel about this approach, however, is its topically organized and seasonally framed presentation of materials that correspond to the cycle of the academic year. According to a description of how it works, each day "the site posts a theme relevant to a college audience, like *Tailgate Saturday*, *Library Shenanigans* or *My Pet is Better Than Yours*. Students then post photos on the site that relate in some way to the theme. Those photos receive 'snaps'—equivalent to 'likes' on Facebook—from others on the app, and those snaps can be redeemed for gift cards to brands that advertise on the platform" (Zimmerman, 2014). In addition, as fall term blends into winter and spring gives way to summer, different retailers are brought onto the site, once approved by student representatives. As of February 2014, Blend reported that it was being used on 1,000 college campuses by more than 50,000 daily active users (*New York Times*, February 6, 2014).

Whatever the future holds for social networking in higher education, it is almost a given that some form of it will continue to be part of the mix of the college experience. The appeal of these platforms lies in their ability to capitalize on the psychosocial dynamics of the college years in a way that matches students' needs to belong to and participate in community, albeit a digital one. Just as growing up is inherently a social experience, so, too, is learning. Social networking, however, is not without its challenges. Several high-profile cases in recent years (see Parker, 2012) suggest that its potential for breaches of privacy, ethics, and truth is considerable (Clemmitt, 2013). Recent concerns have also been expressed over the use of new anonymous sites (e.g., YikYak, Erodr) to post derogatory and offensive comments (Loftin, 2014). Nonetheless, to the extent that it facilitates students' connections to one another and their engagement with learning, it will undoubtedly remain a significant feature of going to college.

The Future of Things to Come

The integration of mobile technology and learning in higher education has been one of the most exciting and transformational changes in how colleges and universities attend to their work of teaching, research, and service. The past ten years in particular have witnessed a revolution in how educators construct the processes of learning and how to engage students in them. Referring specifically to online learning, one observer described this as a paradigm shift that presents "an uncharted set of challenges for academic institutions, most of which are much more familiar with the traditional classroom setting" (Borden, 2011). This shift will reflect both how we fundamentally approach learning as well as the role of instructors. The author suggested:

> Higher education institutions will increasingly rely on learning management systems that enable "prescriptive content"—meaning the systems define appropriate content for each student, according to their measured abilities, and employ learning modalities and techniques that are proven to drive achievement. This method of online learning challenges the student while allowing them to progress at their own pace—ultimately resulting in increased academic success and satisfaction.

This will entail further,

> a higher standard of excellence, driving increased demand for quality, tech-savvy instructors ... [who] will be called on to use technology in the fully online and blended learning classrooms, thereby changing the way courses are taught. Instead of demanding memorization

> and feedback, instructors will employ tools that enable application of knowledge to real-life problems and real-time collaboration with peers.

These shifts are not minor adjustments; they are in fact fundamental changes to the way we do things now. Traditionally, knowledge is delivered, but the success of its use depends on it being engaged. Conventionally, knowledge is accessed through standardized methods for all to use, yet learning is certainly a function of individual student differences, preferences, and resources. Customary practices of teaching are for the most part place-bound, but in an age of mobile learning, does that approach make sense anymore? In an age of lifelong learning, does it make sense to package learning in time-bound blocks (semesters), just to be able to generate a distribution of outcomes to which one can assign grades? What if time and technique were varied but mastery of relevant learning outcomes or competencies held constant? The Gates Foundation is doing exactly that, for example, in supporting innovative competency-based degree programs at Southern New Hampshire University. Perhaps they recognize that the outcomes of learning are at least as important as the means to achieve them. Rather than standardize the inputs to college, doesn't it make more sense to standardize the outcomes and allow individuals to exercise their own strengths to maximize their mastery? Isn't success about results? These are the kinds of questions that will continue to emerge in the future as new technologies and methods challenge the assumptions and expectations we hold in the mix of student success.

The canvassing of 2,558 experts and technology builders about where we will stand by the year 2025 in terms of our digital future yielded some very interesting assessments. Observing that "the world is moving rapidly towards ubiquitous connectivity that will further change how and where people associate, gather and share information, and consume media" (Pew Research Center, 2014), the panel foresaw the development of

> an ambient information environment where accessing the Internet will be effortless and most people will tap into it so easily it will flow through their lives "like electricity" ... mobile, wearable, and embedded computing will be tied together in the Internet of Things, allowing people and their surroundings to tap into artificial intelligence-enhanced cloud-based information storage and sharing.

Among the fifteen theses about the digital future, one spoke directly to the work of educators: "An Internet-enabled revolution in education will spread more opportunities, with less money spent on real estate and teachers." Citing the Google economist Hal Varian (Pew Research Center, 2014):

> The biggest impact on the world will be universal access to all human knowledge. The smartest person in the world currently could well be stuck behind a plow in India or China. Enabling that person—and the millions like him or her—will have a profound impact on the development of the human race. Cheap mobile devices will be available worldwide, and educational tools like the Khan Academy will be available to everyone. This will have a huge impact on literacy and numeracy and will lead to a more informed and more educated world population.

Finally, as one expert commented, "the Internet has already made it possible for us to use one of our unique graces—the ability to share knowledge–for good, and to a degree never before possible." As an institution dedicated to the generation, preservation, communication, and critique of knowledge, higher education must continue to embrace these new tools of understanding while keeping sight of its core mission—to include, secure, engage, and invite students into the learning community.

Whether a replacement for or complement to traditional methods of teaching and learning, it is clear that the mobility, engagement, and individualization possibilities of digital technology have raised the ante significantly in the discourse on educational reform. While not a panacea to all the limitations of the current system, the digital revolution in higher education has changed the conversation about the quality of teaching and will continue to lead the enterprise to new forms and models of learning. Prensky (2001) presaged, "As a result of this ubiquitous environment [of technology] and the sheer volume of their interaction with it, today's students think and process information fundamentally different from their predecessors" (p. 1). As a result, "students have come to expect a high level of engagement in their learning" (Martin & Ertzberger, 2013, p. 77). Whether we can deliver that through the trappings of our traditional system is in doubt, but the promise of the new technology to do so in the future is compelling.

Questions for Discussion

1. How is social media used at your institution to support the inclusion and security of students?
2. To what extent is mobile learning integrated into opportunities for student engagement beyond the classroom at your college or university?
3. How can technology serve to increase availability of personal learning environments on your campus?
4. What mobile apps contribute to student learning and success at your institution?
5. How are uses of technology incorporated into the academic curriculum of your college or university?

9

Assessing and Creating Designs for Student Learning and Success

Reviews of theories and models of student development during the college years have abounded in the higher education and student affairs literature over the past several decades (Evans, Forney, & Guido-DiBrito, 1998; Evans, Forney, Guido, Patton, & Renn, 2010; Rodgers, 1980, 1990, 1991; Strange, 1994; Strange & King, 1990). Concurrent to this has emerged a parallel but limited body of research (e.g., Baird, 1988; Conyne & Clack, 1981; Harper, 2008; Huebner & Lawson, 1990; Moos, 1979, 1986; Pascarella, 1985; Renn & Reason, 2012b; Strange, 1991b, 1993; Strange & Banning, 2001) on the nature, dynamics, and assessment of campus environments and how their various features influence student learning and success. As Evans et al. (1998) pointed out in their first summary of student development theory, the principal focus of the behavioral sciences has limited our perspective, in that "developmental theory has its base in the field of psychology. As such, internal developmental processes tend to be emphasized and insufficient attention is paid to the role of environmental forces that influence development" (p. 283). Without such attention, our ability to explain students' experiences remains, at best, incomplete. Thus, we have attempted in this volume once again to further fill the gap by organizing a descriptive overview of extant theories and models within a conceptual template that addresses their application to the design of campus learning environments.

Toward an Ecology of Learning

We now understand some of the basic features of human environments, and we are beginning to appreciate more clearly their meaning for the design of higher education systems, policies, and practices. In summary, it appears that environments exert their influence on behavior through an array of natural and synthetic physical features, through the collective characteristics of inhabitants, the manner in which they are organized and mediated through the collective social constructions of their inhabitants. Our analysis also suggests that a measure of any educational institution's environmental capacity to encourage and sustain learning is the degree to which it provides the conditions (in real and virtual form) for students' inclusion, safety, engagement, and full membership in the learning community. In effect, these conditions constitute an ecology of learning, that is, a state of dynamic balance when student characteristics synergize with institutional features (physical, aggregate, organizational, and socially constructed) in support of the outcomes of learning. Campus environments set conditions that affect student learning; in turn, students influence the shape of campus environments.

The perspective that the relationship between student and campus is a transactional one was articulated first in the form of a campus ecology model (Aulepp & Delworth, 1976; Banning, 1978; Banning & Kaiser, 1974; Huebner, 1979; Western Interstate Commission for Higher Education, 1973). This model begins with the assumption that students and campus are mutually shaping forces in the complex balance of institutional design. As Kaiser (1975, p. 33) and others originally framed this ecological approach, eight themes comprised its conceptual core:

- A campus environment consists of all the stimuli that impinge upon the students' sensory modalities, including physical, chemical, biological, and social stimulation.

- A transactional relationship exists between college students and their campus environment; that is, the students shape the environment and are shaped by it.
- For purposes of environmental design, the shaping properties of the campus environment are focused on; however, the students are still viewed as active, choice-making agents who may resist, transform, or nullify environmental influences.
- Every student possesses the capacity for a wide spectrum of possible behaviors. A campus environment may facilitate or inhibit any one or more of those behaviors. The campus should be intentionally designed to offer opportunities, incentives, and reinforcements for growth and development.
- Students will attempt to cope with any educational environment in which they are placed. If the environment is not compatible with the students, the students may react negatively or fail to develop desirable qualities.
- Because of the wide range of individual differences among students, fitting the campus environment to the student requires the creation of a wide variety of campus subenvironments. There must be an attempt to design for the wide range of individual characteristics found among students.
- Every campus has a design, even if the administration, faculty, and students have not planned it or are not consciously aware of it. A design technology for campus environments, therefore, is useful for both the analysis of existing campus environments and the design of new ones.

- Successful campus design depends on input from all campus members including students, faculty, staff, administration, and trustees or regents.

These assumptions underscore the point that college and university environments are complex, dynamic entities; any change in one component will likely manifest in other components. Likewise, failure to attend to other components may jeopardize attempts to change only one.

These core themes also emphasize the point that campuses exert their effects whether we want them to or not. Campus design is not a matter of choice; a design already exists. The more important question is whether such designs serve intended purposes. In the context of the present discussion, how do they promote student learning and success, or how do they inhibit it? Designs prohibitive of learning need to be altered or eliminated; facilitative designs need to be supported and enhanced. Furthermore, these assumptions suggest that our best intentions will do little in those directions unless campus constituents affected by these designs are involved in their creation and implementation. Campus environments cannot be molded simply to specification for outcomes to emerge on cue. At best, we can hope only to create conditions that set broad limits on behaviors (Michelson, 1970), encouraging those consistent with institutional mission and supportive of educational purposes. However, providing leadership for this ongoing challenge requires a broad understanding of the various design elements capable of contributing to that goal and of how students interact with those components in pursuit of their learning.

Presented first is a matrix of campus design that connects environmental components to their purposes and impacts. This framework is helpful for evaluating the overall designs of any campus as they relate to certain institutional impacts and outcomes. Second is a model of developmental ecology (Bronfenbrenner, 1977, 1979; Bronfenbrenner & Morris, 2006; Renn & Arnold,

2003) that focuses on the dynamics of person-environment interactions as they relate to the concentric influences, from proximate to distant layers, on individual student's learning, growth, and development during the college experience.

A Campus Design Matrix

Drawing from materials presented in the preceding chapters, Figure 9.1 integrates these environmental concepts into a three-dimensional model or matrix of campus design for purposes of assessment and action. Three essential questions are addressed in this matrix:

- What components are involved in this particular environmental assessment or action?
- What is the impact of the current design?
- What is the intended focus or purpose of this design?

Answers can alert educators to conditions of current campus environments and to intended design of environments yet to be created.

Concerning the first question, any campus assessment or action must identify the environmental components of concern. Are the physical components of the campus involved, natural (terrain), synthetic (layout), or both? Is the composition of particular aggregates (e.g., campus affinity groups) at issue? Are there concerns related to the organizational components of the setting (e.g., decision-making structures)? How do participants construct this condition or phenomenon of interest (social climate or press)?

With respect to the impact of current design, the second focus of this matrix, it is helpful to consider a continuum of possible effects (Moos, 1986) (Exhibit 9.1). At one end of the continuum

Figure 9.1. Campus Design Matrix

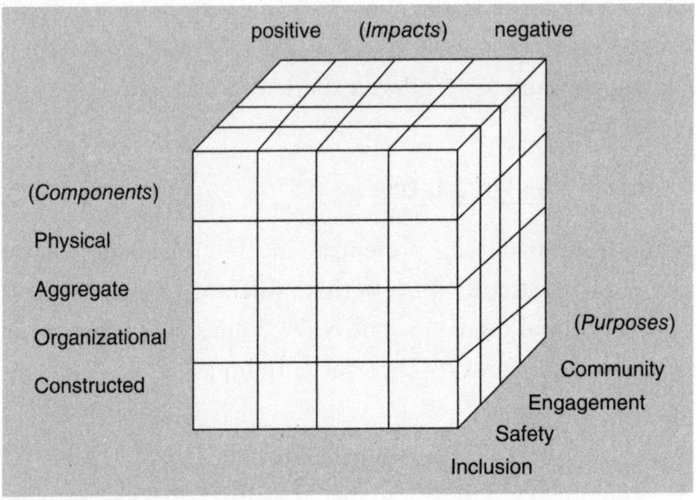

Revised from: Strange, C., & Banning, J. (2001). *Educating by design: Creating campus learning environments that work.* San Francisco, CA: Jossey-Bass.

are environments seen as essentially negative, including those that are actively stressful or limiting, resisting, and inhibiting. At the other end are environments seen as essentially positive, that is, those that release capacities, allowing behaviors to occur, and those that actively stimulate and challenge individuals toward growth and development. In the middle are environments that neither enhance nor inhibit individuals but rather select favored characteristics.

Of course, as discussed further herein, the nature of the impact depends on the characteristics of the individual or persons experiencing the particular environmental condition (Lewin, 1936). For example, a highly differentiated affinity group, such as a student organization or club, may be a very positive force for individuals who share much in common with the group but may be actively stressful for those who don't. Also, it makes sense that environmental selection of certain characteristics depends on what is favored by the environment in question. Again, those who exhibit certain characteristics (e.g., high academic test scores on an honors program application) are most favored in the selection process. Higher education environments in particular are vested in selecting winners along some measure of achievement.

Exhibit 9.1. Five Conceptions of Environmental Impact

\+ Environments are active and *positive* forces

- Stimulate and challenge individuals toward growth
- Release capacities, allow behaviors to occur
- Select favored characteristics
- Limit, resist, or inhibit behaviors
- Actively engender stress

– Environments are essentially *negative* and stressful

Source: From *The human context: Environmental determinants of behavior,* by R. H. Moos, 1986, Malabar, FL: Robert E. Krieger Publishing Company, pp.29–30.

Third, this campus design matrix identifies the intended purposes of the environmental condition. Is the concern one of inclusion or exclusion of certain participants in campus life? Is the question of safety and security at stake, physical or psychological? Are the environmental components and impacts related in some way to aspects of engagement? To what extent, if any, does the environmental assessment or planned action relate to the establishment and maintenance of campus community?

Identification and assessment of environmental components, impacts, and purposes are important first steps in campus design. The value of this matrix in the process is that it requires consideration of the larger campus ecology with reference to current impacts and intended purposes. As an evaluative tool, use of this matrix can alert educational planners to conditions that warrant particular attention. For example, a campus retention committee may focus on the role of small orientation groups (an aggregate/organizational component) in having a powerful positive impact toward purposes of inclusion and safety in the campus environment. The lack of engagement structures and opportunities in a particular department (an organizational component) might signal the limiting, resisting, and inhibiting impact on students who wish to become involved.

Institutional leaders can also use this matrix to systematically plan the design of new or renovated campus environments, considering their impact and purpose. For example, if plans for a new or renovated student union invoke images of a facility for building campus community, then the impact of its current location and proposed design must be considered carefully in light of its capacity for including, securing, and engaging all students. Such projects have been completed at any number of institutions in recent years (e.g., University of Wisconsin, Eastern Michigan University, Bowling Green State University, Ohio State University, Angelo State University, Boston University, and University of North Florida) where plans for new construction or renovation were attached to the institutions' Web pages to allow observers to take a virtual tour of the building before the first brick was laid. In this way, intended users can consider the impact and purposes of the facility while there may yet be time for adjustments. Do the plans suggest a facility that is accessible to all (a physical component)? What student groups might be located in the building for purposes of increasing campus-wide involvement (an aggregate component)? What rules or guidelines will govern the use of this facility (an organizational component)? What images of the facility are conveyed to students as they consider the facility's space and layout (socially constructed component)? At each point, campus planners can consider whether the intended designs will add to the stress of some students (such as students with disabilities) and ultimately whether it will serve as a powerful positive force in campus life. This kind of analysis can assist institutions in anticipating environmental challenges and conditions that, if impervious to alteration or redesign, can at least be responded to in supportive ways.

A Personal Ecology of Student Development

The assessment of campus environments and their effects can be understood not only in terms of overall institutional designs but also from the perspective of individuals encountering those designs. While overall campus features (e.g., physical layout, profile of students, faculty, and staff, institutional culture and climate) exert an influence regardless, the degree of their impact on specific individuals or groups of students is most immediately a function of students' developmental status. This observation lies at the center of an ecological model of student development articulated by Renn and Arnold (2003), extending and applying Bronfenbrenner's (1977, 1979) earlier work on ecological systems theory. From this perspective, the student is situated "at the center of concentric rings of environments, ranging from immediate (*microsystem*) to most distal (*macrosystem*) contexts" (Renn & Arnold, 2003, p. 261) (Figure 9.2).

Students' most immediate experience of the campus environment is through the components of the so-named mesosystem, which, according to Bronfenbrenner (1977, p. 515), "comprises the interrelations among major settings containing the developing person at a particular point in his or her life." Thus, as Renn and Arnold (2003) applied the concept to college students, those settings might include job, roommates, friendship groups, and classes. To those can be added family, formalized task groups such as student clubs and organizations, and certainly now online social networks. It is the dynamic of these components interacting with each other that creates the overall quality and force of students' immediate experience of any particular setting. For example, performance in one mesosystem component (e.g., a

Figure 9.2. Ecology of Individual Students

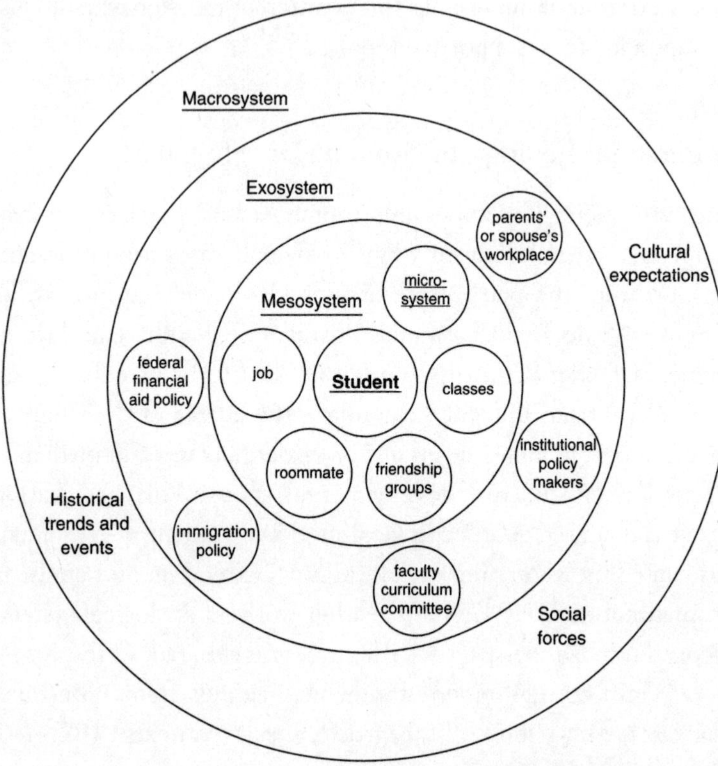

Source: Renn, K.A., & Arnold, K.D. (2003). Reconceptualizing research on college student peer culture. *Journal of Higher Education*, 74(3). © 2003 The Ohio State University. Reprinted with permission.

late-night job at Taco Bell) may well impact participation in another mesosystem component (e.g., an early-morning lecture class). More compatible interests with a particular friendship group (another component) might diminish interactions with a roommate who shares little in common with that group. Likewise, attention of significant family members might encourage certain friendship or task groups, just as a skeptical or benign response from them might discourage interest in certain classes or majors. The importance of these settings and their interaction is their potential for creating "developmental instigators and inhibitors, depending on the nature of the values and expectations that are being amplified, contested, supported, and challenged" (Renn & Reason, 2012a, p. 128). A change in one setting (for example, unanticipated difficult interpersonal dynamics in a work setting) might upset the balance in another setting, such as a friendship group also affiliated with that same work setting. Each setting might also allow the individual to exercise certain interests and skills (such as creative free expression and artistic applications) that may or may not be relevant or appreciated in another setting (for example, a science laboratory class). Furthermore, as intersecting identities (e.g., race and ethnicity, sexual orientation, age, religious belief) acquire different saliences for the individual (Abes, Jones, & McEwen, 2007; Renn, 2004), some influences may exert greater impact than others. Ultimately the combined impact of such influences creates a constellation of effects that promote or diminish the student's learning, growth, and development. As this differential interactionist perspective (Hunt & Sullivan, 1974) suggests, the particular combination of settings, or collective mesosystems, for one student will likely have an effect that differs from that of another student. Nevertheless, Renn and Arnold (2003) concluded that it is at the mesosystem level where the most immediate effects of peer culture are apparent. Recall, from the opening scenario in Chapter Two, that both Phil (a theater arts major) and Mike (a social work transfer student) were excited about the peer groups (aggregates) they encountered at Midwestern University, but each for different reasons. On one hand, for Phil it was an opportunity to engage with others who shared his interests and for Mike it was the diversity of others that most excited him. Felix, on the other hand, was discouraged by not encountering others who shared his ethnic culture. All three students were influenced by human aggregate components in their respective mesosystems, but results differed for each. In the case of the first two students, a sense of inclusion was apparent, but for the third both inclusion and security seemed to be at risk. The ecological model of student development recognizes person-environment interaction as an important explanation in understanding students' campus experiences.

Bronfenbrenner's (1977) model continues with the inclusion of the *exosystem*, that is, "an extension of the mesosystem embracing other specific social structures, both formal and informal, that do not themselves contain the developing person, but impinge upon or encompass the immediate settings in which that person is found, and thereby influence, delimit, or even determine what goes on there" (p. 515). This definition was later amended to include (as cited in Renn & Reason, 2012b, p.129) "the linkages and processes between two or more settings, at least one of which does not contain the developing person, but in which events occur that indirectly influence processes within the immediate setting in which the developing person lives" (Bronfenbrenner, 1993, p. 24).

For example, institutional policies, government regulations, campus organizational structures, and local communities are all potential components of a student's exosystem. Whether private or public, small or large, in an urban or rural setting, institutional characteristics converge to shape the context of any college or university, resulting in a particular array of exosystem components. Although students are not immediately a part of those components, they experience their effects in various indirect ways. For example, anticipating implementation of the Affordable Care Act has led many campuses to restrict the number of hours students can serve in a campus work setting, an important mesosystem component, especially for students of limited financial resources. Some local communities also regulate housing densities to restrict the number of unrelated individuals who can occupy any given rental property, in turn affecting patterns of demand for on-campus residences and affordability of off-campus housing. Transportation systems too can influence preferred locations and access to campus events during certain hours of the day.

Enveloping all this is the *macrosystem*, which includes "general prototypes, existing in the culture or subculture, that set the pattern for the structures and activities occurring at the concrete level." These are mostly "informal and implicit—carried, often unwittingly, in the minds of the society's members as ideology made manifest through custom and practice in everyday life" (Bronfenbrenner, 1977, p. 515). Thus, tacit norms of independence and individuality in the broader American culture, for example, may shape preferred approaches to learning (Do your own work!), and socialization patterns, attributed traditionally to males and females, may influence gender-splitting (Levinson & Levinson, 1996) performances in response to autonomous versus collaborative expectations. These, in turn, affect every aspect of the college campus, from the physical layout of a theater-style lecture hall to the constitutional structures of student clubs and organizations (Forrest, Hotalling, & Kuk, 1986). Like other societal institutions, higher education is framed fundamentally by the cultural context in which it functions. Thus, competitive individualism is one such cultural value (a socially constructed component of the environment) that contains much of what ensues on any given campus in American higher education, where a premium is placed on finishing at the top—the best class section, the solo author, the first person awarded, and the highest merit score achieved. What would a campus organization spring banquet be without the bestowal of plaques, certificates, and trophies upon its attendees? The macrosystem is an insidious layer of all institutions that cannot be divorced from the influence of campus environments. Rather than ignoring such influence (as if one can), it is important to acknowledge and understand it.

To these spheres of influence, Bronfenbrenner (1995) later added the dimension of time (*chronosystem*), suggesting that the historical period through which the person lives, the point in a person's lifespan when such influences are encountered, and the evolution of one's life over time all contribute to the complex algorithms of person-environment interactions. For example, college attendance in the 1960s was influenced by a very different cultural mix from what exists today. Attending postsecondary education for the first time at age forty attunes one to a different set of influences from what is typically experienced by traditional-age students. Finally, as students of all ages progress through the college experience they develop capacities and interests that sensitize them to new sources of influence and lessen the impact of others. This ebb and flow over time produces chronosystem effects unique to each individual but also to some extent shared by common cohorts.

Ultimately, this ecological model of student development reveals the campus environment as a complex web of influences that shape and are in turn shaped by the students who encounter them. Evaluating their degree of influence entails an understanding of these concentric layers, as well as the developmental status of students affected by them. For example, developmental differences related to hierarchical cognitive structures (e.g., dualistic vs. relativistic or conventional vs. principled reasoning) might predispose some students more than others to the influence of a tightly organized setting (high formalization) versus one that is more ambiguous or unclear. Expectations of certainty may leave one student especially frustrated by an open-ended seminar, while another more autonomous student might thrive in such an environment or become easily bored by a more passive mode of learning. In this case, the same mesosystem component results in two different outcomes depending on who experiences it. Likewise, heterogeneous differences (e.g., MBTI, StrengthsQuest talents, and Holland Vocational Interest profiles) might oversensitize some students more than others to the relational influences of different human aggregates or the varying patterns of different organizational structures (e.g., dynamic vs. static). Thus, Myers-Briggs extroverts and Holland Social types might be more attuned to personality differences in their mesosystem components as potential sources of frustration or satisfaction, given their particular orientations. Similarly, a student whose strengths include those of an achiever, activator, and maximizer (Clifton & Anderson, 2002), for purposes of illustration, might benefit from a more stratified hierarchical organizational environment, where competitive performance and upward mobility are stressed, versus an egalitarian setting, which might appeal more to a student whose profile includes strengths of adaptability, connectedness, and consistency. Rather than components of students' environmental systems exerting an even degree of influence, they are much more variable in their impact. In the parlance of college outcomes research, these are conditional effects (Pascarella & Terenzini, 1991, 2005) in that they are a function of the interaction of both the person and the environment. Thus, the impact of any environmental condition is contingent on the status and characteristics of the individual experiencing it.

Campus Policies and Practices

As campus environments are understood in terms of their impact and purpose and their design components, implications for campus policies and practices become clearer. Applications to the college campus of the environmental knowledge base presented here might be considered in terms of five basic strategies (Moos, 1979): maximizing educational information, facilitating and evaluating environmental change, implementing educational consultation, formulating ecologically relevant case descriptions, and enhancing environmental competence. Each of these strategies is considered in light of the policies, functions, and practices of campus educators who, as administrators and staff, faculty, or student affairs professionals, contribute to the learning, growth, and development of students.

Maximizing Educational Information

The knowledge base on human environments presented in this volume offers a conceptual framework for guiding assessment, organization, and communication of information about an institution and its various subenvironments. This framework might also prove useful for giving and taking feedback from students with respect to various campus environments. College and university promotional materials and institutional websites and apps are full of images and descriptions of campus life, focusing mostly on academic departments, majors, and interest areas, and of requisite snapshots of the college experience. Although such information is certainly important, whether this is the best information to offer prospective students as they make the decision to enroll in an institution is debatable, especially if it is the only source of information.

Technical data about departments and curricula rarely convey the qualities of environmental conditions most likely to have a significant effect on students' satisfaction and success. Perhaps communicating the nature of overall institutional social climate (its relationship, personal development, system maintenance, and change dimensions), for example, from student, faculty, and staff perspectives, might better serve to inform them about important institutional dynamics. Presentation of an institutional profile of the National Survey of Student Engagement (Kuh, 2003) might offer yet another means for assisting in making a college choice, as they reflect potential sources and patterns of student involvement. Such information could also be prepared and distributed for various institutional subenvironments, such as specific academic departments, classes (Winston et al., 1994), residential learning centers, and various student clubs and organizations (Winston et al., 1997). The importance of this type of information is that it offers opportunities for individuals to consider sources of compatibility or incongruence in their selection of campus environments.

Another aspect of maximizing educational information concerns what might be done with the data already collected on campus from year to year. Too often we gather responses from students through various surveys but rarely take the time to feed this information back to them for purposes of discussion and insight as to potential understandings and actions. For instance, how these environmental models might be used to communicate to students their collective perceptions of a particular campus environment to facilitate their initial adjustment to college can be illustrated in the context of residence life.

A residence director could administer the *University Residence Environment Scale* (URES) (Form E—expected environment, or Form I—ideal environment) (Moos & Gerst, 1988) to assigned residents prior to their arrival or during the orientation to campus. This could offer planners an understanding of what students consider their ideal expectations of on-campus living. Such a profile might serve as an important source of information for organizing programming that is likely to meet students' needs or, where necessary, for correcting expectations that may be unrealistic. Following up such an assessment six to eight weeks into the term with the URES (Form R—realistic environment, or simply engaging in a guided group discussion of the URES subscale framework and definitions) might help identify sources of discrepancy between what the students expected (or ideally sought) and what they actually found.

This give-and-take of information, which can also be organized by floors or wings, accomplishes several important learning goals. First, students learn about the design and dynamic of their present living environments in terms of a conceptual framework that will continue to prove helpful to them as they make decisions about selecting living environments in the future. Second, students learn how they may differ from or share perspectives with peers on what they perceive to be the desirable aspects of living environments. Third, staff members gain an important source of information for purposes of planning and programming to address any discrepancies students perceive between what they expected and what they found. For example, a significant discrepancy on the emotional support scale of the URES (a relationship dimension with consequences for inclusion and safety) might warrant an intervention of a team-building, service, or human relations kind. Finally, as student residents learn that staff value their perspectives in the planning and experience of a residential learning environment, they are encouraged to become involved in the processes of community change and goal setting.

Other applications might be explored by faculty in departmental and classroom settings as well. Seeking systematic feedback from students with regard to their sense of inclusion, safety, engagement, and experience of community in an academic program or course could prove helpful in maximizing the learning potential of those settings. Perhaps this kind of information, in concert with the usual technical descriptions, can assist students in gaining a broader understanding of environmental impact, again an important lesson for subsequent life choices.

Facilitating and Evaluating Environmental Change

The knowledge base on human environments, Moos (1986) argued, is helpful in facilitating and evaluating the consequences of environmental change on campus, whether that involves changing social climate, for example, or changing architectural and organizational characteristics. Campus change is sometimes unexpected and at other times intentional; it can be both evolutionary and revolutionary. The importance of these environmental models lies in their descriptions of the nature and direction of those changes. In concert with some of the long established environmental process models (Aulepp & Delworth, 1976; Huebner, 1979; Western Interstate Commission for Higher Education, 1973) they can serve as powerful tools in facilitating desired changes. For example, the ecosystem design model (Aulepp & Delworth, 1976) "is utilized to identify environmental shaping properties in order to eliminate dysfunctional features and to incorporate features that facilitate student academic and personal growth" (p. ix), either at the macro level (involving the entire campus community) or micro level (involving subenvironments for groups within the campus community). Additional understanding of the impact of changes on individual students can also be informed by application of the aforementioned ecological model of student development (Renn & Arnold, 2003).

The ecosystem design process itself encompasses seven steps that should be viewed as interacting components. Design work may begin with any of the steps, but unless an institution is just being created or wants to initiate an entirely new environment, it will find entry into the model is most natural at step 5. The seven interdependent steps are as follows:

1. Designers, in conjunction with community members, select educational values.
2. Values are then translated into specific goals.
3. Environments are designed that contain mechanisms to reach the stated goals.
4. Environments are fitted to students.
5. Student perceptions of the environments are measured.
6. Student behavior resulting from environmental perceptions is monitored.
7. Data on the environmental design's successes and failures, as indicated by student perceptions and behavior, are fed back to the designers in order that they may continue to learn about student/environment fit and design better environments. (p. ix)

An illustration of the utility of this model on the macro level is found in the series of women's climate studies (Seeger, 1994) that were conducted at Grand Valley State University in Michigan, for example. This ongoing, campus-wide effort was recognized by the American Association of University Women with its Progress in Equity Award and resulted in significant institutional changes ranging from construction of a new Children's Center (a physical environment change) to the formation in 1996 of a twenty-two-member Grand Valley Women's Commission (an organizational environment change) that continues to this day in its commitment to its "legacy of creating dialogue, celebrating women's leadership, and exploring issues of advocacy" (retrieved from http://www.gvsu.edu/wcommission/). By focusing first on assessing faculty, staff, and student perceptions of the degree of support for women on campus (step 5 in the model), various campus constituents have a common basis in the data generated for a discussion of campus values and purposes (inclusion, safety, engagement, and community) and for the planning of any environmental intervention or redesign.

Construction and renovation of campus unions, residence halls, classroom buildings, and recreation centers are also offering increasing numbers of institutions the opportunity to take advantage of these concepts and practices at the micro level, as values and goals of campus community building are pursued with current innovations in aesthetics and design. The recent conception, construction, and expansion of Greek Villages at Bowling Green State University, University of Central Arkansas, High Point University, and University of South Carolina are but a few examples of how holistic principles of campus ecology can serve to improve specific campus subenvironments through application of the campus neighborhood concept in support of student engagement.

Again, the environmental theories and models reviewed in this volume can sensitize campus planners and renovators to questions about various design components, their impact, and their intended purposes. An integrated environmental perspective suggests that each of these questions must be considered if whole change is to be brought about in the functioning of a setting. Changing one element without altering others may diminish the intended impact of the planned design. Many a campus, at one time or another, for example, has attempted to alter the environment of a particularly troublesome residence hall unit on campus (the proverbial zoo) with a housecleaning of new paint, carpet, and furniture. While such cosmetics may freshen up the general atmosphere of the facility, rarely is any significant change in student behavior observed until the influences of the human aggregate (e.g., all male residents) and organizational features (e.g., few involvement structures) are also taken into consideration. In addition to physical improvements, hall composition perhaps can be reconfigured to include females (an aggregate change strategy), and residents can be invited to participate in opportunities of self-governance and territorial design (organizational change strategies). Such changes may more effectively and positively influence the overall social climate of the hall, while attracting, satisfying, and sustaining new aggregates of students who create, over time, an organizational culture supportive of student engagement and community.

Implementing Educational Consultation

As educators we are often called on to consult with others concerning the functioning of various institutional environments, at both the macro level of an entire institution and the micro level of a particular campus subenvironment, such as a student organization or an administrative work group. Understanding the design components, potential impact, and purposes of an environment can help shape the assessment and feedback steps of these consultations. Upcraft and Schuh (1996) referenced a number of process models used in the environmental assessment steps of a typical consultation, including the ecosystem model (Aulepp & Delworth, 1976); ecomapping (Huebner & Corrazini, 1975–1976) involving the integration of questionnaire, interview, and observational data;

and the culture audit (Kuh et al., 1991; Whitt, 1993), focusing on artifacts of institutional culture as constructed by various campus constituents. These process models usually offer a step-by-step framework for action, but they do not necessarily indicate what needs to be assessed or for what purpose. Again, this environmental knowledge base can serve to guide such efforts. As suggested in the theoretical synthesis, for example, gathering information specific to the sense of inclusion and safety of a particular campus group (e.g., gay, lesbian, bisexual, and transgendered students) may be an important prelude to understanding why a campus environment fails to encourage engagement or the experience of community for some.

The inventory of design components contained in this knowledge base may also suggest strategies that could be applied to the particular problem for which consultation was sought. For example, from a work environment-social climate profile generated in the context of a staff development initiative (see Figure 9.3) it is clear by examining the ideal-real discrepancies on the subscales measured that issues of lack of supervisor support, too much work pressure, too little innovation, and limitations of physical comfort abound.

This provides a targeted source of information for purposes of environmental intervention and redesign. For example, the need to address more specifically (perhaps through interviews and focus groups) issues of physical layout, space usage, and amenities is obvious, since physical comfort is the largest source of discrepancy in the profile. In addition, the lack of innovation perceived in the work setting immediately invokes the organizational conceptual framework of Hage and Aiken (1970), suggesting that an emphasis on quantity of production in an environment will diminish the dynamics supportive of innovation. In this case, the staff members' desire to reduce work pressure serves as a proxy for this organizational parameter, indicating that more emphasis on quality (rather than quantity) of work is warranted. Finally, issues of supervisor support also indicate some changes in the organizational dimensions of the work environment. Two possible leads implicated in the assessment may be related to the high degrees of centralization and stratification perceived by participants, either of which could discourage innovation. In the event that this turns out to be the case, interventions in the form of staff team-building, decision-making, and supervisory relationships may also improve the dynamic of this work setting. The template of social climate, with its identification of relationship, personal growth, and system maintenance dimensions as important aspects of the environment, serves to guide the analysis of the problem as well as the solution (Figure 9.3).

Figure 9.3. Real (Form R) Versus Ideal (Form I) Work-Environment Scale Profile

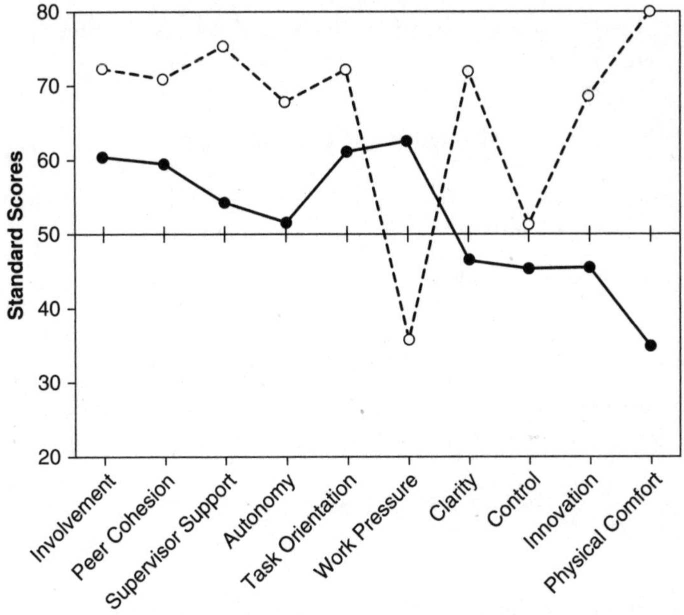

Exhibit 9.2. Work Environment Scale (WES) Dimensions and Subscales

Relationship Dimensions

Involvement—Extent to which employees are concerned about and committed to their jobs.

Coworker cohesion—How much employees are friendly and supportive of one another.

Supervisor support—Extent to management is supportive of employees and encourages employees to be supportive of one another.

Personal Growth Dimensions

Autonomy—How much employees are encouraged to be self-sufficient and to make their own decisions.

Task orientation—Emphasis on good planning, efficiency, and getting the job done.

Work pressure—Degree to which high work demands and time pressure dominate the job milieu.

System Maintenance and Change Dimensions

Clarity—Whether employees know what to expect in their daily routine and how explicitly rules and policies are communicated.

Control—How much management uses rules and pressures to keep employees under control.

Innovation—Emphasis on variety, change, and new approaches.

Physical comfort—Extent to which the physical surroundings contribute to a pleasant work environment.

Source: Moos, 1994b. Used by permission.

Formulating Ecologically Relevant Case Descriptions

Regardless of their circumstances, students arrive on campus, bringing with them an intact life ecology of interacting systems of family, peers, culture, and hometown. To that is joined the existing ecology of the campus, which in many cases may include a residence hall environment, various classroom environments, a social or task group environment, and very often a work environment. In the parlance of the ecological student development model (Renn & Arnold, 2003), these constitute the mesosystem, macrosystem, and exosystem layers of each student's experience at a given moment in time (chronosystem). Thus, these concepts offer a framework for advisors and counselors to understand the nature of each student's experience.

For students expressing transitional adjustment concerns the various social climate dimensions listed in Exhibit 4.3, for example, catalog specific concerns and issues relevant to personal functioning in any of these environments. Combined with dynamics identified in Exhibit 9.1, addressing the nature of the environment's impact, an ecological inventory emerges in the form of an integrated social climate picture relevant to that student's life. Is the presenting issue primarily a relationship dimension concern? Which subenvironments are involved? Family? Which aspects of family relationships are involved? Cohesiveness? Expressiveness? Is the concern one of active stress (a powerful negative influence) requiring immediate relief, or a matter of normal anxiety and frustration in the context of developmental challenge (a powerful positive influence)? In concert with environmental purposes addressed in this volume—inclusion, safety, engagement, community), information about each of these social climate dimensions comprising students' ecology, and the source in their mesosystem, macrosystem, or exosystem—might also serve as a guide for enhancing its overall learning potential, either by adjusting the design of a current environment or seeking out new ones. Such probes and strategies can help advisors and counselors build a more complete and relevant picture of how individual students are adapting to and coping with various institutional environments.

Enhancing Environmental Competence

In this final application, Moos (1979) recommends teaching students how to create, select, and transcend environments, how to maximize person-environment congruence when support is the goal, or how to seek an appropriate amount of incongruence and challenge when the goal is personal growth. The overall intent is to help students understand more fully the impact of the environment on their lives.

Enhancing environmental competence is a goal that encompasses the fundamental purposes and outcomes of higher education. From a developmental perspective, it can be argued that a person who possesses a simplistic, authority-bound, and categorical view of the world (Perry's [1970] dualist or King and Kitchener's [1994] pre-reflective thinker), typical of many entering students, lacks both the motivation and skill for self-directed learning and is ineffective in a world where little is certain and change is constant. Through general education core courses, students are challenged to examine the world environment in all its contexts (historical, cultural, physical, and interpersonal) and to develop the basic tools of inquiry and communication to be able to examine further a select part of that environment through completion of an academic major. The college outcome research (Pascarella & Terenzini, 2005) consistently supports the finding that students who persist in this process emerge with a more complex view of the world, are more appreciative of its subtleties, and are more capable of sorting through the maze of opinions, facts, and interpretations necessary for making good judgments about life and the environment surrounding them. Sensitizing students to the key components, design characteristics, dynamics, and purposes of human environments, through campus experiences and academic course work, will likely enhance their capacity for making wise choices about environments as they progress through life. Creating a better world begins with understanding more clearly what works well (or not so well) in their current world.

Environmental competence is an important tool in shaping such an understanding.

President James A. Garfield, referring to the renowned educator who taught philosophy and rhetoric for fifty-seven years at Williams College and served as its president from 1836 to 1872, described the ideal college as "Mark Hopkins on one end of a log and a student on the other" (Kunitz & Haycraft, 1938, p. 384). Obviously, much has changed in American higher education since Garfield evoked this image of a powerful educational environment. The simple log has grown to an enormous academic edifice of stone, brick, mortar, steel, concrete, and now online websites, reflecting a gallery of real and virtual designs, functions, and purposes. From the log's one end the consummate gentleman scholar, in the person of Professor Hopkins, has given way to a catalog of faculty roles in support of the multifaceted missions of teaching, research, and service. From the log's other end the singular, receptive student sitting in awe of Professor Hopkin's wisdom is now a chorus of active learners voicing an ever rich variety of liberal, technical, and vocational educational interests and goals (Strange, 1996). Higher education in America has indeed changed significantly and dramatically in a relatively short period of time. The promise of even greater change lies in the not too distant future as the digital world evolves.

The effects of such changes have been especially evident over the past fifty years, as many institutions have witnessed a profound revolution in scale, purpose, and clientele. Once a relatively homogeneous system serving the few who could afford it for purposes of developing character, good moral habits, and social status, American higher education is now a multiplex of institutional types serving a vast number of students for as many different reasons. The mixture and variety of students have changed as well. Those Cross (1971) once dubbed new students—many underprepared—are rapidly becoming the new majority student and continue to bring a greater range of expectations of what colleges and universities can and should do for them. Returning adult learners look for assistance in responding to changing life goals and circumstances (Cross, 1981; Knowles, Holton, & Swanson, 2012; Schlossberg, Lynch, & Chickering 1989). Previously disenfranchised racial and ethnic groups seek channels of opportunity and access to social change, and students everywhere expect marketable skills, a career-oriented curriculum, and a secure position upon completion of a degree program or certificate. To all that is added growing demands for online flexible accessibility to learning.

This revolution in American higher learning has given rise to a maze of state, private, proprietary, online, and community-based institutions that is as difficult to comprehend for students who must choose between them as it is challenging for faculty and administrators who work within them. What is the best college to attend? A conveniently located community college? A small private institution assuring more personalized attention? A large multiversity promising the excitement of cutting-edge research and a diversity of student types? A proprietary institution with a direct line to the job market? An online learning option that focuses on competencies rather than courses? What about the choices once within an institution? Should one commute to campus or live in a residence hall? Is a single-sex arrangement or a coed residential learning center best? What are the consequences of not committing immediately to a major?

From the viewpoints of faculty and administrators the task may be equally daunting. What sort of institutional images will attract the types of students who will do well? What can make an institution more attractive and fulfilling to students of differing cultural and ethnic backgrounds? What can be done to increase the student retention rate, especially during the first year? Will teaching strategies for traditional students be as effective with new and different students? What is the potential for creating exciting learning environments in classrooms that hold larger numbers of students? What will assist students in making better decisions about the many campus resources and opportunities available to them?

An essential challenge facing postsecondary educators today is the creation and maintenance of campus environments (both proximate and distant) that attract, satisfy, and sustain students in the achievement of their educational goals. That responsibility lies in the hands of all institutional constituents: campus enrollment managers and orientation directors who recruit and acclimate new students to the college environment; directors of online learning who serve nontraditional students with complex schedules and needs; residence hall directors who assist many students in engaging the challenges of communal living and learning; faculty in foundational courses who introduce students to the concepts and methods of the disciplines; directors of adult and commuter students who enhance the sense of mattering (Schlossberg, 1989) and belonging among them; coordinators of multicultural affairs and directors of international student advising who create and shape welcoming environments for those whose racial, ethnic, or national heritage differs from the dominant campus constituent; student activity and organization advisers who engage students in opportunities for campus engagement and leadership; personal counselors who aid students in understanding the adjustments required of life transitions; and academic, career, and vocational advisers who assist students choosing a personally fulfilling academic and occupational goal. What is needed to guide these functions and practices is a comprehensive model of the college environment that describes its various features and assists campus participants in understanding how such factors can either encourage or inhibit student learning, growth, and development (Strange, 1983; Strange & King, 1990). We trust that the conceptual frameworks offered here will prove to be a helpful start in that direction.

Questions for Discussion

1. What data are available to inform the profile of your institution with respect to its principal environmental components, impacts, and purposes served?
2. What are the greatest environmental assets of your college or university in regard to its support of student success?
3. What environmental components of your institution are most negative and stressful for students?
4. What immediate design changes would you recommend most to strengthen the ecology of learning at your college or university?
5. To what extent are students, faculty, and staff included in making decisions about the designs of campus environments at your institution?

References

Abes, E. S., Jones, S. R., & McEwen, M. K. (2007). Reconceptualizing the model of multiple dimensions of identity: The role of meaning-making capacity in the construction of multiple identities. *Journal of College Student Development*, 48(1), 1–22.

Abras, C., Maloney-Krichmar, D., & Preece, J. (2004). User-centered design. W. Bainbridge, *Encyclopedia of Human-Computer Interaction*, *37*(4), 445–56. Thousand Oaks, CA: Sage Publications.

Adler, R. B., & Proctor II R. F. (2014). *Looking out looking in* (14th edition). Boston, MA: Wadsworth, Cengage Learning.

Amar, A. F., & Gennaro, S. (2005). Dating violence in college women: Associated physical injury, healthcare usage, and mental health symptoms. *Nursing Research*, 54(4), 235–242.

American Council on Education. (1985). *Achieving reasonable campus* security self-regulation initiatives: Resources. Washington, DC: Documents for Colleges and Universities, No. 2.

Anderson, P. (1971). The school as an organic teaching aid. In R. McClure (Ed.), *National society for the study of education yearbook, Part 1. The curriculum: Retrospect and prospect*. Chicago, IL: University of Chicago Press.

Arao, B., & Clemens, K. (2013). From safe spaces to brave spaces: A new way to frame dialogue around diversity and social justice. In L. Landreman (Ed.), *The art of effective facilitation: Reflections from social justice educators* (pp. 135–150). Sterling, VA: Stylus.

Arthur, P., & Passini, R. (1992). *Wayfinding*. New York, NY: McGraw-Hill.

Aslanian, C. B., & Brickell, H. M. (1980). *Americans in transition:* Life changes as reasons for adult learning. New York, NY: College Entrance Examination Board.

Astin, A. W. (1968). *The college environment*. Washington, DC: American Council on Education.

Astin, A. W. (1985). *Achieving educational excellence: A critical assessment of priorities and practices in higher education*. San Francisco, CA: Jossey-Bass.

Astin, A. W. (1993). An empirical typology of college students. *Journal of College Student Development, 34*, 36–46.

Astin, A. W., & Panos, R. J. (1966). A national research databank for higher education. *Educational Record, 47*, 5–17.

Aulepp, L., & Delworth, U. (1976). *Training manual for an ecosystem* model: Assessing and designing campus environments. Boulder, CO: Western Interstate Commission for Higher Education.

Baird, L. L. (1988). The college environment revisited: A review of research and theory. In J. C. Smart (Ed.), *Higher education: Vol.* 4. Handbook of theory and research (pp. 1–52). New York, NY: Agathon Press.

Banning, J. (1992). Visual anthropology: Viewing the campus ecology for messages of sexism. *Campus Ecologist, 10*(1), 1–4.

Banning, J. (1997). Designing for community: Thinking "out of the box" with porches. *Journal of College and University Student Housing, 26*(2), 3–7.

Banning, J., & Bartels, S. (1993). A taxonomy for physical artifacts: Understanding campus multiculturalism. *Campus Ecologist, 11*(3), 2–3.

Banning, J. H. (1989). Impact of college environments on freshman students. In M. L. Upcraft, J. N. Gardner, & Associates (Eds.), *The freshman year experience* (pp. 53–62). San Francisco, CA: Jossey-Bass.

Banning, J. H. (1995). Campus images: Homoprejudice. *Campus Ecologist, 13*(3), 3.

Banning, J. H. (Ed.). (1978). *Campus ecology: A perspective for student affairs*. Cincinnati, OH: NASPA Monograph.

Banning, J. H., Clemons, S., McKelfresh, D., & Gibbs, R. W. (2010). Special places for students: Third place and restorative place. *College Student Journal, 44*(4), 906–912.

Banning, J. H., & Cunard, M. (1986). The physical environment supports student development. *Campus Ecologist, 4*(1), 1–3.

Banning, J. H., & Kaiser, L. (1974). An ecological perspective and model for campus design. *Personnel and Guidance Journal, 52*(6), 370–375.

Banning, J .H., & Luna, F. (1992). Viewing the campus ecology for messages about Hispanic/Latino culture. *Campus Ecologist, 10*(4), 1–4.

Banning, J. H., McGuire, F. D., & Stegman, J. (1996) Housing that makes a difference. *College Services Administration, 19*(1), 53–58.

Banning, J. H., Middleton, V., & Deniston, T. (2008). Using photographs to assess equity climate: A taxonomy. *Multicultural Perspectives, 10*(1), 1–6.

Barker, R. (1968). *Ecological psychology*. Palo Alto, CA: Stanford University Press.

Baum, A., & Valins, S. (1977). *Architecture and social behavior: Psychological studies of social density*. Hillsdale, NY: Erlbaum.

Bechtel, R. B. (1997). *Environment and behavior: An introduction*. Thousand Oaks, CA: Sage.

Bechtel, R. B., & Zeisel, J. (1987). Observations: The world under a glass. In R. Becthel, R. Marans, & W. Michelson (Eds.), *Methods in environmental and behavioral research* (pp. 11–40). New York, NY: Van Nostrand Reinhold.

Beeler, K., Bellandese, S., & Wiggins, C. (1991). *Campus safety: A survey of administrative perceptions and strategies* (Report No. HE 024 821). Washington, DC: NASPA. (ERIC Document Reproduction Service No. 336 001)

Beetham, H., & Sharpe, R. (Eds.). (2013). *Rethinking pedagogy for a digital age: Designing for 21st century learning*. New York, NY: Routledge.

Bell, D. (2009). Learning from second life. *British Journal of Educational Technology, 40*(3), 515–525.

Bell, P. A., Greene, T. G., Fisher, J. D., & Baum, A. (2001). *Environmental psychology* (5th ed.). Orlando, FL: Harcourt Brace.

Bellah, R. N., Madsen, R., Sullivan, W. M., Swidler, A., & Tipton, S. M. (1985). *Habits of the heart*. New York, NY: Harper & Row.

Bennett, M., & Benton, S. (2001). What are the buildings saying? A study of first-year undergraduate students' attributions about college campus architecture. *NASPA Journal, 38*(2), 159–177.

Bennett, S. (2007). First questions for designing higher education learning spaces. *Journal of Academic Librarianship, 33*(1), 14–26.

Bers, M., & Chau, C. (2010). The virtual campus of the future: stimulating and simulating civic actions in a virtual world. *Journal of Computing in Higher Education, 22*(1), 1–23.

Birnbaum, R. (1988). *How colleges work: The cybernetics of academic organization and leadership*. San Francisco, CA: Jossey-Bass.

Blau, P. M. (1973). *The organization of academic work*. New York, NY: Wiley.

Blimling, G. S. (1988). *The influence of college residence halls on students: A meta-analysis of the empirical research, 1966–1985* (Unpublished doctoral dissertation). Ohio State University, Columbus, OH.

Blimling, G. S. (2015). *Student learning in college residence halls: What works, what doesn't, and why*. San Francisco, CA: Jossey-Bass.

Bolman, L. G., & Deal, T. E. (2011). *Reframing organizations: Artistry, choice, and leadership* (4th ed.). San Francisco, CA: Jossey-Bass.

Bonner, T. N. (1976, September–October). The unintended revolution in America's colleges since 1940. *Change, 18*, 44–51.

Borden, J. (2011, August). The future of online learning. *elearn Magazine*. Retrieved from http://elarningmag.acm.org/featured.cfm?aid=2024704.

Bott, S. E. (2000). *The development of psychometric scales to measure sense of place* (Unpublished doctoral dissertation). Colorado State University, Fort Collins, CO.

Bott, S. E., Banning, J., Wells, M., Haas, G., & Lakey, J. (2006). Sense of place: A framework and its application to campus ecology. *College Services*, 6(5), 42–47.

Boyer, E. (1987). *College: The undergraduate experience in America*. New York, NY: Harper & Row.

Brandon, A., Hirt, J., & Cameron, T. (2008). Where you live influences who you know: Differences in student interaction based on residence hall design. *Journal of College and University Student Housing*, 35(2), 62–79.

Bransford, J. (2000). *How people learn: Brain, mind, experience, and school*. Washington, DC: National Academy Press.

Braskamp, L. (2008). *StrengthsQuest on the college campus: From concept to implementation*. Princeton, NJ: Gallup Organization.

Bronfenbrenner, U. (1977). Toward an experimental ecology of human development. *American Psychologist, 32*(7), 513.

Bronfenbrenner, U. (1979). *The ecology of human development: Experiments by nature and design*. Cambridge, MA: Harvard University Press.

Bronfenbrenner, U. (1993). The ecology of cognitive development: Research models and fugitive findings. In R. H. Wozniak & K. W. Fischer (Eds.), *Development in context: Acting and thinking in specific environments* (pp. 3–44). Hillsdale, NJ: Erlbaum.

Bronfenbrenner, U. (1995). Developmental ecology through space and time: A future perspective. In P. Moen & G. H. Elder, Jr. (Eds.), *Examining lives in context: Perspectives on the ecology of human development* (pp. 619–647). Washington, DC: American Psychological Association.

Bronfenbrenner, U. (1999). Environments in developmental perspective: Theoretical and operational models. In S. L. Friedman & T. D. Wachs (Eds.), *Measuring environment across the life span: Emerging methods and concepts* (pp. 3–28). Washington, DC: American Psychological Association.

Bronfrenbrenner, U., & Morris, P. A. (2006). The ecology of developmental processes. In R. Lerner & W. E. Damon (Eds.), *Handbook of child psychology: Theoretical models of human development* (6th ed., Vol. 1) (pp. 793–828). Hoboken, NJ: John Wiley.

Brooks, D. C. (2012). Space and consequences: The impact of different formal learning spaces on instructor and student behavior. *Journal of Learning Spaces, 1*(2). Retrieved from: http://libjournal.uncg.edu/ojs/index.php/jls/article/view/285.

Brower, A. M., & Dettinger, K. M. (1998, November–December). What is a learning community? *About Campus*, 3(5), 15–21.

Brower, A. M., & Inkelas, K. K. (2010). Living-learning programs: One high-impact educational practice we now know a lot about. *Liberal Education*, 96(2), 36–43.

Budin, D. (2009, Spring). John Carroll gets a second life. *John Carroll Magazine*. University Heights, OH: John Carroll University.

Burgstahler, S. (2008). Universal design in higher education. In S. Burgstahler & R. Cory (Eds.), *Universal design in higher education: From principles to practice* (pp. 3–20). Cambridge, MA: Harvard Education Press.

Carnegie Foundation for the Advancement of Teaching. (1990). *Campus life: In search of community*. Princeton, NY: Carnegie Foundation for the Advancement of Teaching.

CAST (2011). *Universal design for learning guidelines version 2.0*. Retrieved from http://www.udlcenter.org/aboutudl/udlguidelines.

Ceglarek, S. L., & Brower, A. (2007). Changing the culture of high-risk drinking. In J. F. Jackson & M. C. Terrell (Eds.), *Creating and maintaining safe college campuses: A sourcebook for evaluating and enhancing safety programs* (pp. 15–33). Sterling, VA: Stylus.

Center for Universal Design (1997). *The principles of universal design, version 2.0*. Raleigh, NC: North Carolina State University.

Chaffee, E. E., & Tierney, W. G. (1988). *Collegiate culture and leadership strategies*. New York, NY: American Council on Education and Macmillan.

Chambliss, D. F., & Takacs, C. G. (2014). *How college works*. Cambridge, MA: Harvard University Press.

Champagne, D. E. (2007). Elements of a comprehensive safety plan. In J. F. L. Jackson & M. C. Terrell (Eds.), *Creating and maintaining safe college campuses* (pp. 261–274). Sterling, VA: Stylus.

Chan, T. W. (1995). A tutorial on social learning systems. In T. W. Chan & J. A. Self (Eds.), *Emerging computer technologies in education*, 71–69. Charlottesville, VA: Association for the Advancement of Computing in Education.

Chapman, M. P. (2006). *American places: In search of the twenty-first century campus*. Portsmouth, NH: Greenwood Publishing Group.

Chen, B., & Denoyelles, A. (2013, October 7). Exploring students' mobile learning practices in higher education. *Educause Review*. (Retrieved from http://www.educause.edu/ero/article/exploring-students-mobile-learning-practices-higher-education.)

Chen, P. S. D., Lambert, A. D., & Guidry, K. R. (2010). Engaging online learners: The impact of Web-based learning technology on college student engagement. *Computers & Education*, *54*(4), 1222–1232.

Cheng, D. X. (2004). Students' sense of campus community: What it means, and what to do about it {Computer File}. *NASPA Journal (Online)*, *41*, 216–234. Retrieved August 19, 2008 from Education Full Text database.

Chism, N. V. N., & Bickford, D. J. (Eds.). (2002). The importance of physical space in creating supportive learning environments. *New Directions for Teaching & Learning*. No. 92. San Francisco, CA: Jossey-Bass.

Chickering, A. W. (1969). *Education and identity*. San Francisco, CA: Jossey-Bass.

Chickering, A. W., & Reisser, L. (1993). *Education and identity* (2nd ed.). San Francisco, CA: Jossey-Bass.

Christensen, C. M., & Eyring, H. J. (2011). *The innovative university: Changing the DNA of higher education from the inside out*. San Francisco, CA: Jossey-Bass.

Clark, B., & Trow, M. (1966). The organizational context. In T. Newcomb & E. Wilson (Eds.), *College peer groups: Problems and prospects for research* (pp. 17–70). Chicago, IL: Aldine.

Clemmitt, M. (2013, January 25). Social media explosion: Do social networking sites threaten privacy rights? *CQ Researcher*, *23*(4), 81–104. Retrieved from http://photo.pds.org:5012/cqresearcher/document.php?id=cqresrre2013012500.

Clifton, D. O. (1997). *The self-reflection scale*. Princeton, NJ: Gallup Organization.

Clifton, D. O., & Anderson, E. (2002). *StrengthsQuest: Discover and develop your strengths in academics, career, and beyond*. Washington DC: Gallup Organization.

Clifton, D. O., & Harter, J. K. (2003). Strengths investment. In K. S. Cameron, J. E. Dutton, & R. E. Quinn (Eds.), *Positive organizational scholarship* (pp. 111–121). San Francisco, CA: Berrett-Koehler.

Cole, D. G., Orsuwan, M., & Sam, A. A. (2007). Violence and hate crimes on campus: Uncovering the mystique. In J. F. Jackson & M. C. Terrell (Eds.), *Creating and maintaining safe college campuses: A sourcebook for evaluating and enhancing safety programs* (pp. 34–57). Sterling, VA: Stylus.

comScore. *(2014, August)*. *U.S. Mobile App Report*. (2014, August). Reston, VA: Author.

Conyne, R. K., & Clack, R. J. (1981). *Environmental assessment and design: A new tool for the applied behavioral scientist*. New York, NY: Praeger.

Cottrell, L. S., Jr. (1983). The competent community. In R. L. Warren & L. Lyon (Eds.), *New perspectives on the American community* (pp. 401–411). Homewood, IL: Dorsey Press.

Council of Ontario Universities. (1991). *Women's campus safety audit Guide.* Toronto, Ontario: Ontario Ministry of Colleges and Universities. (ERIC Document Reproduction Service No. ED 338 129)

Cox, M. D., & Richlin, L. (Eds.). (2004). Building faculty learning communities. *New Directions for Teaching and Learning, 97(15).* San Francisco, CA: Jossey-Bass.

Cresswell, T. (2004). *Place: A short introduction.* Malden, MA: Blackwell Publishing.

Crockett, E. (2011). *Results of the University of Arizona Safe Zone Program impact evaluation.* (Prepared for the University of Arizona Office of LBGTQ Affairs). Retrieved from http://lgbtq.arizona.edu//sites/lgbtq.arizona.edu/images/Condensed_Internship_Report.pdf.

Cronon, W. (1992). Kennecott journey: The paths out of town. In W. Cronon, G. Miles, & J. Gitlin (Eds.), *Under an open sky* (pp. 28–51). New York, NY: Norton.

Crook, C., & Mitchell, G. (2012). Ambience in social learning: Student engagement with new designs for learning spaces. *Cambridge Journal of Education, 42*(2), 121–139.

Crookston, B. B. (1974). A design for an intentional democratic community. In D. A. DeCoster & P. Mable (Eds.), *Student development and education in college residence halls* (pp. 55–67). Washington, DC: American College Personnel Association.

Cross, K. P. (1971). *Beyond the open door: New students to higher education.* San Francisco, CA: Jossey-Bass.

Cross, K. P. (1981). *Adults as learners.* San Francisco, CA: Jossey-Bass.

Cross, K. P. (1998). Why learning communities? Why now? *About Campus,* 3(3), 4–11.

Cunningham, H. V., & Tabur, S. (2012). Learning space attributes: Reflections on academic library design and its use. *Journal of Learning Spaces, 1*(2). Retrieved from https://libjournal.uncg.edu/index.php/jls/article/view/392/287.

Curtis, P., & Nicholas, D. A. (1993). MUDs grow up: Social virtual reality in the real world. In *Proceedings of 3rd International Conference on Cyberspace.*

Cuseo, J. (2007). The empirical case against large class size: Adverse effects on the teaching, learning, and retention of first-year students. *Journal of Faculty Development, 21*(1), 5–21.

Cychosz, C. (2007). The incompatibility of weapons and college campuses. In J. F. Jackson & M. C. Terrell (Eds.), *Creating and maintaining safe college campuses: A sourcebook for evaluating and enhancing safety programs* (pp. 188–204). Sterling, VA: Stylus.

D'Augelli, A. R. (1989). Lesbians' and gay men's experience of discrimination and harassment in a university community. *American Journal of Community Psychology*, *17*, 317–321.

Dabbagh, N., & Kitsantas, A. (2012). Personal learning environments, social media, and self-regulated learning: A natural formula for connecting formal and informal learning. *Internet and Higher Education*, *15*(1), 3–8.

Davis III, C., Deil-Amen, R., Rios-Aguilar, C., & Gonzalez Canche, M. (2012). *Social media in higher education: A literature review and research directions*. Report printed by the University of Arizona and Claremont Graduate University. Retrieved from http://works.bepress.com/cgi/viewcontent.cgi?article=1003&contexthfdavis.

DeAndrea, D. C., Ellison, N. B., LaRose, R., Steinfield, C., & Fiore, A. (2012). Serious social media: On the use of social media for improving students' adjustment. *Internet and Higher Education*, *15*, 15–23.

De Lucia, A., Francese, R., Passero, I., & Tortora, G. (2009). Development and evaluation of a virtual campus on Second Life: The case of SecondDMI. *Computers & Education*, *52*(1), 220–233.

Dede, C., Nelson, B., Ketelhut, D. J., Clarke, J., & Bowman, C. (2004, June). Design-based research strategies for studying situated learning in a multi-user virtual environment. In *Proceedings of the 6th international conference on Learning sciences* (pp. 158–165). International Society of the Learning Sciences.

Devlin, A. S. (2012). Environmental perception: Wayfinding and spatial cognition. In S. Clayton (Ed.), *The Oxford handbook of environmental and conservation psychology* (pp. 41–64). Oxford, UK: Oxford University Press.

Devlin, A. S., Donovan, S., Nicolov, A., Nold, O., & Zandan, G. (2008). Residence hall architecture and sense of community: Everything old is new again. *Environment and Behavior*, 40(4), 487–521.

Dewey, J. (1916). *Democracy and education*. New York, NY: Free Press.

Dewey, J. (1933). *How we think: A restatement of the relation of reflective thinking to the educative process*. New York, NY: D.C. Heath.

Dieterle, E., & Clarke, J. (2007). Multi-user virtual environments for teaching and learning. In M. Pagani (Ed.), *Encyclopedia of multimedia technology and networking* (2nd ed.) (pp. 1033–1044).

Dietz-Uhler, B., & Murrell, A. (1992). College student's perceptions of sexual harassment: Are gender differences decreasing? *Journal of College Student Development*, 33(6), 540–546.

Dober, R. (1992). *Campus design*. New York, NY: John Wiley & Sons.

Duggan, M., & Smith, A. (2013, December). *Pew Research Internet Project: Social Media Update 2013*. Retrieved from http://www.pewinternet.org/2013/12/30/social-media-update-2013/.

Dukes, C. M., & Harris, T. (2007). Safety in the community college environment. In J. F. Jackson & M. C. Terrell (Eds.), *Creating and maintaining safe college campuses: A sourcebook for evaluating and enhancing safety programs* (pp. 136–149). Sterling, VA: Stylus.

Dunbar, R. I. M. (1992). Neocortex size as a constraint on group size in primates. *Journal of Human Evolution, 22*(6), 469–493.

Dunne, J. (1986). Sense of community in l'Arche and in the writings of Jean Vanier. *Journal of Community Psychology, 14*, 41–54.

Dyer, W. G., Jr. (1986). The cycle of cultural evolution in organizations. In R. Kilman, M. Saxton, R. Serpa, & Associates (Eds.), *Gaining control of the corporate culture* (pp. 200–229). San Francisco, CA: Jossey-Bass.

Dziech, B. W., & Weiner, L. (1984). *The lecherous professor: Sexual harassment on campus*. Boston, MA: Beacon Press.

Eckert, E. L. (2013, January–February). The tale of three campuses: A case study in outdoor campus assessment. *Facilities Manager*, 32–37.

Eckman, P. (1985). *Telling lies: Clues to deceit in the marketplace, politics, and marriage*. New York, NY: Norton.

Etzioni, A. (1964). *Modern organizations*. Englewood Cliffs, NJ: Prentice-Hall.

Etzioni, A. (1993). *The spirit of community: Rights, responsibilities and the communitarian agenda*. New York, NY: Crown Publishers, Inc.

Evans, N. J., Forney, D. S., Guido, F. M., Patton, L. D., & Renn, K. A. (2010). *Student development in college: Theory, research, and practice*. San Francisco, CA: Jossey-Bass.

Evans, N. J., Forney, D. S., & Guido-DiBrito, F. (1998). *Student development in college: Theory, research and practice*. San Francisco, CA: Jossey-Bass.

Evans, N. J., & Rankin, S. (1998). Heterosexism and campus violence: Assessment and intervention strategies. In A. M. Hoffman, J. H. Schuh, & R. H. enske (Eds.), *Violence on campus: Defining the problems, strategies for action* (pp. 169–186). Gaithersburg, MD: Aspen.

Evans, N. J., & Wall, V. A. (Eds.). (1991). *Beyond tolerance: Gays, lesbians, and bisexuals on campus*. Alexandria, VA: American College Personnel Association Media Publication.

Evans, D. (2012). The internet of everything: How more relevant and valuable connections will change the world. *Internet Business Solution Group: USA*.

Ezeh, C., & Harris, L. C. (2007). Servicescape research: A review and a research agenda. *Marketing Review, 7*(1), 59–78.

Feldman, K. A., & Newcomb, T. M. (1969). *The impact of college on students*. San Francisco, CA: Jossey-Bass.

Felix, E. (2011). Learning space service design. *Journal of Learning Spaces, 1*(1). Retrieved from http://libjournal.uncg.edu/index.php/jls/article /view/284.

Felix, E., & Brown, M. (2011). The case for a learning space performance rating system. *Journal of Learning Spaces, 1*(1). Retrieved from http://libjournal.uncg.edu/index.php/jls/article/viewArticle/287/154.

Fink, L. D. (2013). *Creating significant learning experiences: An integrated approach to designing college courses*. San Francisco, CA: Jossey-Bass.

Finley, C., & Corty, E. (1993). Rape on campus: The prevalence of sexual assaults while enrolled in college. *Journal of College Student Development, 34*(2), 113–117.

Fisher, B., & Nasar, J. L. (1992). Fear of crime in relation to three exterior site features: Prospect, refuge, and escape. *Environment and Behavior, 24*(1), 35–65.

Ford, R. C., & Heaton, C. P. (2000). *Managing the guest experience in hospitality*. Albany, NY: Delmar-Thornton.

Forrest, L., Hotalling, K., & Kuk, L. (1986). *The elimination of sexism in the university environment*. Pingree Park, CO: Student Development through Campus Ecology Second Annual Symposium. (ERIC Document Reproduction Service # ED 267 348)

Francis, J., Giles-Corti, B., Wood, L., & Knuiman, M. (2012). Creating sense of community: The role of public space. *Journal of Environmental Psychology, 32*, 401–409.

Freire, P. (1972). *Pedagogy of the oppressed.* 1968. Trans. Myra Bergman Ramos. New York, NY: *Herder*.

Friedman, M. (1983). *The confirmation of otherness*. New York, NY: Pilgrim Press.

Fry, T. (Ed.). (1981). *RB 1980: The rule of St. Benedict*. Collegeville, MN: Liturgical Press.

Gabr, H. S., & Al-Sallal, K. A. (2003). Post occupancy evaluation of university educational buildings. In G. Moser, E. Pol, Y. Bernard, M. Bonnes, J. A. Corraliza, & M. V. Giuliana (Eds.), *People, places, and sustainability* (pp. 229–242). Kirkland, WA: Hogrefe & Huber Publishers.

Gallup. (2008). *A framework for strengths programming*. Lincoln, NE: Author.

Garbarino, J. (1978). *The human ecology of school crime*. Hackensack, NJ: National Council on Crime and Delinquency.

Gardner, H. (1985). *Frames of mind: The theory of multiple intelligences*. New York, NY: Basic Books.

Gardner, H. (1999). *Intelligence reframed: Multiple intelligences for the 21st century*. New York, NY: Basic Books.

Gardner, J. W. (1990). *On leadership*. New York: Free Press.

Garrison, D. R., & Vaughan, N. D. (2008). *Blended learning in higher education: Framework, principles, and guidelines*. San Francisco, CA: Jossey-Bass.

Gasman, M. & Drezner, N. D. (2007). A call for community-based education: The state of public safety issues at minority-serving institutions. In J. F. Jackson & M. C. Terrell (Eds.), *Creating and maintaining safe college campuses: A sourcebook for evaluating and enhancing safety programs* (pp. 173–187). Sterling, VA: Stylus.

Gehl, J., & Svarre, B. (2013). *How to study public life*. Washington, DC: Island Press.

Gerald, S., & Antonacci, D. M. (2009). Virtual world learning spaces: Developing a Second Life operating room simulation. *EDUCAUSE Quarterly*, *32*(1). Retrieved from http://www.webcitation.org/5k8IXDmdI

Gikas, J., & Grant, M. (2013). Mobile computing devices in higher education: Student perspectives on learning with cellphones, smartphones & social media. *Internet and Higher Education*, *19*, 18–26.

Gilligan, C. (1982). *In a different voice: Psychological theory and women's development*. Cambridge, MA: Harvard University Press.

Gifford, R. (2007). The consequences of living in high-rise buildings. *Architectural Science Review*, *50*(1), 2–17.

Giuliani, M. V., & Feldman, R. (1993). Place attachment in a developmental and cultural context. *Journal of Environmental Psychology*, *13*(3), 267–274.

Gladwell, M. (2006). *The tipping point: How little things can make a big difference*. New York, NY: Hachette Digital, Inc.

Goldman, N. (1961). Socio-psychological study of school vandalism. *Crime and Delinquency*, *7*, 221–230.

Goldstein, A. P. (1996). *The psychology of vandalism*. NY: Plenum Press.

Graham, R. (2015). The modern megachurch can't really die (Retrieved from: slate.com).

Gregory, D. E., & Janosik, S. M. (2013). Research on the Clery Act and crime reporting: Its impact on the literature and administrative practice in higher education. In B. Fisher & J. J. Sloan (Eds.), *Campus crime: Legal, social, and policy perspectives* (3rd ed.) (pp. 45–64). Springfield, IL: Charles C. Thomas Publishers.

Griffin, K. A., Nichols, A. H., Perez II, D., & Tuttle, K. D., (2008). Making campus activities and student organizations inclusive for racial/ethnic minorities. In S. R. Harper (Ed.), *Creating inclusive campus environments for cross-cultural learning and student engagement* (pp. 121–138). Washington, DC: NASPA.

Griffith, J. C. (1994). Open space preservation: An imperative for quality campus environments. *Journal of Higher Education, 65*, 645–669.

Gunnings, B. B. (1982). Stress and minority student on a predominantly white campus. *Journal of Non-White Concerns in Personnel and Guidance, 11*, 11–16.

Gustafson, P. E. R. (2001). Meaning of place: Everyday experiences and theoretical conceptualizations. *Journal of Environmental Psychology, 21*, 5–16.

Hage, J. (1980). *Theories of organizations: Forms, process, and transformation*. New York, NY: Wiley.

Hage, J., & Aiken, M. (1970). *Social change in complex organizations*. New York, NY: Random House.

Hall, E. T. (1976). *Beyond culture*. Garden City, NY: Doubleday.

Hall, R. M., & Sandler, B. R. (1982). *The campus climate: A chilly one for women: Report of the project on the status and education of women*. Washington, DC: Association of American Colleges.

Hall, R. M., & Sandler, B. R. (1984). *Out of the classroom: A chilly campus climate for women: Report of the project on the status and education of women*. Washington, DC: Association of American Colleges.

Hancock, E. (1990). Zoos, tunes, and gweeps—A dictionary of campus slang. *Journal of Higher Education, 61*, 98–106.

Hansen, W. B., & Altman, I. (1976). Decorating personal places: A descriptive analysis. *Environment and Behavior, 8*, 491–505.

Harper, S. R. (Ed.). (2008). *Creating inclusive campus environments for cross-cultural learning and student engagement*. Washington, DC: NASPA.

Harper, S. R., & Quaye, S. J. (2009). Beyond sameness, with engagement and outcomes for all. In S. Harper & S. Quaye (Eds.), *Student engagement in higher education: Theoretical perspectives and practical approaches for diverse populations* (pp. 1–15). New York, NY: Routledge.

Harrington, R., & Loffredo, D. A. (2010). MBTI personality type and other factors that relate to preference for online versus face-to-face instruction. *Internet and Higher Education, 13*(1), 89–95.

Hawkins, B. C. (1989). Students on predominantly white campuses: The need for a new commitment. *NASPA Journal, 26*(3), 175–179.

Heilweill, M. (1973). The influence of dormitory architecture on resident behavior. *Environment and Behaviors, 5*, 337–412.

Hemphill, B. O., & LaBlanc, B. H. (Eds.). (2010). *Enough is enough*. Sterling, WV: Stylus.

Henshaw, R. G., Edwards, P. M., & Bagley, E. J. (2011). Use of swivel desks and aisle space to promote interaction in mid-sized college classrooms. *Journal of Learning Spaces, 1*(1). Retrieved from http://libjournal.uncg.edu/ojs/index.php/jls/article/view/277.

Hill, C., & Silva, E. (2005). *Drawing the line: Sexual harassment on campus.* Washington, DC: AAUW Educational Foundation.

Hill, D. C., & Magolda, P. M. (2008). Enacting multicultural and democratic ideals on campus: Challenges and possibilities. In S. R. Harper (Ed.), *Creating inclusive campus environments for cross-cultural learning and student engagement.* (pp. 235–261). Washington, DC: NASPA.

Hodges, T. D., & Clifton, D. O. (2004). Strengths-based development in practice. In P. A. Linley & S. Joseph (Eds.), *International handbook of positive psychology in practice: From research to application* (pp. 256–268). New York, NY: Wiley.

Holland, J. L. (1973). *Making vocational choices: A theory of careers.* Englewood Cliffs, NJ: Prentice Hall, Inc.

Hopkins, R. D. (1994). *The mythical ivory tower: Student perceptions of safety in residence halls* (Unpublished master's thesis). Colorado State University, Fort Collins, CO.

Horowitz, H. L. (1984). *Alma mater: Design and experience in women's colleges from their nineteenth century beginnings to the 1930s.* New York, NY: Knopf.

Horowitz, H. L. (1987). *Campus life: Undergraduate cultures from the end of the eighteenth century to the present.* New York, NY: Knopf.

Hostettler, J. A. (1993). *Amish society* (4th ed.). Baltimore, MD: The Johns Hopkins University Press.

Howard, J. (2008). Design for service: Sociofugal vs. sociopetal space [Blog post]. Retrieved from http://designforservice.wordpress.com/2008/02/09/sociofugal-and-sociopetal-space/

Hu, P. J. H., & Hui, W. (2012). Examining the role of learning engagement in technology-mediated learning and its effects on learning effectiveness and satisfaction. *Decision Support Systems,* 53(4), 782–792.

Hu, S., & Li, S. (Eds.) (2011). Using typological approaches to understand college student experiences and outcomes. *New Directions for Institutional Research, Assessment Supplement 2011.* San Francisco, CA: Jossey-Bass.

Hu, S., & McCormick, A. C. (2012). An engagement-based student typology and its relationship to college outcomes. *Research in Higher Education,* 53(7), 738–754.

Huebner, L. A. (1979). *Redesigning campus environments. New Directions for Student Services, No. 8*. San Francisco, CA: Jossey-Bass.

Huebner, L. A., & Corrazini, J. (1975–1976). Eco-mapping: A dynamic model for intentional campus design. *Student Development Staff Papers*, 6(2), Colorado State University.

Huebner, L. A., & Lawson, J. M. (1990). Understanding and assessing college environments. In D. G. Creamer & Associates (Eds.), *College student development: Theory and practice for the 1990s* (pp. 127–151). Alexandria, VA: American College Personnel Association.

Huerta, M., Cortina, L. M., Pang, J. S., Torges, C. M., & Magley, V. J. (2006). Sex and power in the academy: Modeling sexual harassment in the lives of college women. *Personality and Social Psychology Bulletin, 32*(5), 616–628.

Hunt, D. E., & Sullivan, E. V. (1974). *Between psychology and education*. Hinsdale, IL: Dryden Press.

Inkelas, K. K., Daver, Z. E., Vogt, K. E., & Leonard, J. B. (2007). Living–learning programs and first-generation college students' academic and social transition to college. *Research in Higher education*, 48(4), 403–434.

Internet World Stats. (2014). Usage and population statistics. (Retireved from http://www.internetworldstats.com).

Ithaca College. (2014). Mission statement. (Retrieved from http://www.ithaca.edu/about/mission/).

Jackson, G. S., & Schroeder, C. (1977). Behavioral zoning for stimulation seekers. *Journal of College and University Student Housing*, 7(1), 7–10.

Jackson, J. F., & Terrell, M. C. (Eds.). (2007). *Creating and maintaining safe college campuses: A sourcebook for evaluating and enhancing safety programs*. Sterling, VA: Stylus.

Jang, H., Kang, J. H., Dierenfeldt, R., & Lindsteadt, G. (2014). Weapon possession among college students: A study from a midwestern university. *International Journal of Offender Therapy and Comparative Criminology*, 0306624X14536371. Retrieved from http://ijo.sagepub.com/content/early/2014/06/03/0306624X14536371.abstract.

Janosik, S. M., & Gregory, D. E. (2009). The Clery Act, campus safety, and the perceptions of senior student affairs officers. *Journal of Student Affairs Research and Practice*, 46(2), 499–736.

Jeffery, C. R. (1977). *Crime prevention through environmental design*. Thousand Oaks, CA: Sage.

Jenkins, T. S., & Walton, C. (2008). Student affairs and cultural practice: A framework for implementing culture outside the classroom. In S. R. Harper

(Ed.), *Creating inclusive campus environments for cross-cultural learning and student engagement* (pp. 87–101). Washington, DC: NASPA.

Jin, Q. (2002). Design of a virtual community based interactive learning environment. *Information Sciences, 140*(1), 171–191.

Johnson, D., Soldner, M., Leonard, J., Alvarez, P., Inkelas, K., Rowan-Kenyon, H., & Longerbeam, S. (2007). Examining sense of belonging among first-year undergraduates from different racial/ethnic groups. *Journal of College Student Development, 48*(5), 525–542.

Johnson, L., Adams, S., & Haywood, K. (2011). *The MNC horizon report: 2011 K–12 edition*. Austin, TX: New Media Consortium. Retrieved from http://www.nmc.org/pdf/2011-Horizon-Report-K12.pdf.

Jones, S., Johnson-Yale, C., Millermaier, S., & Perez, F. (2009). U.S. college students' internet use: Race, gender and digital divides. *Journal of Computer-Mediated Communication, 14*, 244–264.

Jones, S. R. (1996). Toward inclusive theory: Disability as social construction. *NASPA Journal, 33*(4), 347–354.

Jones, S. R. (2008). Student resistance to cross-cultural engagement: Annoying distraction or site for transformative learning? In S. R. Harper (Ed.), *Creating inclusive campus environments for cross-cultural learning and student engagement* (pp. 67–85). Washington, DC: NASPA.

Junco, R. (2014). *Engaging students through social media: Evidence-based practices for use in student affairs*. San Francisco, CA: Jossey-Bass.

Junco, R., Heiberger, G., & Loken, E. (2011). The effect of Twitter on college student engagement and grades. *Journal of Computer Assisted Learning, 27*(2), 119–132.

Jung, C. G. (1971). *Psychological types*. Bollingen Series XX. The Collected Works of C. G. Jung, vol. 6. Princeton, NJ: Princeton University Press. (Original work published 1923.)

Kaiser, L. R. (1975). Designing campus environments. *NASPA Journal, 13*, 33–39.

Kaplan, R., Kaplan, S., & Ryan, R. (1998). *With people in mind: Design and management of everyday nature*. Washington, DC: Island Press.

Kaminer, A. (2014). Student-built apps teach colleges a thing or two. *New York Times*, August 27, 2014.

Kaminski, R. J., Koons-Witt, B. A., Thompson, N. S., & Weiss, D. (2010). The impacts of the Virginia Tech and Northern Illinois University shootings on fear of crime on campus. *Journal of Criminal Justice, 38*(1), 88–98.

Kanter, R. M. (1972). *Commitment and community: Communes and utopias in sociological perspective* (Vol. 36). Cambridge, MA: Harvard University Press.

Katel, P. (2011, February 4). Crime on campus: Are colleges doing enough to keep students safe? *CQ Researcher, 21*, 97–120. Retrieved from http://photo.pds.org:5012/cqresearcher/document.php?id=cqresrre2011020409&action=print.

Keller, J. (2007, July 6). No stirrings of pride. *Chronicle of Higher Education: Notes from Academe.*

Kenney, D. R., Dumont, R., & Kenney, G. (2005). *Mission and place: Strengthening learning and community through campus design.* Westport, CT: Praeger.

Keup, J.R. & Stolzenberg, E.B. (2004). Your First College Year Survey: Exploring the Academic and Personal Experiences of First-Year Students. Columbia, SC: University of South Carolina, National Resource Center for the First Year Experience and Students in Transition.

Kilmartin, C. T. (1996, May–June). The white ribbon campaign: Men working to end men's violence against women. *Journal of College Student Development, 37*, 347–8.

Kimbrough, W. K. (2007). Why students beat each other: A developmental perspective for a detrimental crime. In J. F. Jackson & M. C. Terrell (Eds.), *Creating and maintaining safe college campuses: A sourcebook for evaluating and enhancing safety programs* (pp. 58–74). Sterling, VA: Stylus.

King, P. M., & Kitchener, K. S. (1994). *Developing reflective judgment.* San Francisco, CA: Jossey-Bass.

Kinzie, J., & Mulholland, S. (2008). Transforming physical spaces into inclusive multicultural learning environments. In S. R. Harper (Ed.), *Creating inclusive campus environments for cross-cultural learning and student engagement* (pp. 103–120). Washington, DC: NASPA.

Knez, I. (2005). Attachment and identity as related to place and its perceived climate. *Journal of Environmental Psychology, 25*, 207–218.

Knowles, M. S., Holton III, E. F., & Swanson, R. A. (2012). *The adult learner.* New York, NY: Routledge.

Kolb, A. Y., & Kolb, D. A. (2005). Learning styles and learning spaces: Enhancing experiential learning in higher education. *Academy of Management Learning & Education*, 4(2), 193–212.

Kolb, A. Y., & Kolb, D. A. (2012). Kolb's learning styles. In *Encyclopedia of the Sciences of Learning* (pp. 1698–1703). New York, NY: Springer.

Kolb, D. A. (1984). *Experiential learning: Experience as the source of learning and development.* Englewood Cliffs, NJ: Prentice-Hall.

Kopec, D. (2012). *Environmental psychology for design* (2nd Edition). New York: Fairchild Books.

Koss, M. P., Gidycz, C. A., & Wisniewski, N. (1987). The scope of rape: Incidence and prevalence of sexual aggression and victimization in a national survey of higher education students. *Journal of Consulting and Clinical Psychology*, 55(2), 162–170.

Krehbiel, L. E., & Strange, C. C. (1991). Checking of the truth: The case of Earlham College? In G. D. Kuh & J. H. Schuh (Eds.), *The role and contribution of student affairs in involving colleges* (pp. 148–167). Washington, DC: National Association of Student Personnel Administrators.

Krier L., & Thadani D. (2009). *The architecture of community*. Washington, DC: Island Press.

Kuh, G. D. (1996). *Organizational theory*. In S. R. Komives, D. B. Woodard, & Associates (Eds.), *Student services: A handbook for the profession* (pp. 269–294). San Francisco, CA: Jossey-Bass.

Kuh, G. D. (2003). *The National Survey of Student Engagement: Conceptual framework and overview of psychometric properties*. Retrieved from http://nsse.iub.edu/pdf/conceptual_framework_2003.pdf.

Kuh, G. D. (2008). *Excerpt from "High-Impact Educational Practices: What They Are, Who Has Access to Them, and Why They Matter."* Washington, DC: Association of American Colleges and Universities.

Kuh, G. D. (Ed.). (1993). Cultural perspectives in student affairs work. Landham, MD: American College Personnel Association.

Kuh, G. D., & Hall, J. E. (1993). Using cultural perspectives in student affairs. In G. D. Kuh (Ed.), *Cultural perspectives in student affairs work* (pp. 1–20). Lanham, MD: American College Personnel Association.

Kuh, G. D., Hu, S., & Vesper, N. (2000). "They shall be known by what they do": An activities-based typology of college students. *Journal of College Student Development, 41*(2), 228–44.

Kuh, G. D., Kinzie, J., Schuh, J. H., Whitt, E. J., & Associates. (2005). *Student success in college: Creating conditions that matter*. San Francisco, CA: Jossey-Bass.

Kuh, G. D., Schuh, J. H., Whitt, E. J., Andreas, R. E., Lyons, J. W., Strange, C. C., Krehbiel, L. E., & MacKay, K. A. (1991). *Involving colleges: Encouraging student learning and personal development through out-of-class experiences*. San Francisco, CA: Jossey-Bass.

Kuh, G. D., & Whitt, E. J. (1988). The invisible tapestry: Cultures in American colleges and universities. *ASHE-ERIC Higher Education Report Series, No. 1*. Washington, DC: Association for the Study of Higher Education.

Kuk, L., Banning, J. H., & Thomas, D. (2009). Enhancing student organizations as agents for community development and civic engagement. *Journal of Student Affairs, 18*, 98–106.

Kuk, L., Thomas, D., & Banning, J. (2008). Student organizations and their relationship to the institution. *Journal of Student Affairs*, *17*, 9–20.

Kunitz, S., & Haycraft, H. (1938). *American authors 1600–1900*. New York, NY: H.W. Wilson.

Lave, J., & Wenger, E. (1991). *Situated learning: Legitimate peripheral participation.* Cambridge, UK: Cambridge University Press.

Lawless, J. W. (2012). Residence hall design in the success of student learning. Retrieved from http://www.treanorarchitects.com/ news/sector /treanor-architects/2012–01–30/residence-hall-design-success-student -learning/.

Lenning, O. T., Hill, D. M., Saunders, K. P., Solan, A., & Stokes, A. (2013). *Powerful learning communities: A guide to developing student, faculty, and professional learning communities to improve student success and organizational effectiveness*. Sterling, VA: Stylus.

Levine, A., & Dean, D. R. (2012). *Generation on a tightrope: A Portrait of today's college student*. San Francisco, CA: Jossey-Bass.

Levinson, D. J. (1978). The seasons of a man's life. New York, NY: Ballantine.

Levinson, D. J., & Levinson, J. D. (1996). *The seasons of a woman's life*. New York, NY: Alfred A. Knopf.

Levy, J. (2009, May). Then & now: Architecture of community. *Bulletin*, *77*(3), 10.

Lewicka, M. (2011). Place attachment: How far have we come in the last 40 years? *Journal of Environmental Psychology*, *31*, 270–230.

Lewin, K. (1936). Principles of topological psychology. New York, NY: McGraw-Hill.

Lippincott, J., & Greenwell, S. (2011). *7 things you should know about the modern learning commons*. EDUCAUSE. Retrieved from http://www.educause.edu /Resources/7ThingsYouShouldKnowAbouttheMo/227141.

Loftin, R. B. (2014). Message from chancellor Loftin. Retrieved from http:// chancellor.missouri.edu/news/message-from-chancellor-loftin-12–2–14/.

Louis, M. C. (2012). *The Clifton StrengthsFinder and student strengths Development: A review of research*. Omaha, NE: Gallup Organization.

Love, P. G., & Guthrie, V. L. (Eds.). (1999). *Understanding and applying cognitive development theory. New Directions for Student Services, Number* 88 (27). San Francisco, CA: Jossey Bass.

Lowery, J. W. (2007). The legal implications of campus crime for student affairs professionals. In J. F. Jackson & M. C. Terrell (Eds.), *Creating and maintaining safe college campuses: A sourcebook for evaluating and enhancing safety programs* (pp. 205–222). Sterling, VA: Stylus.

Lundberg, C. C. (1985). On the feasibility of cultural intervention in organizations. In P. J. Frost, L. F. Moore, M. R. Louis, C. C. Lundberg, & J. Martin (Eds.), *Organizational culture* (pp. 169–186). Beverly Hills, CA: Sage.

Lyndon, D. (2005). Caring for places: Caring for thought. *Places*, *17*(1), 3.

Lyons, J. (1993). The importance of institutional mission. In M. J. Barr (Ed.), *The Handbook of Student Affairs Administration* (3–15). San Francisco, CA: Jossey-Bass.

McClenney, K. M., & Greene, T. (2005). A tale of two students: Building a culture of engagement in the community college. *About Campus*, *10*(3), 2–7.

McCormick, A. C., Gonyea, R. M., & Kinzie, J. (2013). Refreshing engagement: NSSE at 13. *Change: The Magazine of Higher Learning*, *45*(3), 6–15.

McGill, L. (2011). *Curriculum innovation: Pragmatic approaches to transforming learning and teaching through technologies*. Bristol, UK: JISC.

McGloughlin, C., & Lee, M. J. W. (2010). Listen and learn: A systematic review of the evidence that podcasting supports learning in higher education. In C. Montgomerie & J. Seale (Eds.), *Proceedings of World Conference on Educational Multimedia, Hypermedia and Telecommunications* (pp. 1669–1677). Chesapeake, VA: AAC.

McHaney, R. (2011). *The new digital shoreline: How web 2.0 and millennials are revolutionizing higher education*. Sterling, VA: Stylus.

McMillan, D. W., & Chavis, D. M. (1986). Sense of community: A definition and theory. *Journal of Community Psychology*, *14*, 6–23.

McMullen, S. (2008). US academic libraries: Today's learning commons model. *Librarian Publications*. *Paper 14*. Retrieved from http://docs.rwu.edu/librarypub/14

McPherson, M., Smith-Lovin, L., & Cook, J. M. (2001). Birds of a feather: Homophily in social networks. *Annual Review of Sociology*, *27*, 415–444.

Magolda, P. M. (2000). The campus tour: Ritual and community in higher education. *Anthropology & Education Quarterly*, *31*(1), 24–46.

Magolda, P. M. (2001). What our rituals tell us about community on campus: A look at the campus tour. *About Campus*, *5*(6), 2–8.

Mallory-Hill, S., Preiser, W. F. E., & Watson, G. G. (2012). *Enhancing building performance* (2nd ed.). Hoboken, NJ: Blackwell Publishing, Ltd.

Mandell, J. I. (1981). *The psychological sense of community and the small college campus: A community psychology perspective on the role of deans of students* (Unpublished doctoral dissertation). University of Massachusetts, Amherst, MA.

Manning, K. (2013). *Organizational theory in higher education*. New York, NY: Routledge.

Mark, N. P., & Harris, D. R. (2012). Roommate's race and the racial composition of white college students' ego networks. *Social Science Research, 41*(2), 331–342.

Marsick, V. J., & Watkins, K. E. (2001). Informal and incidental learning. *New Directions for Adult and Continuing Education, No.* 89 (pp. 25–34). San Francisco, CA: Jossey-Bass.

Martin, F., & Ertzberger, J. (2013). Here and now mobile learning: An experimental study on the use of mobile technology. *Computers & Education*, 68, 76–85.

Martin, P. Y., & O'Connor, G. G. (1989). *The social environment: Open systems application*. New York, NY: Longman.

Masland, A. T. (1985). Organizational culture in the study of higher education. *Review of Higher Education*, 8, 157–168.

Maslow, A. H. (1968). *A psychological of being*. New York, NY: D. Van Nostrand Company, Inc.

Maslow, A. H., & Mintz, N. (1956). Effects of those aesthetic surroundings: Initial effects of those aesthetic surroundings upon perceiving "energy" and "well-being" in the faces. *Journal of Psychology*, *41*, 247–254.

Masters, N. T. (2010). "My strength is not for hurting": Men's anti-rape websites and their construction of masculinity and male sexuality. *Sexualities*, *13*(1), 33–46.

Matthews, A. (1997). *Bright college years: Inside the American campus today*. New York, NY: Simon & Schuster.

Matthews, K. E. (2010). Engaging students in their space—designing and managing social learning spaces to enhance student engagement. In *Proceedings of the International Society for the Scholarship of Teaching and Learning Conference*. International Society for the Scholarship of Teaching and Learning Conference, Liverpool, UK, October 19–22.

Matthews, K. E., Adams, P., & Gannaway, D. (2009). The impact of social learning spaces on student engagement. In *Preparing for tomorrow today: The first year experience as foundation: First Year in Higher Education Conference Proceedings*. Townsville, Queensland, Australia.

Matthews, K. E., Andrews, V., & Adams, P. (2011). Social learning spaces and student engagement. *Higher Education Research & Development*, *30*(2), 105–120.

Max-Neef, M. A. (1989). *Human scale development*. New York, NY: Apex Press.

Mehrabian, A. (1981). *Silent messages* (2nd ed.). Belmont, CA: Wadsworth.

Meyer, A., Rose, D., & Gordon, D. (2014). *Universal design for learning: Theory and practice*. Wakefield, MA: CAST Professional Publishing.

Miami University. (2014). Mission statement. (Retrieved from http://www.miami.edu/index.php/about_us/leadership/mission_statement/).

Miami University Center for Enhancement of Learning, Teaching and University Assessment. (2014). What is a faculty and professional learning community? (Retrieved from: http://www.units.miamioh.edu/flc/whatis.php).

Michelson, W. (1970). *Man and his urban environment: A sociological approach.* Reading, MA: Addison-Wesley.

Miller, T. E., Bender, B. E., & Schuh, J. (2005). *Promoting reasonable expectations: Aligning student and institutional views of the college experience*. San Francisco, CA: Jossey–Bass.

Miller, T. E., & Sorochty, R. W. (2015). *Risk management in student affairs*. San Francisco, CA: Jossey-Bass.

Moffatt, M. (1989). *Coming of age in New Jersey: College and American culture.* New Brunswick, NJ: Rutgers University Press.

Moore, R. M. (2004). The rising tide: "Branding" in the academic marketplace. *Change: The Magazine of Higher Learning*, 36(3), 56–61.

Moos, R. H. (1974). *Family environment scale-Form R*. Palto Alto, CA: Consulting Psychologist Press.

Moos, R. H. (1979). *Evaluating educational environments*. San Francisco, CA: Jossey-Bass.

Moos, R. H. (1986). *The human context: Environmental determinants of behavior.* Malabar, FL: Robert E. Krieger Publishing Company.

Moos, R. H. (1994a). *The social climate scales: A user's guide*. Palo Alto, CA: Consutling Psychologists Press.

Moos, R. H. (1994b). Work environment scale manual, 3rd ed., Palo Alto, CA: Consulting Psychologists Press.

Moos, R. H., & Gerst, M. (1988). *The university residence environment scale manual.* 2nd ed. Palo Alto, CA: Consulting Psychologists Press.

Moos, R. H., & Trickett, E. J. (1974). *Classroom environment scale: Manual.* Palo Alto, CA: Consulting Psychologists Press.

Moran, E., & Gonyea, T. (2003). *The influence of academically-focused peer interaction on college students' development* (ED478773). Washington, DC: United States Department of Education/ERIC.

Morrill, C., Snow, D. A., & White, C. H. (Eds.). (2005). *Together alone: Personal relationships in public places*. Berkeley, CA: University of California Press.

Murray, H. (1938). *Exploration in personality*. New York, NY: Oxford University Press.

Museus, S. (2008). Focusing on institutional fabric: Assessing campus cultures to enhance cross-cultural engagement. In S. R. Harper (Ed.), *Creating inclusive campus environments for cross-cultural learning and student engagement* (pp. 205–234). Washington, DC: NASPA.

Myers, I. B. (1980). *Gifts differing*. Palo Alto, CA: Consulting Psychologists Press.

Myers, I. B., & McCaulley, M. H. (1985). *Manual: A guide to the development and use of the Myers-Briggs Type Indicator*. Palo Alto, CA: Consulting Psychologists Press.

Narum, J. L. (Ed.). (2013). *A guide planning for assessment 21st century spaces for 21st century learners*. Washington, DC: Learning Spaces Collaboratory.

Nasar, J. L., & Fisher, B. (1992). Design for vulnerability: Uses and reactions to fear of crime. *Social and Social Research*, *76*(2), 48–58.

National Institute of Education. (1984). *Involvement in learning*. Washington, DC: National Institute of Education.

Newbrough, J. R., & Chavis, D. M. (1986). Psychological sense of community. *Journal of Community Psychology*, *14*, 3–4.

Newman, J. H. (1982). *The idea of a university*. Notre Dame, IN: University of Notre Dame Press.

Newman, O. (1972). *Defensible space: Crime prevention through urban design*. New York, NY: Collier Books.

Nicoletti, J., Spencer-Thomas, S., & Bollinger, C. M. (Eds.). (2010). *Violence goes to college: The authoritative guide to prevention and intervention*. Springfield, IL: Charles C. Thomas Publisher.

Nock, A. J. (1943). *Memories of a superfluous man*. New York, NY: Harper & Brothers.

Oakland Community College. (2014). 2014 Mission statement. (Retrieved from https://www.oaklandcc.edu/diversity/Mission.aspx).

Oblinger, D. (2006). *Learning spaces* (Vol. 2). Washington, DC: Educause.

O'Callaghan, (2007). A growing concern: Sexual violence against women on college campuses. In J. F. Jackson & M. C. Terrell (Eds.), *Creating and maintaining safe college campuses: A sourcebook for evaluating and enhancing safety programs* (pp. 99–134). Sterling, VA: Stylus.

Okoli, D. T. (2013). *Sense of place and student engagement among undergraduate students at a major public research university* (Unpublished doctoral dissertation). Colorado State University, Fort Collins, CO.

Oldenburg, R. (1989). *The great good place*. New York, NY: Marlowe & Company.

Oldenburg, R. (1997). Making college a great place to talk. In G. Keller (Ed.), *The best of planning for higher education*. Ann Arbor, MI: Society for College and University Planning.

Osmond, H. (1957). Function as the basis of psychiatric ward design. *Mental Hospitals (Architectural Supplement)*, 8, 23–29.

Pablant, P., & Baxter, J. C. (1975). Environmental correlates of school vandalism. *Journal of the American Institute of Planners, 41*, 270–279.

Pace, C. R. (1969). College and university environment scales: Technical manual. 2nd ed. Princeton, N.J.: Educational Testing Service.

Pace, C. (1990). *The undergraduates: A report of their activities and progress in college in the 1980s.* Los Angeles, CA: Center for the Study of Evaluation, University of California.

Pace, C. R. (1984). *Measuring the quality of college student experience.* Los Angeles, CA: Higher Education Research Institute, The University of California.

Pace, C. R., & Kuh, G. D. (1998). *College Student Experiences Questionnaire: CSEQ.* Bloomington, IN: Indiana University Center for Postsecondary Research and Planning, School of Education.

Pace, C. R., & Stern, G. G. (1958). An approach to the measurement of psychological characteristics of college environments. *Journal of Educational Psychology, 49*, 269–277.

Painter, S., Fournier, J., Grape, C., Grummon, P., Morelli, J., Whitmer, S., & Cevetello, J. (2013). *Research on learning space design: Present state, future directions* (Report from the Recipients of the 2012 Perry Chapman Prize). Published by the Society of College and University Planning. Retrieved from http://www.scup.org.

Palmer, C. J. (1996). Violence and other forms of victimization in residence halls: Perspectives of resident assistants. *Journal of College Student Development, 37*(3), 268–277.

Palmer, P. J. (1977). *A place called community.* Wallingford, PA: Pendle Hill.

Palmer, P. J. (1987, September–October). Community, conflict, and ways of knowing. *Change, 19*(5), 20–25.

Palmer, P. J. (1998). *The courage to teach: Exploring the inner landscape of a teacher's life.* San Francisco, CA: Jossey-Bass.

Palmer, P. J. (2002). Afterword: The quest for community in higher education. In W. M. McDonald (Ed.), *Creating campus community: In search of Ernest Boyer's legacy* (pp. 179–192). San Francisco, CA: Jossey-Bass.

Palmer, P. J., Zajonc, A., & Scribner, M. (2010). *The heart of higher education: A call to renewal.* San Francisco, CA: Jossey-Bass.

Parker, I. (2012, *February* 6). The story of a suicide. New Yorker.

Parks, S. D. (2000). *Big questions worthy dreams: Mentoring young adults in their search for meaning, purpose, and faith.* San Francisco, CA: Jossey-Bass.

Parsons, T. (1960). *Structure and process in modern societies.* Glencoe, IL: Free Press.

Pascarella, E. T. (1985). College environmental influences on learning and cognitive development: A critical review and synthesis. In J. C. Smart (Ed.), *Higher education: Vol. 1. Handbook of theory and research* (pp. 1–61). New York, NY: Agathon Press.

Pascarella, E. T., & Terenzini, P. T. (1991). *How college affects students.* San Francisco, CA: Jossey-Bass.

Pascarella, E. T., & Terenzini, P. T. (2005). *How college affects students* (Vol. 2). San Francisco, CA: Jossey-Bass.

Passini, R. (2002). Wayfinding research and design. In J. Frascara (Ed.), *Design and the Social Sciences: Making Connections* (pp. 1–8). London, UK: Taylor & Francis.

Patton, L. D. (Ed.). (2010). *Culture centers in higher education: Perspectives on identity, theory, and practice.* Sterling, VA: Stylus.

Patton, L. D., & Hannon, M. D. (2008). Collaboration for cultural programming: Engaging culture centers, multicultural affairs, and student activities offices as partners. In S. R. Harper (Ed.). *Creating inclusive campus environments for cross-cultural learning and student engagement* (pp. 139–154). Washington, DC: NASPA.

Pearson Learning Solutions. (2013). The *student mobile device survey 2013: National report on college students.* New York, NY: Pearson.

Peck, M. S. (1987). *The different drum.* New York, NY: Simon & Schuster.

Perrotti, J. A. (2007). The role of campus police and security department in the 21st century: An essay based on 30 years of experience. In J. F. Jackson & M. C. Terrell (Eds.), *Creating and maintaining safe college campuses: A sourcebook for evaluating and enhancing safety programs* (pp. 173–187). Sterling, VA: Stylus.

Perry, W. G. (1970). *Forms of intellectual and ethical development in the college years: A scheme.* New York, NY: Holt, Rinehart, & Winston.

Pew Research Center. (2014, August). Pew Research Internet Project: Mobile technology fact sheet. Retrieved from http://www.pewinternet.org/fact-sheets/mobile-technology-fact-sheet/.

Pew Research Center. (2014). World wide web timeline. Retrieved from http://www.pewinternet.org/2014/03/11/world-wide-web-timeline/.

Pew Research Center. (2014). Digital life in 2025. Retrieved from http://www.pewinternet.org /2014/03/11/digital-life-in-2025/.

Phelps, L.A. (1990). High-rise residence halls: A response to the uniqueness of these buildings. Unpublished master's thesis, Colorado State University, Fort Collins, CO.

Phillips, G. H. (1982). *Rural vandalism.* Washington, DC: National Institute of Justice Vandalism Prevention Workshop.

Pike, G. R., & Kuh, G. D. (2005). A typology of student engagement for American colleges and universities. *Research in Higher Education*, 46, 185–210.

Pittenger, D. J. (1993). The utility of the Myers-Briggs Type Indicator. *Review of Educational Research*, 63, 467–488.

Pittenger, D. J. (2005). Cautionary comments regarding the Myers-Briggs Type Indicator. *Consulting Psychology Journal: Practice and Research*, 57(3), 210.

Pocket Gamer.biz. (2014). Apps store metric summary report (Retrieved from http://www.pocketgamer.biz/metrics/app-store/).

Preiser, W. F. E. (1989). *Building evaluation*. New York, NY: Springer.

Prensky, M. (2001). Digital natives, digital immigrants. *On the Horizon*, 9(5), 1–6.

Price, D. (2005). *Learning communities and student success in postsecondary education: A background paper*. New York, NY: Manpower Demonstration Research Corporation.

Price, J. L. (1972). *Handbook of organizational measurement*. Lexington, MA: Heath.

Progressive Education Network. (2014). History and principles (Retrieved from http://progressiveeducationnetwork.com/history/).

Proshansky, H. M., Fabian, A. K., & Kaminoff, R. (1983). Place-identity: Physical world socialization of the self. *Journal of Environmental Psychology*, 3(1), 57–83.

Provost, J. A., & Anchors, S. (1987). *Applications of the Myers-Briggs type indicator in higher education*. Palo Alto, CA: Consulting Psychology Press.

Prown, J. D. (1982). Mind in matter: An Introduction to material culture theory and method. *Winterthur Portfolio*, 17(1), 1–19.

Quinn, C. (2000, Fall). mLearnings: Mobile, wireless, in-your-pocket learning. *LineZine*. Retrieved from http://www.linezine.com/2.1/features/cqmmwiyp.htm.

Randall, M., & Wilson, G. (2009). Making it my street: The Bond University "street" area. In *Learning Spaces in Higher Education: Positive Outcomes by Design. Proceedings of the Next Generation Learning Spaces 2008 Colloquium*, October 1–2 (pp. 107–110). University of Queensland, Brisbane, Australia.

Rankin, S. R. (2005). Campus climates for sexual minorities. *New Directions for Student Services*, Number 111 (pp. 17–23). San Francisco, CA: Jossey-Bass.

Rankin, S. R., Millar, E. A. R., & Matheis, C. (2007). Safe campuses for student: Systemic transformation through re(a)wakened senior leaders. In J. F. Jackson & M. C. Terrell (Eds.), *Creating and maintaining safe college campuses: A sourcebook for evaluating and enhancing safety programs* (pp. 75–98). Sterling, VA: Stylus.

Rapoport, A. (1982). *The meaning of the built environment.* Thousand Oaks, CA: Sage Publications.

Rapoport, A. (1994). A critical look at the concept of "place." *National Geographical Journal of India, 40*, 31–45.

Rapoport, A. (2005). *Culture, architecture, and design.* Chicago, IL: Locke Science Publishing Company.

Reason, R. D., & Lutovsky, B. R. (2007). You are not alone: Resources for the college administrator. In J. F. Jackson & M. C. Terrell (Eds.), *Creating and maintaining safe college campuses: A sourcebook for evaluating and enhancing safety programs* (pp. 241–260). Sterling, VA: Stylus.

Reeve, J. R., & Kassabaum, D. G. (1997). A sense of place master plan. Linking mission and place. *1997 APPA Proceedings*, 219–228.

Regoeczi, W. (2008). Crowding in context: An examination of the differential responses of men and women to high-density living environments. *Journal of Health and Social Behavior, 49*, 254–268.

Rendon, L. I. (1994). Validating culturally diverse students: Toward a new model of learning and student development. *Innovative Higher Education, 19*(1), 33–51.

Renn, K.A. (2004). *Mixed race students in college: The ecology of race, identity, and community on campus.* Albany, NY: State University of New York Press.

Renn, K. A., & Arnold. (2003). Reconceptualizing research on college student peer culture. *Journal of Higher Education, 74*(3), 261–291.

Renn, K. A., & Reason, R. D. (2012a). *College students in the United States: Characteristics, experiences, and outcomes.* San Francisco, CA: Jossey-Bass.

Renn, K. A., & Reason, R. D. (2012b). College environments. In K. A. Renn & R. D. Reason, *College students in the United States: Characteristics, experiences, and outcomes* (pp. 82–113). San Francisco, CA: Jossey-Bass.

Rheingold, H. (1991). *Virtual reality: Exploring the brave new technologies.* New York, NY: Simon & Schuster.

River City Project. (2014). Retrieved from http://muve.gse.harvard.edu/ rivercityproject/index.html.

Rocconi, L. M. (2011). The impact of learning communities on first year students' growth and development in college. *Research in Higher Education, 52*(2), 178–193.

Rodger, S., Johnson, A., & Wakabayashi, P. (2005). The impact of residence design on freshman outcomes: Dormitories versus suite-style residences. *Canadian Journal of Higher Education, 35*(3), 83–99.

Rodgers, R. F. (1980). Theories underlying student development. In D. G. Creamer (Ed.), *Student development in higher education: Theories, practices and future.* (ACPA Media Publications, No. 27). Alexandria, VA: ACPA Media.

Rodgers, R. F. (1990). Recent theory and research underlying student development. In D. G. Creamer & Associates (Eds.), *College student development: Theory and practice for the 1990s* (pp. 27–29). Alexandria, VA: American College Personnel Association.

Rodgers, R. F. (1991). Using theory in practice in student affairs. In T. K. Miller, R. B. Winston, Jr., & Associates (Eds.), *Administration and leadership in student affairs: Actualizing student development in higher education* (pp. 203–251). Muncie, IN: Accelerated Development.

Rose, D. H., Harbour, W. S., Johnston, C. S., Daley, S. G., & Abarbanell, L. (2006). Universal design for learning in postsecondary education: Reflections on principles and their application. *Journal of Postsecondary Education and Disability, 19*(2), 135–151.

Rosenberg, M., & McCullough, B. C. (1981). Mattering: Inferred significance and mental health. *Research in Community and Mental Health, 2*, 163–182.

Rubin, N. (2010). *Creating a user-centric learning environment with Campus Pack personal learning spaces.* PLS Webinar, Learning Objects Community. Retrieved from http://community.learningobjects.com/Users/Nancy.Rubin/Creating_a _User-Centric_Learning.

Sandeen, A., & Rhatigan, J. J. (1990). New pressures for social responsiveness and accountability. In M. J. Barr & M. L. Upcraft (Eds.), *New Futures for Student Affairs* (pp. 98–113). San Francisco, CA: Jossey-Bass.

Sanford, N. (1966). *Self and society: Social change and individual development.* New York, NY: Atherton Press.

Sanoff, H. (2000). *Community participation methods in design and planning.* New York, NY: John Wiley & Sons.

Saunders, D. R. (1969). A factor analytic study of the AI and CCI. *Multivariate Behavioral Research, 4*, 329–346.

Scannell, L., & Gifford, R. (2014). Comparing the theories of interpersonal and place attachment. In L. Manzo & P. Devine-Wright (Eds.). *Place attachment: Advances in theory, methods and research* (pp. 23–36). New York, NY: Routledge.

Schein, E. H. (1985). *Organizational culture and leadership.* San Francisco, CA: Jossey-Bass.

Schein, E. H. (1992). *Organizational culture and leadership* (2nd ed.). San Francisco, CA: Jossey-Bass.

Schlossberg, N. K. (1989). Marginality and mattering: Key issues in building community. *New Directions for Student Development Services*, 48 (pp. 5–15). San Francisco, CA: Jossey-Bass.

Schlossberg, N. K., Lynch, A., & Chickering, A. W. (1989). *Improving higher education environments for adults*. San Francisco, CA: Jossey-Bass.

Schneekloth, L. H., & Shibley, R. G. (1995). *Placemaking: The art and practice of building communities*. New York, NY: John Wiley & Sons, Inc.

Schroeder, C.C. (1978–1979). Territoriality: Conceptual and methodological issues for residence educators. *Journal of College and University Student Housing*, 8, 9–15.

Schroeder, C. C. (1993). Creating residence life programs with student development goals. In R. B. Winston, Jr., S. Anchors, & Associates (Eds.), *Student housing and residential life* (pp. 517–534). San Francisco, CA: Jossey-Bass.

Schroeder, C. C. (1994). Developing learning communities. In C. C. Schroeder, P. Mable, & Associates (Eds.), *Residence halls and the college experience: Past and present*. San Francisco, CA: Jossey-Bass.

Schuh, J. (1991). Making a large university feel small: The Iowa State University story. In G. D. Kuh & J. H. Schuh (Eds.), *The role and contribution of student affairs in involving colleges* (pp. 30–41). Washington, DC: NASPA.

Schuh, J. H. (1980). Housing. In W. H. Morrill, J. C. Hurst, & E. R. Oetting (Eds.), *Dimensions for intervention for student development*. (pp. 189–205). New York, NY: Wiley & Sons.

Schuh, J. H. (1993). Fiscal pressures on higher education and student affairs. In M. J. Barr (Ed.), *The handbook of student affairs administration* (pp. 49–68). San Francisco, CA: Jossey-Bass.

Schuh, J. H., Andreas, R. E., & Strange, C. C. (1991). Students at metropolitan universities: Viewing involvement through different lenses. *Metropolitan University*, 2(3), 64–74.

Scott-Webber, L., Strickland, A., & Kapitula, L. R. (2013). Built environments impact behaviors: Results of an active learning post-occupancy evaluation. *Planning for Higher Education Journal*, *42*(1), 1–12.

Seeger, M. A. (1994). *Women's climate study: A report to the Grand Valley campus community*. Allendale, MI: Grand Valley State University, Academic Resources and Special Programs.

Seligman, M. E. P., & Csikszentmihalyi, M. (2000). Positive psychology: An introduction. *American Psychologist*, *55*(1), 5–14.

Selznick, P. (1992). *The moral commonwealth: Social theory and the promise of community*. Berkeley, CA: University of California Press.

Sheehy, K. (2014). 5 must-download apps for college students. U.S. News and World Report: Education. (Retrieved from http://www.usnews.com/education/best-colleges/articles/2014/08/21/5-must-download-apps-for-college-students?int=993008.

Sipple, S., & Lightner, R. (2013). *Developing faculty learning communities at two-year colleges: Collaborative models to improve teaching and learning*. Sterling, VA: Stylus.

Skinner, B. F. (1953). *Science and human behavior*. New York, NY: Simon and Schuster.

Sköld, O. (2011). The effects of virtual space on learning: A literature review. *First Monday*, *17*(1). Retrieved from http://journals.uic.edu/ojs/index.php/fm/article/view/3496.

Sloan III, J. J., & Fisher, B. S. (2010). *The dark side of the ivory tower: Campus crime as a social problem*. Cambridge, UK: Cambridge University Press.

Smart, J. C., Feldman, K. A., & Ethington, C. A. (2000). *Academic disciplines: Holland's theory and the study of college students and faculty*. Nashville, TN: Vanderbilt University Press.

Smith, A., Rainie, L., & Zickuhr, K. (2011). *College students and technology*. Pew Research Internet & American Life Project. Retrieved from http://www.pewinternet.org/2011/07/19/college-students-and-technology/.

Smith, B. L., & MacGregor, J. (2009). Learning communities and the quest for quality. *Quality Assurance in Education*, *17*(2), 118–139.

Smith, B. L., MacGregor, J., Matthews, R.S., & Gabelnick, F. (2004). *Learning communities: Reforming undergraduate education*. San Francisco, CA: Jossey-Bass.

Smith, M. C. (1988). *Coping with crime on campus*. New York, NY: American Council on Education and Macmillan.

Smith, M. C., & Fossey, R. (1995). *Crime on campus: Legal issues and campus administration*. Phoenix, AZ: American Council on Education and Oryx Press.

Sommer, R. (1978). *Personal space: The behavioral basis of design*. Englewood Cliffs, NJ: Prentice Hall.

Spitzberg, I. J., Jr., & Thorndike, V. V. (1992). *Creating community on college campuses*. Albany, NY: State University of New York Press.

Stantasiero, E. (2002). The "third place": Essential for campuses and for communities. *Lawlor Review*, Fall, 10–13.

Staats, H. (2012). Restorative environments. In S. Clayton (Ed.), *The Oxford handbook of environmental and conservation psychology* (pp. 276–294). Oxford, UK: Oxford University Press.

Stearns, E., Buchmann, C., & Bonneau, K. (2009). Interracial friendships in the transition to college: Do birds of a feather flock together once they leave the nest? *Sociology of Education*, 82(2), 173–195.

Stern, G. (1970). *People in context: Measuring person-environment congruence in education and industry*. New York: Wiley & Sons.

Stern, R. A. (1986). *Pride of place: Building the American dream*. New York, NY: Houghton Mifflin.

Stevens, D., & Kitchenham, A. (2011). An analysis of mobile learning in education, business and medicine. In A. Kitchenham (Ed.), *Models for interdisciplinary mobile learning: Delivering information to students* (pp. 1–25). Hershey, PA: IGI Global Publication.

Stewart, J. D., & Schuh, J. H. (2007). Exemplar programs and procedures: Best practices in public safety. In J. F. L. Jackson & M. C. Terrell (Eds.), *Creating and maintaining safe college campuses* (pp. 223–240). Sterling, VA: Stylus.

Stockdale, S. (2011). *Muraling myths: A research prospectus*. Retrieved from http://thisisnotthat.com/wordpress/2011/muraling-myths-a-research-prospectus/.

Strange, C. (2010). Theoretical foundations of student success. In D. Cox & C. Strange (Eds.) *Achieving student success: Effective student services in Canadian higher education* (pp. 18–30). Montreal, Quebec: McGill Queen's University Press.

Strange, C. C. (1983). Human development theory and administrative practice in student affairs: Ships passing in the daylight? *NASPA Journal*, *21*, 2–8.

Strange, C. C. (1991a). Emergence of a metroversity: The university of Louisville case. In George D. Kuh & John H. Schuh (Eds.), *The role and contribution of student affairs in involving colleges* (pp. 72–89). Washington, DC: NASPA.

Strange, C. C. (1991b). Managing college environments: Theory and practice. In T. K. Miller, R. B. Winston, Jr., & Associates (Eds.), *Administration and leadership in student affairs: Actualizing student development in student affairs* (2nd ed.) (pp. 159–199). Muncie, IN: Accelerated Development, Inc.

Strange, C. C. (1993). Theories and concepts of campus living environments. In R. B. Winston, Jr., S. Anchors, and Associates (Eds.), *Student housing and residential life: A handbook for the professional committed to student development goals* (pp. 134–166). San Francisco, CA: Jossey-Bass.

Strange, C. C. (1994). Student development: The evolution and status of an essential idea. *Journal of College Student Development*, 35(6), 399–412.

Strange, C. C. (2000). Creating environments of ability. In H. Belch, *Serving students with disabilities*. *New directions in student services, 91* (pp. 19–30). San Francisco, CA: Jossey-Bass.

Strange, C. C. (2014, June). *Navigating campus spaces to promote engagement: It's about bricks and stones!* Presentation at the Canadian Association of College and University Student Services Annual Conference, Halifax, NS.

Strange, C. C., & Banning, J. H. (2001). *Educating by design: Creating colleges and universities that work.* San Francisco, CA: Jossey-Bass.

Strange, C. C., & Hagan, H. (1998). Benedictine values and building campus community. *The Cresset: A Review of Literature, Arts and Public Affairs, Special Lilly Issue*, 5–12.

Strange, C. C., & Hannah, D. (1994, March). *The learning university: A model for the twenty-first century.* Paper presented at the meeting of the American College Personnel Association, Indianapolis, IN.

Strange, C. C., & King, P. M. (1990). The professional practice of student development. In D. Creamer & Associates (Eds.), *College student development: Theory and practice for the 1990s* (American College Personnel Association Media Publication No. 49, (pp. 9–24). Alexandria, VA: American College Personnel Association.

Sturner, W. F. (1972). Environmental code: Creating a sense of place on the college campus. *The Journal of Higher Education, 43*(2), 97–109.

Sucher, D. (1995). *City comforts: How to build an urban village.* Seattle, WA: City Comfort Press.

Sugerman, D., & Hotaling, G. (1989). Dating violence: Prevalence, context and risk markers. In M. Priog-Good & J. Stets (Eds.), *Violence in dating relationships: Emerging social issues* (pp. 3–32). New York, NY: Praeger.

Taming campus vandals. (1980). *American School and University, 53*(2), 44–45, 48.

Territo, L. (1983). Campus rape: Determining liability. *Trial, 19*, 100–103.

Thang, D. C. L., & Tan, B. L. B. (2003). Linking consumer perception to preference of retail stores: An empirical assessment of the multi-attributes of store image. *Journal of Retailing and Consumer Services, 10*, 193–200.

Thayer-Bacon, B. J., & Bacon, C. S. (1998). *Philosophy applied to education: Nurturing a democratic community in the classroom.* Upper Saddle River, NJ: Merrill.

Thelin, J. R., & Yankovich, J. (1987). Bricks and mortar: Architecture and the study of higher education. In J. C. Smart (Ed.), *Higher education: Handbook of theory and research* (Vol. 3) (pp. 57–83). New York, NY: Agathon Press.

Thomas, D. F. (2004). Toward an understanding of place building in communities (Unpublished doctoral dissertation). Colorado State University, Fort Collins, CO.

Thomas, D. F., & Cross, J. (2007). Organizations as place builders. *Journal of Behavioral and Applied Management*, 9(1), 33–61.

Thornburg, D. D. (2001). Campfires in cyberspace: Primordial metaphors for learning in the 21st century. *Education at a Distance*, *15*(6), 1–10.

Thornton, C. H., & Jaeger, A. J. (2007, March–April). *The ceremonies and symbols of citizenship*. *About Campus*, 15–20.

Tierney, W. G. (1993). *Building communities of difference: Higher education in the twenty-first century*. Westport, CT: Bergin & Garvey.

Tinto, V. (2003). Learning better together: The impact of learning communities on student success. *Higher Education Monograph Series*, *2003*(1), 1–8. Higher Education Program, School of Education, Syracuse University. http://soeweb.syr.edu/academics/grad/higher_education/Copy%20of%20Vtinto/Files/LearningBetterTogether.pdf

Toffler, A. (1970). *Future shock*. New York, NY: Random House.

Treanor Architects (2011). *Survey results: What to watch in 2012 & beyond*. Results of Treanor Architects' Survey on Student Life Facility Trends. Retrieved from http://treanorarchitects.com.

Tribe, C. (1982). *Profile of three theories: Erikson, Maslow, Piaget*. Dubuque, IA: Kendal/Hunt.

Troyer, D. (2005). Imagine if we could start over: Designing a college from scratch. *About Campus*, *10*(4), 4–9.

Turner, P. V. (1995). *Campus: An American planning tradition*. Cambridge, MA: MIT Press.

University of Arizona Campus Health Service (2010). Health & Wellness Survey Data [Powerpoint slides]. Author: Salafsky, D., Pring, L. Vaughan, N. D., Cleveland-Innes, M., & Garrison, D. R. (2014). *Teaching in blended learning environments*. Edmonton, AB: Athabasca University Press.

Upcraft, M. L., & Schuh, J. H. (1996). *Assessment in student affairs: A guide for practitioners*. San Francisco, CA: Jossey-Bass.

U.S. Department of Education. (2012). Campus safety and security data (Retrieved from http://www.ope.ed.gov/security/).

Van Der Werf, M. (2014). MOOCs haven't killed higher ed: Will online learning finish the job? (Retrieved from http://collegeof2020.com/moocs-havent-killed-higher-ed-will-online-learning-finish-the-job).

Vaughan, N. D., Cleveland-Innes, M., & Garrison, D. R. (2013). Teaching in blended learning environments. Edmonton, AB: Athabasca University Press.

Vescio, V., Ross, D., & Adams, A. (2008). A review of research on the impact of professional learning communities on teaching practice and student learning. *Teaching and Teacher Education*, *24*(1), 80–91.

Vinu, P., Sherimon, P., & Krishnan, R. (2011). Towards pervasive mobile learning–the vision of 21st century. *Procedia-Social and Behavioral Sciences, 15*, 3067–3073.

Virginia Tech Division of Student Affairs Housing and Residence Life. (2014). Living learning communities (Retrieved from http://www.housing.vt.edu/llc/ index.html).

Vye, C., Scholljegerdes, K., & Welch, I. (2007). *Under pressure and overwhelmed.* Westport, CT: Prager.

Walsh, W. B. (1973). *Theories of person-environment interaction: Implications for the college student.* Iowa City, IA: American College Testing Program.

Wang, F., & Burton, J. K. (2013). Second life in education: A review of publications from its launch to 2011. *British Journal of Educational Technology, 44*(3), 357–371.

Warren, R. L., & Lyon, L. (Eds.). (1983). *New perspectives on the American community.* Homewood, IL: Dorsey Press.

Warsaw, R. (1988). *I never called it rape.* New York, NY: Harper & Row.

Weber, M. (1947). *The theory of social and economic organization.* (A. M. Henderson & Talcott Parsons, Trans.). Glencoe, IL: Free Press.

Webopedia. (2014). Web 2.0 (Retrieved from http://www.webopedia.com/TERM/W/Web_2_point_0.html).

Weinmayer, V. M. (1969). Vandalism by design: A critique. *Landscape Architecture, 59*, 286.

Wells, R. L. (1996). *Leadership for community: A case study of individuals perceived as creators and maintainers of a psychological sense of community in a university* (Unpublished doctoral dissertation). Temple University, Philadelphia, PA.

Western Interstate Commission for Higher Education (1973). *The ecosystem model: Designing campus environments.* Boulder, CO: Author.

Whitaker, L. C., & Pollard, J. W. (Eds.). (1993). *Campus violence: Kinds, causes, and cures.* New York, NY: Haworth Press.

Whitt, E. J. (1993). Making the familiar strange: Discovering culture. In G. D. Kuh (Ed.), *Using cultural perspectives in student affairs* (pp. 81–94). Alexandria, VA: ACPA Media.

Wicker, A. W. (1973). Undermanning theory and research: Implications for the study of psychological and behavioral effects of excess populations. *Representative Research in Social Psychology, 4*, 184–206.

Wicker, A. W. (1984). *An introduction to ecological psychology.* Cambridge, UK: Cambridge University Press.

Widick, C., Knefelkamp, L., & Parker, C. (1975). The counselor as developmental instructor. *Counselor Education and Supervision, 14*, 286–296.

Wikipedia. (2014). Progressive education (Retrieved from http://en.wikipedia.org/wiki/Progressive_education).

Wilson, G., & Randall, M. (2012). The implementation and evaluation of a new learning space: a pilot study. *Research in Learning Technology, 20*, 1–17.

Wilson, R. G., Lasala, J. M., & Sherwood, P. C. (2009). *Thomas Jefferson's academical village: The creation of an architectural masterpiece*. Charlottesville, VA: University of Virginia Press.

Winston, R. B., Jr., Bledsoe, T., Goldstein, A. R., Wiseby, M. E., Street, J. L., Brown, S. R., Goyen, K. D., & Rounds, L. E. (1997). Describing the climate of student organizations: The student organization environment scales. *Journal of College Student Development, 38*, 417–427.

Winston, R. B., Jr., Vahala, M. E., Nichols, E. C., Gillis, M. E., Wintrow, M., & Rome, K. D. (1994). A measure of college classroom climate: The college classroom environment scales. *Journal of College Student Development, 35*, 11–18.

Zeisel, J. (1976). Stopping school property damage. *CEFP Journal, 15*, 6–11, 18–21.

Zeisel, J. (2006). *Inquiry by design: Environment/behavior/neuroscience in architecture, interiors, landscape, and planning*. New York, NY: W.W. Norton & Company.

Zhao, C. M., Gonyea, R. M., & Kuh, G. D. (2003, May). *The psychographic typology: Toward higher resolution research on college students*. Paper presented at the Annual Forum of the Association for Institutional Research, Tampa, FL.

Zhao, C., & Kuh, G. (2004). Adding value: Learning communities and student engagement. *Research in Higher Education, 45*(2), 115–138.

Zimbardo, P. G. (1969). The Human Choice: Individuation, reason, and order versus deindividuation, impulse, and chaos. In W. J. Arnold & D. Devine (Eds.), *Nebraska Symposium on Education* (pp. 237–307). Lincoln, NE: University of Nebraska Press.

Zimmerman, E. (2014). A social network that's just for college students. New York Times (February 6). Retrieved from boss.blogs.nytimes.com/2014/ … /a-social-network-thats-just-for-college-s …

Zimmerman, B. J. (2000). Attainment of self-regulation: A social cognitive perspective. In M. Boekaerts, P. Pintrich, & M. Zeidner (Eds.), *Self-regulation: Theory, research, and applications* (pp. 13–39). Orlando, FL: Academic Press.

Zipp, Y. (2013). Western Michigan University to redesign campus living around "neighborhoods" by 2015. Retrieved from: retrieved from http://www.mlive.com/news/kalamazoo/index.ssf/2013/ 07/western_michigan_university_to_44.html.

Name Index

A

Abes, E. S., 281
Abras, C., 251
Adams, A., 233
Adams, P., 31, 35
Adams, S., 257
Adler, R. B., 15, 17
Aiken, M., 88, 89, 90, 91, 92, 94, 97, 99, 100, 101, 204, 292
Al-Sallal, K. A., 44
Altman, I., 16
Amar, A. F., 154
Anchors, S., 57
Anderson, E., 62, 248, 285
Anderson, P., 17
Andrews, V., 31
Antonacci, D. M., 261
Arao, B., 171
Arnold, K. D., 274, 279, 281, 289, 295
Arthur, P., 38
Astin, A. W., 52, 53, 63, 64, 72, 188, 189, 220
Aulepp, L., 272, 288, 291

B

Bacon, C. S., 235
Baird, L. L., 271
Banning, J. H., 12, 19, 20, 25, 31, 33, 34, 40, 41, 109, 148, 154, 175, 180, 239, 271, 272
Barker, R., 17
Bartels, S., 154
Baum, A., 14, 148
Baxter, J. C., 160
Bechtel, R. B., 21, 174
Beckmann, 255
Beeler, K., 181
Beetham, H., 244
Bell, 160, 174, 179
Bell, D., 263
Bell, P. A., 14, 148, 152
Bellah, R. N., 216
Bellandese, S., 181
Bender, B. E., 33
Bennett, M., 16, 29
Benton, S., 16
Bers, M., 245
Bickford, D. J., 25
Birnbaum, R., 83, 85
Blau, P. M., 108, 109, 111
Blimling, G. S., 162, 220
Bollinger, C. M., 145, 177
Bolman, L. G., 83, 85
Bonneau, K. 151
Bonner, T. N., 23
Borden, J., 267
Bott, S. E. 12
Bowman, C., 261
Boyer, E., 13, 107, 108, 155, 216
Brandon, A., 147
Bransford, J., 255
Braskamp, L., 63
Briggs, K., 56

Bronfenbrenner, U., 274, 279, 282, 283
Brooks, D. C., 29
Brower, A., 177, 227, 232
Brown, M., 35, 36
Buchmann, C., 151
Budin, D., 262
Burton, J. K., 261

C

Cameron, T., 147
Ceglarek, S. L., 177
Chaffee, E. E., 126, 127
Chambliss, D. F., 51
Champagne, D. E., 178
Chan, T. W., 248
Chapman, M. P., 12, 25
Chau, C., 245
Chavis, D. M., 215, 216
Chen, B., 252
Chen, P.S.D., 260
Cheng, D. X., 229
Chickering, A. W., 34, 76, 108, 110, 202, 214, 227, 234, 298
Chism, N.V.N, 25
Churchill, W., 14
Clack, R. J., 271
Clark, B., 53
Clark, K., 17
Clarke, J., 261, 263
Clemens, K., 172
Clemmitt, M., 266
Clemons, S., 33
Cleveland-Innes, 239
Clifton, D. O., 53, 61, 62, 169, 248, 285
Cole, D. G., 177
Conyne, R. K., 271
Cook, J. M., 74
Corrazini, J., 291
Cortina, L. M.l, 155
Corty, E., 163
Cottrell, L. S., Jr., 216, 217
Cox, M. D., 232
Cresswell, T., 12, 39
Crockett, E., 171
Cronon, W., 39
Crook, C., 31
Crookston, B. B., 104, 214, 215
Cross, K. P., 39, 107, 213, 297, 298
Csikszentmihalyi, M., 61
Cunard, M., 25
Cunningham, H. V., 29, 30
Curtis, P., 260
Cuseo, J., 148
Cychosz, C., 178

D

Dabbagh, N., 256, 257, 259
D'Augelli, A. R., 150
Daver, Z. E., 232
Davis III, C., 247
De Lucia, A., 261
Deal, T. E., 83, 85
DeAndrea, D. C., 245
Dede, C., 261
Deil-Amen, R., 247
Delworth, U., 272, 288, 291
Deniston, T., 31
Denoyelles, A., 252
Dettinger, K. M., 227
Devlin, A. S., 37, 147
Dewey, J., 235, 249
Dierenfeldt, R., 145, 177
Dieterle, E., 261, 263
Dietz-Uhler, B., 163
Dober, R., 38, 39
Donovan, S., 147
Drezner, N. D., 177
Duggan, M., 256
Dukes, C. M., 177
Dumont, R., 34, 41, 45
Dunbar, R., 111
Dunne, J., 216
Dyer, W. G., Jr., 127
Dziech, B. W., 155

E

Eckert, E. L., 13
Eckman, P., 17
Edwards, P. M., 28
Ellison, N. B., 245

Ertzberger, J., 253, 254, 255, 270
Ethington, C. A., 74
Etzioni, A., 82, 213, 216
Evans, N. J., 150, 155, 251
Ezeh, C., 43

F

Fabian, A. K., 13
Feldman, K. A., 74, 220
Feldman, R., 13
Felix, E., 35, 36
Finley, C., 163
Fiore, A., 245
Fisher, B., 144, 161
Fisher, J. D., 14, 148
Ford, R. C., 43
Forney, D. S., 155, 271
Forrest, L., 104, 283
Fossey, R., 144, 175
Francese, R., 261
Francis, J., 40
Freire, P., 236
Friedman, M., 216
Fry, T., 218

G

Gabelnick, F., 214
Gabr, H. S., 44
Gannaway, D., 35
Garbarino, J., 163
Gardner, H., 215, 216, 217, 248
Garfield, J. A., 297
Garrison, D. R., 239
Gasman, M., 177
Gee, G., 44
Gehl, J., 40
Gennaro, S., 154
Gerald, S., 261
Gerst, M., 287
Gibbs, R. W., 33
Gidycz, C. A., 163
Gifford, R., 146
Gikas, J., 247
Giles-Corti, B., 40
Gilligan, C., 104
Giuliani, M. V., 13
Gladwell, M., 240
Goldman, N., 163
Goldstein, A. P., 153, 162, 179
Gonyea, R. M., 68, 148, 192
Gonyea, T., 148
Gonzalez Canche, M., 247
Gordon, D., 170
Graham, R., 204
Grant, M., 247
Greene, T. G., 14, 148, 196
Greenwell, S., 30
Gregory, D. E., 145, 177
Griffin, K. A., 176, 263
Guido-DiBrito, F., 155, 271
Guidry, K. R., 260
Gunnings, B. B., 150
Gustafson, P.E.R., 15

H

Haas, G., 12
Hagan, H., 218
Hage, J., 88, 89, 90, 91, 92, 94, 97, 99, 100, 101, 105, 204, 292
Hall, E. T., 221, 222
Hall, J. E., 126, 127, 128, 129
Hall, R. M., 150, 155
Hancock, E., 127
Hannah, D., 109
Hannon, M. D., 176
Hansen, W. B., 16
Harper, S. R., 176, 201, 271
Harrington, R., 242
Harris, D. R., 151
Harris, L. C., 43
Harris, T., 177
Harter, J. K., 53, 61, 169
Hawkins, B. C., 150
Haycraft, H., 297
Haywood, K., 257
Heaton, C. P., 43
Heiberger, G., 264
Heilweil, M., 147, 162
Hemphill, B. O., 153
Henshaw, R. G., 28
Hill, C., 154
Hill, D. C., 176

Hill, D. M., 232
Hirt, J., 147
Hodges, T. D., 62
Holland, J. L., 51, 53, 54, 55, 70, 72, 73, 74, 75, 104, 169, 200
Holton III, E. F., 298
Hopkins, M., 297
Hopkins, R. D., 144
Horowitz, H. L., 126
Hostettler, J. A., 206, 221, 222, 223
Hotaling, G., 155
Hotalling, K., 104, 283
Howard, J., 42
Hu, P.J.H., 247
Hu, S., 53, 63, 65, 68, 75, 192
Huebner, L. A., 271, 272, 288, 291
Huerta, M., 155
Hui, W., 247
Hunt, D. E., 281

I

Inkelas, K. K., 232

J

Jackson, G. S., 162
Jackson, J. F., 145, 177
Jaeger, A. J., 126
Jang, H., 145, 177
Janosik, S. M., 145, 177
Jeffery, C. R., 174
Jenkins, T. S., 176
Jin, Q., 248, 260, 261
Johnson, A., 147
Johnson, D., 150, 173
Johnson, L., 257
Johnson-Yale, C., 242
Jones, S., 242
Jones, S. R., 149, 150, 176, 281
Junco, R., 244, 264
Jung, C. G., 56

K

Kaiser, L. R., 272
Kaminer, A., 264
Kaminoff, R., 13
Kaminski, R. J., 145, 177
Kang, J. H., 145, 177
Kanter, R. M., 217
Kapitula, L. R., 12, 27
Kaplan, R., 34
Kaplan, S., 34
Kassabaum, D. G., 12
Katel, P., 145, 177
Keller, J., 44
Kenney, D. R., 34, 41, 45
Kenney, G., 34, 41, 45
Ketelhut, D. J., 261
Keup, J. R., 33
Kilmartin, C. T., 163
Kimbrough, 177
King, P. M., 104, 197, 271, 296, 299
Kinzie, J., 68, 126, 176, 192, 195
Kitchener, K. S., 104, 197, 296
Kitchenham, A., 254
Kitsantas, A., 256, 257, 259
Knefelkamp, L., 110
Knez, I., 13
Knowles, M. S., 298
Knuiman, M., 40
Kolb, A. Y., 57, 58, 248
Kolb, D. A., 53, 57, 58, 61, 73, 169, 248
Koons-Witt, 145, 177
Kopec, D., 26
Koss, M. P., 163
Krehbiel, L. E., 128, 129
Krier, L., 219
Krishnan, R., 251, 254
Kuh, G. D., 53, 63, 65, 67, 68, 75, 76, 87, 117, 119, 126, 127, 128, 129, 131, 132, 151, 169, 177, 190, 191, 194, 195, 196, 198, 199, 205, 207, 208, 230, 232, 233, 236, 286, 292
Kuk, L., 40, 104, 283
Kunitz, S., 297

L

LaBlanc, B. H., 153
Lakey, J., 12
Lambert, A. D., 260
LaRose, R., 245
Lave, J., 254

Lawless, J. W., 32, 149
Lawson, J. M., 271
Lee, M. J.W., 257
Lenning, O. T., 232
Leonard, J. B., 232
Levinson, D. J., 234, 283
Levinson, J. D., 234, 283
Levy, J., 219
Lewicka, M., 12, 36
Lewin, K., 276
Li, S., 63
Lightner, R., 232
Lindsteadt, G., 145, 177
Lippincott, J., 30
Loffredo, D. A., 242
Loftin, R. B., 266
Loken, E., 264
Lowery, J. W., 178
Luna, F., 20, 154
Lundberg, C. C., 127
Lutovsky, B. R., 178
Lynch, A., 298
Lyndon, D., 39
Lyon, L., 216
Lyons, M., 132, 151

M

Mace, R. L., 165
MacGregor, J., 214
Magley, V. J., 155
Magolda, P. M., 126, 176
Mallory-Hill, S., 44
Maloney-Krichmar, D., 251
Mandell, J. I., 218
Manning, K., 85
Mark, N. P., 151
Marsick, V. J., 29
Martin, F., 253, 254, 255, 270
Martin, P. Y., 160
Masland, A. T., 128
Maslow, A. H., 16
Masters, N. T., 163
Matheis, C., 177
Matthews, A., 35, 126
Matthews, K. E., 31
Matthews, R. S., 214
Maurrell, A., 163
Max-Neef, M. A., 111
McCaulley, M. H., 56, 169
McClenney, K. M., 196
McCormick, A. C., 68, 192
McCullough, B. C., 155
McEwen, M. K. 281
McGill, L., 244
McGloughlin, C., 257
McGuire, F. D., 175
McHaney, R., 240
McKelfresh, D., 33
McMillan, D. W., 215
McMullen, S., 30
McPherson, M., 74
Mehrabian, A., 16
Meyer, A., 169
Michelson, W., 19, 274
Middleton, V., 19, 31
Millar, E.A.R., 177
Miller, T. E., 33, 177
Millermaier, S., 242
Mintz, N., 16
Mitchell, G., 31
Moffatt, M., 126, 131
Moore, R. M., 133
Moos, R. H., 52, 109, 116, 117, 119, 120, 124, 125, 159, 162, 201, 202, 205, 206, 271, 275, 285, 287, 288, 296
Moran, E., 148
Morrill, C., 12
Morris, P. A., 274
Mulholland, S., 176
Murray, H., 117
Museus, S., 176
Myers, I., 53, 56, 57, 70, 104, 169

N

Narum, J. L., 26
Nasar, J. L., 161
Nelson, B., 261
Newbrough, J. R., 216
Newcomb, T. M., 220
Newman, J. H., 31, 32
Newman, O., 174, 175

Nicholas, D. A., 260
Nichols, A. H., 176
Nicoletti, J., 145, 177
Nicolov, A., 147
Nock, A. J., 196
Nold, O., 147

O

Oblinger, D., 25
O'Callaghan, 177
O'Connor, G. G., 160
Okoli, D. T., 12
Oldenburg, R., 33, 199
Orsuwan, M., 177
Osmond, H., 42

P

Pablant, P., 160
Pace, C. R., 117, 118, 119, 188, 189, 190, 191
Painter, S., 27, 28, 29
Palmer, C. J., 154
Palmer, P., 214, 216, 234, 235, 248, 249
Pang, J. S., 155
Panos, R. J., 220
Parker, C., 110
Parker, I., 266
Parks, S. D., 31, 32
Parsons, T., 82
Pascarella, E. T., 191, 271, 285, 296
Passero, I., 261
Passini, R., 37, 38
Patton, L. D., 172, 173, 176, 177, 271
Peck, M. S., 216, 217
Perez II, D., 176
Perez, F., 242
Perrotti, J. A., 178
Perry, W. G., 104, 296
Phelps, L. A., 175
Phillips, G. H., 159
Pike, G. R., 67, 76
Pittenger, D. J., 57
Pollard, J. W., 144
Preece, J., 251
Preiser, W.F.E., 44
Prensky, M., 270
Price, D., 153
Price, J. L., 95
Proctor II, R. F. 15, 17
Proshansky, H. M., 13
Provost, J. A., 57
Prown, J. D., 19

Q

Quaye, S. J., 201
Quinn, C., 254

R

Rainie, L., 242
Randall, M., 31
Rankin, S., 150, 153, 177
Rapoport, A., 14, 15, 16, 17, 18
Reason, R. D., 178, 271, 281, 282
Reeve, J. R., 12
Regoeczi, W., 148
Reisser, L., 34, 76, 110, 202, 227, 234
Rendon, L. I., 155
Renn, K. A., 271, 274, 279, 281, 282, 289, 295
Rhatigan, J. J., 150
Rheingold, H., 240
Richlin, L., 232
Rios-Aguilar, C., 247
Rodger, S., 147
Rodgers, R. F., 271
Rose, D. 169
Rosenberg, M., 155
Ross, D., 233
Rubin, N., 257
Ryan, R., 34

S

Sam, A. A., 177
Sandeen, A., 150
Sandler, B. R., 150, 155
Sanford, N., 211
Sanoff, H., 44
Saunders, D. R., 118
Saunders, K. P., 232
Schein, E. H., 126, 127, 129, 130, 131
Schlossberg, N. K., 155, 217, 298, 299

Schneekloth, L. H., 38, 44
Scholljegerdes, K., 34
Schroeder, C. C., 162, 175, 224, 226
Schuh, J., 33, 126, 128, 144, 145, 162, 177, 178, 195, 196, 291
Scott-Webber, L., 12, 27
Scribner, M., 214
Seeger, M. A., 289
Seligman, M., 61
Selznick, P., 216, 217
Sharpe, R., 244
Sheehy, K., 264
Sherimon, P., 251, 254
Shibley, R. G., 38, 44
Silva, E., 154
Sipple, S., 232
Skinner, B. F., 200, 206
Sköld, O., 241
Sloan III, J. J., 144
Smart, J. C., 74
Smith, A., 242, 256
Smith, B. L., 214
Smith, M. C., 144, 175, 180
Smith-Lovin, L., 74
Snow, D. A., 12
Solan, A., 232
Sommer, R., 16
Sorochty, R. W., 177
Spencer-Thomas, S., 145, 177
Spitzberg, I. J., Jr., 201, 210, 213, 223, 224
Staats, H., 34
Stantasiero, E., 33
Stearns, E., 151
Stegman, J., 175
Steinfield, C., 245
Stern, G. G., 117, 118
Stern, R. A., 13
Stevens, D., 254
Stewart, J. D., 178
Stockdale, S., 20
Stokes, A., 232
Stolzenberg, E. B., 33
Strange, C., 25, 102, 105, 109, 128, 129, 149, 150, 151, 159, 162, 196, 218, 239, 271, 297, 299
Strickland, A., 12, 27
Sturner, W. F., 12, 13, 45
Sucher, D., 40
Sugarman, D., 155
Sullivan, E. V., 281
Svarre, B., 40
Swanson, R. A., 298

T

Tabur, S., 29, 30
Takacs, C. G., 51
Tan, B.L.B., 43
Terenzini, P. T., 191, 285, 296
Terrell, M. C., 145, 177
Teter, C., 156
Thadani, D., 219
Thang, D.C.L., 43
Thayer-Bacon, B. J., 235
Thelin, J. R., 13
Thomas, D. F., 39, 40
Thompson, N. S., 145, 177
Thornburg, D. D., 25
Thorndike, V. V., 201, 210, 213, 223, 224
Thornton, C. H., 126
Tierney, W. G., 117, 126, 127, 213
Tinto, V., 214
Toffler, A., 107
Torges, C. M., 155
Tortora, G., 261
Trow, M., 53
Troyer, D., 24, 149
Turner, P. V., 144
Tuttle, K. D., 176

U

Upcraft, M. L., 291

V

Van Der Werf, M., 242
Varian, H., 269
Vaughan, N. D., 239
Vescio, V., 233
Vesper, N., 53, 63, 65, 75
Vinu, P., 251, 254

Vogt, K. E., 232
Vye, C., 34

W

Wakabayashi, P., 147
Wall, V. A., 150
Walsh, W. B., 53, 117
Walton, C., 176
Wang, F., 261
Warren, R. L., 216
Warsaw, R., 163
Watkins, K. E., 29
Watson, G. G., 44
Weber, M., 81
Weiner, L., 155
Weinmayer, V. M., 160, 175
Weiss, D., 145, 177
Welch, I., 34
Wells, M., 12
Wells, R. L., 215, 216, 217, 218, 223
Wenger, E., 254
Whitaker, L. C., 144
White, C. H., 12
Whitt, E. J., 126, 177, 195, 210, 292
Wicker, A. W., 17, 18, 19, 108, 110, 152, 202
Widick, C., 110
Wiggins, C., 181
Wilson, G., 31
Winston, R. B., Jr., 286
Wisniewski, N., 163
Wood, L., 40
Woolf, V., 199

Y

Yankovich, J., 13

Z

Zajonc, A., 214
Zandan, G., 147
Zeisel, J., 21, 22, 23, 160, 175
Zhao, C., 68, 230, 232, 233
Zickuhr, K., 242
Zimbardo, P. G., 153
Zimmerman, E., 257, 266
Zipp, Y., 149

Subject Index

A

Academic major learning communities, 230
Academics (type of student), 192, 193, 194
Accommodating (learning style), 60
Acquaintances, student, 190, 191
Acting (learning style), 59
Active Citizenship Through Technology (ACT), 245–246
Active learning classroom, 28
Affordable Care Act, 282
Alcohol consumption, 162, 163
Americans with Disabilities Act of 1990, 144, 149
Anarchical frame, 83, 84
Apps, mobile, 263–265
Architectural determinism, 14
Artifacts of material culture, 19–21
Artistic personality type, 54
Artists, 64
Assimilating (learning style), 59
Assumptions, and institutional culture, 129–130
Audits, safety, 176–183

B

Balancing (learning style), 60
Behavior settings, 17–19
Behavioral traces, 21–23
Belonging, sense of, 51, 173, 213, 215
Blend (retail marketing platform), 266
Blogs, 258
Bullying, 171. *See also* Harassment
Bureaucratic frame, 83, 84

C

Campus, as a whole, 27
Campus assessment for safety, strategies for, 179–185
Campus culture, 126–132
Campus design matrix, 275–279
Campus learning communities. *See* Communities of learning
Campus location, 194–196
Campus policies and practices, 285–299
CampusQuad app (social media technology), 247, 260
Carry capacity, 153
Centralization, in organized environments, 89–90
Citizenship Through Technology, Active, 245–246
Civil Rights Act of 1964, 143
Classroom Environment Scale (CES) Dimensions and Subscales, 122
Classrooms: active learning, 28; technology-infused, 27; traditional, 27
Clifton Strengths Finder, 61
Coffee shops and bookstores, 33, 41
Collaborative institutions, 67

College and University Environment Scale (CUES), 118
College Characteristics Index (CCI), 118
College Student Experiences Questionnaire (CSEQ), 65, 119, 190
Collegial frame, 83, 84
Comfort and image, 30
Communities: characteristics of, 215–217; dimensions of, 218–223; importance of, 214; successful, 217–218
Communities of learning: assessment of, 233–238; challenges of building, 223–230; four models of, 230–233; importance of, 213–214; seven characteristics of, 228–229
Competition-oriented living environments, 125
Congruence, person-environment, 73–76
Consultation, educational, 291–293
Contingent institutions, 39
Contributive institutions, 39–40
Conventional personality type, 55
Converging learning style, 60
Cooperative Institutional Research Program's (CIRP) national freshman survey, 64
Crime, campus, 144–145, 158–159, 175. *See also* Safety, campus; Vandalism

D

Defensible space, 174–175
Disengaged students, 68, 69
Diverging learning style, 59
Dormitories, low-rise, 197. *See also* Residence halls

E

Ecology of learning: campus design matrix, 275–279; defined, 272; eight themes for, 272–274; and personal ecology of student development, 279–285
Educational consultation, 291–293
Engagement: and institutional assessment, 209–211; physical dimensions of, 194–199; theories of, 188–194. *See also* Involvement
Engagement types, 63–69
Engaging institutions, 67, 207–209
Enhanced learning communities, 230–231
Enterprising personality type, 55
Environmental code, six precepts of, 45–46
Environmental competence, enhancing, 296–299
Environmental differentiation and consistency, 71–73
Escape places, 199
Ethnic culture centers, 172–173
Exosystem, defined, 282
Experiencing (learning style), 58
Experiential learning theory (ELT), 57
Exploitive institutions, 39

F

Facebook, 263, 264, 265, 266
Faculty learning communities, 232–233
Flickr, 258
Formal learning spaces, 27–28
Formalization, in organized environments, 90–92
Freshman interest groups (FIGs), 200
Friendships, 191, 200, 279, 280, 281
Furniture, 28

G

Gay, bisexual, and trans-gendered community, 170–172
Google Calendar, 258
Graffiti, campus, 20, 23, 153–154

H

Harassment, 150, 154–155, 170–172
Hedonists, 64–65
Here-and-now mobile learning, 254–256

Hierarchy of learning space attributes, 29, 30
High-context cultures, 221
Holland Vocational Interest-Personality Types, 54–55, 72, 284
Homophily, principle of, 74
Housing, student, 31–32, 146–148, 197, 231–232
Human Scale Development (H-SD) model, 111
Human-scale design, 196–197

I

Incidental learning, 29
Inclusion, environments for: designing, 146–153; and human aggregate factors, 149–151; and organizational factors, 151–153; and physical factors, 146–149; and psychological inclusion, 153–158; and safety, 143, 158–159; and technology, 245–247
Inclusive spaces, 25, 26
Informal spaces, 27, 31–34
Institutions, types of engaging, 67
Intentional democratic community (IDC), 215
Internet use, facts about, 241–242. *See also* Mobile learning
Investigative personality type, 54
Involvement: aggregate dimensions of, 200–201; and community, 224–225; constructed dimensions of, 205–209; defined, 188–189; importance of, 188; and investment, 225; organizational dimensions of, 201–205
Involvement theory, 189–190
Involving campuses, 207–209
Involving College Audit Protocol, 236

L

Laboratories, 28
Leaders, 65
Learning communities: assessment of, 233–238; challenges of building, 223–230; four models of, 230–233; importance of, 213–214; seven characteristics of, 228–229
Learning signature, 24
Learning space attributes, hierarchy of, 29, 30
Learning styles, 57–61
Learning through mobile technology: apps, 263–265; here-and-now mobile learning, 254–256; mobile learning in general, 251–254; MUDs, 260–263; personal learning environments (PLEs), 256–260
Lecture halls, 27–28
Lesbian, gay, bisexual, trans-gendered, queer, and questioning (LGBTQQ) community, 170–172
Libraries, 29
Location, campus, 194–196
Low-context cultures, 221, 222

M

Mascots, 157, 158
Mattering, five aspects of, 155, 217–218
Maximizers, 193, 194
Mobile learning: apps, 263–265; general description of, 251–254; here-and-now, 254–256; multiuser dimensions (MUDs), 260–263; personal learning environments (PLEs), 256–260
Monastic communities, 218
Morale, and organized environments, 98–99
Multiuser dimensions (MUDs), 260–263
Multiuser virtual environments (MUVEs), 261–263
Murals, 20
Myers-Briggs Type Indicator (MBTI), 56–57, 284

N

National Survey of Student Engagement (NSSE), 191, 249, 286
Native American students, 156–157
Nonverbal communication, conduits of, 17–23

O

Organizational models, synthesis of, 100
Organizational performance, 105–112
Organized environments: anatomy of, 86–88; and centralization, 89–90; complexity of, 88–89; dynamics of, 100–105; efficiency of, 97–98; morale in, 98–99; nature of, 81–86; and production, 93–95; routinization in, 95–97; and size, 106–111; and stratified systems, 92–93
Overmanned settings, 108, 152–153, 202

P

People, environments as, 52
Personal ecology of student development, 279–285
Personal learning environments (PLEs), 256–260
Personal space, 198–199
Personality types: engagement types, 63–65, 192–194; Holland vocational interest, 54–55; and learning styles, 57–61; and Myers-Briggs Type Indicator (MBTI), 56–57
Person-environment congruence, 73–76
Place: campus as, 11–15; function and symbol of, 15–17
Placebuilding, 39–40
Placemaking and placemarking, 36, 38–39
Political frame, 83, 84
Postoccupancy evaluation (POE), 43–44, 179
Power, distribution of, 89–90
Press, environmental, 117–119
Public spaces, 40–42

R

Rape, 162, 163
Realistic personality type, 54
Redundancy, in larger institutions, 108
Reflecting (learning style), 58
Rehabilitation Act of 1973, 143
Relationship dimensions, 120
Relationship-oriented living environments, 124
Relationships, importance of, 51
Residence halls, 31–32, 146–148, 197, 231–232
Residential colleges, 231
Restorative places, 34
Rituals, annual, 13
Rule clarity, and classroom environment, 122

S

Safe and brave spaces, 170–172
Safety, campus: aggregate factors in, 162–163; assessment of, 176–183; and campus crime, 144–145, 158–159; conclusions on, 183–185; designing for, 158–159; five types of, 181; and inclusion, 143, 146–153; organizational factors in, 163–164; physical factors for, 159–162; strategies for, 164–165; and technology, 245–247
Safety audits, 176–183
Scholars, 64
Sense of belonging, 51, 173, 213, 215
Sense of place, importance of, 12
Servicescape and atmospherics of place, 42–43
Sexual assaults, 162–163
Shootings, and campus safety, 158
Signage, 20, 22, 23, 37
Size, organizational, 106–111
Smartphones, tablets, and e-book readers, 251–254. *See also* Learning through mobile technology

Social activists, 64
Social media: and CampusQuad app, 247, 260; Facebook, 263, 264, 265, 266
Social networking sites, 259
Social personality type, 55, 70
Socially constructed environments: and campus culture, 126–132; and environmental press, 117–119; and social climate, 119–126
Sociopetal or socially catalytic spaces, 198
Static organizations, developmental environments versus, 100, 102, 103
Status strivers, 65
Stratified systems, 92–93
Student development, personal ecology of, 279–285
Student engagement: and institutional assessment, 209–211; physical dimensions of, 194–199; theories of, 188–194. *See also* Involvement
Student union, features to consider in designing, 219–220
Students, types of, 192–194. *See also* Personality types
Styles, learning, 57–61
Synomorphic relationship, 19

T

Talents and strengths, 61–63
Target hardening, 179, 184
Technology-infused classrooms, 27
Territoriality, 174–175
Themed housing, 231–232
Thinking (learning style), 59
Transformational institutions, 40

U

Uncommitted students, 65
Unconventional students, 68, 69, 193, 194
Universal design, principles of, 165–170
University Residence Environment Scale (URES), 287–288

V

Values, and campus culture, 128–129
Vandalism, 159, 160–161, 162, 163
Verbal harassment, 150, 154–155, 171
Violence, campus-related, 158–159, 162–163
Vocational Interest-Personality Types, 54–55, 72, 284

W

Wabash National Study of Liberal Arts Education (WNSLAE), 68
Walkways, campus, 34–35
Wayfinding, 36–38
Welcoming spaces, 25
Wikis, 258
Women, support for, 289–290
Women's safety, 155, 162–163, 183
Work Environment Scale (WES), 293, 294
World Wide Internet, facts about, 241–242. *See also* Mobile learning

Y

YouTube, 258